ACLS History E-Book Project

Reprint Series

THE CELTIC PENITENTIALS

PROTAT BROTHERS, PRINTERS, MACON (FRANCE)

THE UNIVERSITY OF CHICAGO

THE CELTIC PENITENTIALS

AND THEIR INFLUENCE ON CONTINENTAL CHRISTIANITY

A DISSERTATION

SUBMITTED TO THE FACULTY
OF THE GRADUATE SCHOOL OF ARTS AND LITERATURE
IN CANDIDACY FOR THE DEGREE OF

DOCTOR OF PHILOSOPHY

DEPARTMENT OF CHURCH HISTORY IN THE GRADUATE DIVINITY SCHOOL

BY

JOHN THOMAS MCNEILL

PARIS
LIBRAIRIE ANCIENNE HONORÉ CHAMPION, EDITEUR
ÉDOUARD CHAMPION
5, QUAI MALAQUAIS, 5

1923

TABLE OF CONTENTS

CHAPTER IV

Special Features of the Celtic Penitentials as Affected by Pre-Christian Customs.

CHAPTER V

The Spread of Celtic Penance on the Continent of Europe.

CHAPTER VI

How the Penitentials affected the Discipline of the Continental Church.

CORRIGENDA

P. 5, l. 20. Omit brackets.
" 9, " 11. After *1841*, begins new title.
" 52, " 7. Omit *with* at end.
" 61, " 2. Quotation mark after *scholars*.
" 104, Note 6. For *Gerigg* read *Gerig*.
" 108, l. 20. For *the of* read *they*.
" 125, " 22. Insert *their* before *crimes*, and add period.
" 129, Note 3, add *p. 64*.
" 137, l. 17. For *fil* read *file*.
" 139, Note 4, l. 2. For *und* read *et*.
" 141, " 2, add *p. 52*.
" 163, l. 30. Insert *to* before *the flames*.
" 180, Note 3. For *Migne, Patrol, Lat.*, read *Mansi, Concil.*

Obvious orthographic corrections should be made in the following:

Page 11, line 6; 32, 2; 41, 18; 43, 18; 44, 23 & 28; 58, 17; 62, 27; 82, 15; 83, 28; 115, 12; 118, 12; 119, 20; 138, note 2, last word; 154, 6; 167, 4; 168, 32; 176, 24; 197, 24; 199, 20.

PREFACE

No phase of mediaeval Christianity was a more vital part of common life than the Penitential System. Through it priest and people had their most significant relationships. It was the foremost agency in the cure of souls, and at the period of fullest institutional development it assumed a very important place in the ecclesiastical frame-work.

The origins of the Penitential System must be sought in the simple customs of the primitive church; but in course of evolution it was profoundly modified by the practice of a branch of the church which developed its characteristics in almost complete isolation from continental influences. This was the Celtic church of Ireland and Wales, whose penitential practice was formulated in the *libri poenitentiales*, a long series of works prescribing acts and seasons of penance for particular offences. The series extends in time from the fifth to the twelfth century, and comprises contributions from a wide continental field. But its original home is undoubtedly to be found in the British Islands, and its earliest and most characteristic exemplars in the closely related group of penitential books written by Irish and Welsh leaders in the fifth and sixth centuries. This early group of penitentials exhibits what may be called the Celtic penitential type. Its historic significance, however, lies in the fact that it was transmitted by Anglo-Saxon and Frankish writers in an ever-growing mass of penitential literature, and that the practices which it fostered were gradually, and not without conflict and modification, incorporated in the organism of the Latin church.

The very wide use of these manuals of penance during the eighth, ninth and tenth centuries is the most striking fact in the development of mediaeval penance. It is undoubtedly to this influence that we are to ascribe, at least in a large degree, the subsequent predominance of private confession and absolution, which became universally obligatory under Innocent III. Not less closely connected with the Celtic tendency in penance stands the practice of indulgences, which emerged in the eleventh century, and for which a theoretic explanation was provided by thirteenth century scholastics. It is in these Celtic codes that we find the first seeds of the rank weed of the indulgence traffic, the importance of which in the decadence of mediaeval Christianity has long been recognized.

The subject of this dissertation is one that has heretofore been treated with undeserved neglect. Penance has been thought of purely as an internal phase of the history of Christianity, and pagan affinities and influences have been left out of consideration. Protestant historians have generally contented themselves with an exposure of the evil fruits of the indulgence system, and have given no attention to its remote roots, or to the historical process that made inevitable these later manifestations. Even Lea, to whose massive researches all students of the history of indulgences must stand indebted, does not wholly escape this criticism. Catholic writers, on the other hand, have either assumed or intemperately asserted the early predominance of Rome in matters of penance, and thus have minimized the Celtic contribution. Writers of treatises on church history covering the mediaeval period, generally reveal a remarkable lack of information on the subject of penance. Only in the work of Hauck and of Lagarde does it receive an attention at all proportional to its importance. Morinus' heavy folio of 1651 and the 98 page historical sketch with which Wasserschleben introduces his documents in his *Bussordnungen der abendländischen Kirche*, 1851, are the treatises on which our church historians mainly rely. These old works are still highly useful. Fragmentary recent work of specialists has illumined many small areas of the field. Efforts have been made by Seebass, Schmitz, and Hauck to solve a number of the literary problems, while Celtic scholars like d'Arbois de Jubainville, Zimmer, K. Meyer, and Whitley Stokes have greatly extended our knowledge of the cultural background, and of the character of Celtic Christianity. In the light of such special studies it should presently be possible to write a satisfactory history of mediaeval penance.

The present treatise was completed to the end of Chapter V in February 1920, before the appearance of

Mr. Oscar D. Watkins' *History of Penance* [1]. A perusal of this work offers no reason for a revision of these chapters. Had Mr. Watkins' book appeared before they were written it would have been laid under contribution, and his valuable selection of documents would in some degree have simplified the task of preparing Chapter II. The ample treatment accorded by Mr. Watkins to the period prior to A. D. 450 (nearly two-thirds of the whole treatise), dwarfs the brief reference to that field which the present work contains. Yet as the latter is in no sense a miniature of the former, designed as it is to establish positions in which Mr. Watkins is not primarily interested, it is here allowed to stand. Nor is any modification made in this section to avoid difference from the conclusions arrived at by Mr. Watkins, as in all such cases the present writer confesses himself still partial to the views he had here expressed.

Mr. Watkins and the present writer are in accord on the major consideration that the Celtic penance was unique and widely different from that of the Ancient Catholic Church. The interests of the two studies are, however, fundamentally different. Mr. Watkins nowhere raises the question : Why had the Celtic penance this unique character ? — the question to the answer of which Chapters III and IV below are intended to make some contribution.

" The Keltic System " fills a space in Mr. Watkins' book proportionally briefer than that accorded to the early church. Two documents which receive consider-

1. O. D. Watkins, *A History of Penance*, two volumes, London, 1920.

able attention below are by him entirely omitted from mention, viz, the canons of St. Patrick and the *Collectio Canonum Hibernensis*. Overlooking recent discussions the author has unfortunately assigned to the canons of the so-called Second Synod of St. Patrick an antiquity which is assuredly unwarranted. In cómmon with the present writer Mr. Watkins recognizes St. Finnian of Clonard as the *Vinniaus* of the Penitential. As he states his common-sense reasons for this in a single sentence, it may be that the more extended argument below will lend greater certainty in the matter. The excerpt which he inserts from the tenth century abbot Adso is a probably valid additional testimony to the expansion among the Franks of the discipline of Columban. Readers of both works will observe its value as supplying an omission from Chapter V below.

Advantage has been taken of Mr. Watkins' discussion of a somewhat puzzling passage in the *Pœnitentiale Columbani*, in a footnote on p. (50). His work has suggested no other change in Chapters I to V. In writing Chapter VI Mr. Watkins Second Volume has been found useful, as a number of references will attest.

At the date of this writing Mr. T. P. Oakley's promised dissertation on the penitentials has not appeared.

The writer of this dissertation sets himself the double task of investigating the character of the Celtic penance and of showing how it was, with modifications, carried over into the continental church. The treatment will be arranged in accordance with the following general outline :

(1) A fresh survey of the literary sources. This will necessarily be confined to published documents. With the aid of a number of recent studies an attempt will be made to establish the authorship, chronology and relationship of the more important of the penitential books.

(2) A study of the formative influences in the development of Celtic penance. Here an effort will be made to show the relative importance of the ecclesiastical and of the national-cultural elements contributing to the rise of the Celtic penitential practice and literature.

(3) An examination of the process by which the Celtic penitential literature and practice gradually obtained recognition on the Continent. This will involve a condensed account of a movement extending over about five centuries, in which the invading penance was promoted and opposed by a variety of agencies and parties. We shall endeavor to estimate its influence upon the papal church, and to show the compromise effected between Celtic and Roman principles in the final formulation of Catholic penance.

It is my duty and pleasure to acknowledge aid received from many sources in the preparation of this volume. First I should mention Dr. Shailer Mathews, Dean of the Divinity school, University of Chicago, and Professors Shirley J. Case and P. G. Mode of the Department of Church History, under whose leadership my general studies in Church History have been pursued. My thanks are likewise due, for many kindnesses, to Professor A. C. MacLaughlin, Head of the Department of History. In the task of research my constant adviser and guide has been Professor James Westphal Thompson, from whose full store of mediaeval reading I was supplied with many references, and who gave generously of his time in frequent conferences. I have also had the benefit of the advice of Professor T. P. Cross of the Department of English, who brought to my notice much material relating to Celtic culture, and corrected a number of errors into which I had fallen. Professor Walter E. Clark of the Department of Comparative Philology was also several times consulted.

I should like to add the names of the late Professor A. R. MacEwen of New College, Edinburgh, who in 1912 first encouraged my studies in the history of the Celtic Church, and of Professor James Stalker of Aberdeen, who, on a visit to Vancouver, Canada, in 1911, first awakened my interest in Church History.

A tribute is due to the valued service of a considerable number of officials and attendants in the Harper, Divinity, Law, Classical and Education Libraries of the University of Chicago, in the Library of McCormick Theological Seminary, and in the Newberry Library, Chicago. Materials have also been utilized in the book which were compiled in the libraries of Union Seminary and Columbia University, New York (1911-12 and 1915), in the Library of New College Edinburgh (1912-13) and (during a brief visit in each case) in the Library of the British Museum (1913) and in that of Harvard University (1919). For courteous assistance in all these institutions I wish to record my thanks.

The Bibliography and footnotes constitute the only

acknowledgement possible of the service rendered by many learned investigators of whose researches I have thankfully availed myself.

John T. McNeill.

Queen's University,
Kingston, Canada.

December 1, 1921.

BIBLIOGRAPHY

I. — Sources

Achéry, Luc d'
Specilegium, sive collectio veterum aliquot scriptorum qui in Galliae bibliothecis delitucrant. 3 vols. Paris 1723.

The Ancient Laws of Ireland.
Pub. by the Commissioners for publishing the ancient laws of Ireland. Ed. W. N. Hancock, T. O'Mahony, A. G. Richey, R. Atkinson. 6 vols. Dublin, 1865-1901.

The Ancient Laws and Institutes of Wales.
Ed. Owen, Aneurin, 2 vols. (Records Series) London 1841. Ancient Laws and Institutes of England comprising laws enacted under the Anglo-Saxon Kings. Ed. Thorpe, Benjamin. 2 vols. (Records Series) 1840.

Bede, Historia ecclesiastica gentis Anglorum. Ed. Plummer, C, 2 vols. Oxf. 1896.

Bernard, Saint, of Clairvaux.
Vita S. Malachiae, Migne, Patrologia, series Latina. Tom. 182, col. 1073 f.

Bernard, John, and Atkinson, Robert.
The Irish Liber Hymnorum, Publications of Henry Bradshaw Society, 2 vols. London 1898.

Bollandus, Joannes, and successors.
Acta sanctorum quotquot orbe coluntur, 3rd ed., 64 vols. Paris and Rome 1863 f.

Chronicon Scottorum.
A Chronicle of Irish Affairs from the Earliest Times to A. D. 1135, ed. with transl. by Wm. H. Hennessy (Rolls Series). London 1866.

Colgan, John.
Acta Sanctorum veteris et majoris Scotiae seu Hiberniae, sanctorum insulae, (fo.). Louvain 1645.

Colgan, John.

Triadis Thaumaturgae seu divorum Patricii, Columbae et Brigidae... acta. (fo.) Louvain 1647.
Dinan, W.
Monumenta Historica Celtica, Vol. I. London 1911.
Fowler, Joseph T.
Admnani vita S. Columbae. Oxf. 1894.
Giraldus Cambrensis.
Opera, ed. J. S. Brewer, 8 vols. Lond. 1861 (Rolls Series).
Historical Works, tr. T. Wright. London 1863.
Gregory of Tours.
Historiae Francorum libri X, in Collection des textes pour servir à l'étude et à l'enseignement de l'histoire, vols. II 1886 and XII 1892. New ed. by R. Poupardin. Paris 1913.
Gwynn, John.
Liber Ardmachanus, The Book of Armagh, ed. with introd. and Appendices by John Gwynn. (Roy. Ir. Acad.) Dub. and Lond. 1913.
Haddan, A. W., and Stubbs, Wm.
Councils and Ecclesiastical Documents relating to Great Britain and Ireland. 3 vols. Oxf. 1869-1878.
Hinschius, F. K. Paul.
Decretales Pseudo-Isidorianae et capitula Angilramni. Leips. 1863.
Jonas, Monk of Bobbio.
Vita S. Columbani, in Monumenta Germ. Hist., Script. rer. merov. Tom. IV, pp. 64-108.
Lightfoot, J. B.
The Apostolic Fathers. Revised texts with short introductions and English translations, ed. and completed by J. R. Harmer. Lond. 1891.
Loth, J.
Les Mabinogion du livre rouge de Hergest. Paris 1913.
Löwenfeld, S.
Epistolae pontificum Romanorum ineditae. Lipsiae, 1885.
Mabillon, Johannes, and Achéry, Lucas d'.
Acta Sanctorum ordinis sancti Benedicti. 9 vols. (fo.) Paris 1668-1701.
Mansi, Joannes.
Sacrorum conciliorum nova et amplissima collectio, 31 vols. Florence, 1759 f. (New ed., Paris 1901 f.)
Martene, Edmund, et Durand, Ursinus.
Thesaurus Novus Anecdotorum. 5 vols. Paris 1717.

Meyer, Kuno.
An Old Irish Treatise *De Arreis*. Rev. Celt. XV, 1894, p. 485 f.

Migne, Jacques Paul.
Patrologiae cursus completus series Latina. 221 vols. Paris 1844-1864, series Graeca, 161 vols. Paris 1857-1886.

Monumenta Germaniae Historica.
. Scriptores, Berl. 1826-1903, Auctores Antiquissimi, 1877-1903, Scriptores Rerum Merovingicarum 1885-1913, Leges, 1835-89.

Müller, F. Max.
The Sacred Books of the East, by various Oriental Scholars, and ed. by F. Max Müller, 50 vols. Oxf. 1879-1910 ; especially vols. II and XXV, containing the Sacred Laws of the Aryas, tr. Bühler, Georg.

O'Clery Michael (d. 1643).
Annals of the Kingdom of Ireland by the Four Masters, ed. O'Donovan, John. Dubl. 1856.

O'Grady, Standish H.
Silva Gadelica, a collection of Tales in Irish, 2 vols. Lond, 1892.

O'Hanlon, John.
Lives of the Irish Saints, Dublin, 1875. Vols. by months, published to Vol. IX. (September).

Petrie, H. and Sharp, I.
Monumenta Historica Britannica. Lond. 1848.

Plummer, C.
Vitae Sanctorum Hiberniae partim hactenus ineditae. 2 vol. Oxf. 1910.

Proceedings of the Royal Irish Academy.
1st ser. Dubl. 1836-1869. 2nd ser. 1870-1888, 3rd ser. 1888 f.

Reeves, Wm.
The Life of St. Columba, founder of Hy, written by Adamnan, ninth abbot of that monastery. Dubl. 1857.

Roberts, Alex. and Donaldson, James.
The Ante-Nicene Fathers, (American Reprint of Edinburgh ed.) 9 vols. Buffalo, 1885 f.

Rozière, Eugène de.
Recueil général des formules usitées dans l'Empire des Francs, v^e^-xe siècle. 3 vols. Paris 1857-1871.

Schaff, Philip, and Wall, Henry.

Nicene and Post-Nicene Fathers of the Christian Church. 14 vols. N. Y. Oxf., Lond. 1890 f.

Seebass, Otto.

Regula monachorum Sancti Columbani Abbatis, Zeitschr. f. Kirchengesch. Bd. XV, p. 366 f.. Gotha 1895.

Skene, Wm. Forbes.

The Four Ancient Books of Wales, 2 vols. Edin. 1868.

De Smedt, C., et de Backer, J.

Acta Sanctorum Hiberniae ex Codice Salmanticensi. Edin. and Lond. 1888.

Smith, Wm., and Cheetham, Samuel.

A Dictionary of Christian Antiquities. 2 vols. Lond. 1875.

Stokes, Whitley.

Lives of Saints from the Book of Lismore, Anecdota Oxoniensia, Mediaeval and Modern Series. Oxf. 1890.

— Three Middle Irish Homilies on the Lives of Saints Patrick, Brigit and Columba. Calcutta 1877.

— The Calendar of Œngus. Dubl. 1880. Republished with translation in Henry Bradshaw Society Publications. Lond. 1906.

— The Saltair na Rann. Anecdota Oxoniensa, mediaeval and modern series. Oxf. 1883. (Tr. in Eleanor Hull, The Poem-Book of the Gael.)

— The Colloquy of the Sages. (10 th Century). Paris 1905.

Wasserschleben, F. W. H.

Bussordungen der Abendländischen Kirche nebst einer rechtsgeschichtlichen Einleitung. Halle 1851.

— Die irische Kanonensammlung. Giessen 1874. 2nd ed. 1885.

White, N. J. D.

Libri Sancti Patricii, or Latin Writings of St. Patrick, in Proceedings of the Royal Irish Academy, vol. XXV, Sect. C., p. 201 f., Dubl. 1905.

Williams, Hugh.

Gildae de Excidio Britanniae, Fragmenta, Liber de Poenitentia, accedit et Lorica Gildae, ed. for Society of Cymmrodorion (Cymmrod. Record Ser. No. 3). Lond. 1899-1901.

Windisch, Ernst W. O., and Stokes, Whitley.

Irische Texte. Berl. 1880 f.

II. — LITERATURE.

(General histories of the Church are omitted from this hist).

Albers, Dom Bruno.
Untersuchungen zu den älteste Mönchsgewohnheiten. Munich, 1905.

Arbois de Jubainville, Henri d'.
Cours de littérature celtique, 12 vols. Paris 1883-1902.
— Études sur le Senchus Mor. Nouvelle rev. hist. de droit français et étranger. 1880, 1881, 1884, 1888.
— Les premiers habitants de l'Europe. 2 vols. Paris 1889.
— La civilisation des Celtes et celle de l'épopée homérique. Paris 1899 (Vol. 6 of Cours de litt. Celt.)
— La procédure du jeûne en Irlande. Rev. Celt. Vol. 7, 1886, p. 245 f.

Arnold, Matthew.
The Study of Celtic Literature, ed. Alfred Nutt. Long Acre 1910.

Babut, E. C.
Saint Martin de Tours. Paris 1912.

Baring-Gould, S., and Fisher, John.
The Lives of the British Saints, the Saints of Wales and Cornwall, and such Irish Saints as have dedications in Britain, 4 vols. Lond. 1907-1913.

Bateson, Mary.
The origin and early History of the Double Monasteries, Royal Hist. Soc., Transactions of. New, (i. e. 2nd) Series, vol. 13, p. 137. London 1899.

Batiffol, Pierre.
History of the Roman Breviary, tr. Baylay. Lond., N. Y., Bombay, Calcutta 1912.

Bertrand, A.
La Religion des Gaulois, Paris 1897.

Borderie, Arthur de la.
La date de la naissance de Gildas. Rev. Celt. T. VI, 1883, p. 1. f.

Boudhinon, A.
Sur l'histoire de la pénitence, à propos d'un ouvrage récent. Revue d'histoire et de la littérature religieuses, T. II (1897), p. 306 f.

Bradshaw, Henry.

The Early Collection of Canons commonly known as the Hibernensis, a letter to Wasserschleben, May 28, 1885, in Collected Papers of Henry Bradshaw, edited for the Syndics of the Press. Cambridge 1889.

— The Early Collection of Canons known as the Hibernensis. Edited for the Syndics of the Press. Cambridge, 1893. (Cf. Review by Turner, C. H., Engl. Histor. Rev. Oct. 1894.)

Brehaut, Ernest.

History of the Franks by Gregory of Tours. New York, 1916.

Bund, J. W. Willis.

The Celtic Church in Wales. Lond. 1897.

Bourke, Ulick. J.

Pre-Christian Ireland. Dubl. 1887.

Bury, J. B.

The Life of St. Patrick. Lond. 1905.

Clarke, W. K. Lowther.

St. Basil the Great, a study in Monasticism. Cambr. 1913.

Coffey, George.

Archaeological Evidence for the Intercourse of Gaul with Ireland before the First Century. Proc. Roy. Ir. Acad., Vol. 28, (1910), sec. C, p. 96 f.

Concannon, Mrs. Thos.

The Life of St. Columban. Dubl. 1915.

Crowe, J. O'Beirne.

The Amra Cholumb Cille of Dallan Forgaill. Dubl. 1871.

Dottin, Georges.

Manuel à servir à l'étude de l'antiquité celtique. Paris, 1906.

— La religion des Celtes, 3rd ed. Paris 1908.

Duchesne, Louis.

Origines du Culte chrétien, 4th ed. Paris 1908.

Dudden, F. Holmes.

Gregory the Great, his Place in History and Thought, 2 vols.. Lond. 1905.

Dunn, Joseph.

The Ancient Irish Epic Tale, Táin Bó Cúalnge. Lond. 1914.

Ermoni, J.

La pénitence dans l'histoire à propos d'un ouvrage récent, Rev. des quest. hist., Jan. 1900, pp. 1-55.

Fournier, Paul.

De l'influence de la collection irlandaise sur la formation des collections canoniques. Nouvelle rev. hist. de droit français et étranger 1899, p. 27 f.

— Le Liber ex lege Moysi. Rev. Celt., T. XXX (1909).

Frank, F.

Die Bussdisciplin der Kirche von den Apostelzeiten bis zum siebenten Jahrhundert. Mainz 1867.

Godkin, James.

The Religious History of Ireland. Lond. 1873.

Gottlob, Adolf.

Kreuzablass und Almosenablass, ein Studie über die Frühzeit des Ablasswesens. Stuttgart, 1896 (in Stutz, Ulrich, Kirchengeschichtliche Abhandlungen).

Gougaud, Dom Louis.

L'œuvre des Scotti dans l'Europe Continentale. Revue d'histoire ecclésiastique, Vol. IX (Louvain 1908.), p. 21 f. and 255 f.

— Les Chrétientés celtiques. Paris 1911.

Green, Alice Stopford.

The Old Irish World. Dubl. and Lond. 1912.

Gromer, George.

Die Laienbeicht im Mittelalter, ein Beitrag zu ihrer Geschichte. Munich 1909. Cf. Review by E. Jordan in Revue historique. Vol. 106, p. 359 f.

Guest, Charlotte.

The Mabinogion. Lond. & N. Y. 1906.

Harnack, Adolf.

History of Dogma, tr. Buchanan, from the 3rd Germ. ed., 7 vols. Lond. 1896.

Hauck, A.

Kirchengeschichte Deutschlands, 4 vols., 3rd ed. Leipz. 1906.

Haverfield, F. R.

Ancient Rome and Ireland. Engl. Hist. Rev., Jan. 1913, p. 1.

Healy, John.

Insula Sanctorum et Doctorum, or Ireland's Ancient Schools and Scholars, 3rd. Ed., Dublin and New York 1897.

Henderson, Geo.

Survivals in Belief among the Celts. Glasg. 1911.

Hinschius, F. K. P.

System des Katholischen Kirchenrechts mit besonderer Rücksicht auf Deutschland, 6 vols. Berlin 1869-1897.

Hogan, J. F.
Irish monasteries in Germany. Ir. Eccles. Record, vol. IV, 1898, p. 265 f.

Holmes, T. R.
Ancient Britain and the Invasion of Julius Caesar. Oxf. 1907.

Holmes, T. S.
The Christian Church in Gaul. Lond. 1911.

Hook, Walter F.
Lives of the Archbishops of Canterbury. 12 vols. Lond. 1865-1884.

Hughes, Wm.
A History of the Church of the Cymry. Revised ed. Lond. 1916.

Jeudwine, J. W.
Tort, Crime and Police in Mediaeval Britain. Lond. 1917.

Jolly, Julius.
Recht und Sitte in Grundriss der Indo-Arische Philologie. Strassburg 1895.

Joyce, P. W.
A Social History of Ancient Ireland. 2 vols. Lond., N. Y., and Bombay 1903.

Keating, Geoffrey.
History of Ireland. 3 vols. Publ. of. Irish Text Society. Lond. 1908.

Kunstmann, Friedrich.
Die Lateinischen Poenitentialbücher der Angelsachsen, mit geschichtlicher Einleitung. Mainz 1844.

Lagarde, André.
The Latin Church in the Middle Ages, tr. Alexander. N. Y. 1915.

— Saint Augustin a-t-il connu la confession ? (with similar studies on Chrysostom, and Gregory the Great.) Revue d'histoire et de la littérature religieuses. 1912, 1913, 1914.

— Le Manuel du confesseur au xie siècle, Rev. d'hist. et de litt. relig. New Series, T. I, 1910, p. 542 f.

Lagrange, Le P. Marie-Joseph.
Études sur les religions sémitiques. Paris 1905.

Lea, Henry Charles.
A Formulary of the Papal Penitentiary in the Thirteenth Century, Phila. 1892.

— A History of Auricular Confession and Indulgences. 3 vols.

Phila. 1896.

Levison, Wilhelm.

Die Iren und die fränkische Kirche, Historische Zeitschrift, 3rd series, Bd. 13. Munich 1912.

Lindsay, W. M.

Notae Latinae ; an acct. of abbreviation in Latin MSS. of the early minuscule Period, c. 700-800. Cambridge 1915.

Lloyd, J. E.

A History of Wales, 2 vols. Lond. 1911.

Loofs, Friedrich.

Antiquae Britonum Scottorumque ecclesiae quales fuerint mores etc. Lond, 1882.

Maine, Sir Henry Sumner.

Lectures on the Early History of Institutions, N. Y. 1888.

— Ancient Law, its Connection with the Early History of Society and its Relation to Modern Ideas. Lond. 1906.

— Dissertation on Early Law and Customs. N. Y. 1886.

Maassen, Friedrich.

Geschichte der Quellen und der Literatur des Kanonischen Rechts, 2 vols. Gratz 1870.

MacCullough, J. A.

The Religion of the Ancient Celts. Edin. 1911.

MacEwen, Alex. R.

A History of the Church in Scotland. Vol. I, Lond., N.Y., Toronto, 1913.

Malorny, A.

Quid Luxovienses monachi, discipuli Sancti Columbani, ad regulam monasteriorum atque ad communem profectum ecclesiae contulerint. Paris 1895. (Cf. A. Molinier, in Revue Historique, vol. LX, pp. 92-98.)

Martin, E.

Saint Colomban. (Les Saints series.) Paris, 1905.

Meyer, Kuno, and Nutts, Alfred.

The Voyage of Bran son of Febal to the Land of the Living, 2 vols. 1895-1897.

— Learning in Ireland in the Fifth Century and the Transmission of Letters. Dublin 1912.

— Aus dem Nachlass Heinrich Zimmers. Zeitschr. f. Celt. Phil. Bd. 9 (1913), p. 117 f.

— An Crīnōg, Sitzungsber. d. Königl. Preuss. Akad. d. Wissenschaften. (philos.-histor. klasse) Apr. 11, 1918.

Miles, George.

The Bishops of Lindisfarne, Hexam, Chester-le-Street and Durham, Lond. 1898.

Montalemlert, C. F. R., Comte de.

Histoire des moines d'Occident depuis S. Benoît jusqu'à S. Bernard, 7 vols. Paris 1860-77. Engl. tr. The Monks of the West. 6 vols. Lond. 1896.

Morinus, Joannis.

Commentarius Historicus de Disciplina in Administratione Sacramenti Poenitentiae tredecim primis seculis (fo.) First published Paris 1651, 2nd ed. Antwerp, 1682.

Morison, E. F.

St. Basil and his Rule, a Study in Early Monasticism. Lond. 1912.

Newell, E. J.

History of the Welsh Church to the dissolution of the Monasteries. Lond. 1895.

Nicholson, E. M.

The Origin of the Hibernian Collection of Canons, Zeitschr. f. celt. Phil., Bd. 3, 1901, p. 99 f.

— Remarks on the Date of the First Settlement of the Saxons in Britain. Zeitschr. f. celt. Phil. Bd. 6, 1908, p. 541.

— The Annales Cambriae and their so-called Exordium. Zeitschr. f. Celt. Phil., Bd. 8, 1910 p. 121 f.

O'Curry, Eugene.

Lectures on the Manuscript Materials of Ancient Irish History. 2nd ed. Dubl. 1873.

— On the Manners and Customs of the Ancient Irish, 3 vols., Lond., N. Y., 1873.

Ozanam, Antoine F.

La civilisation chrétienne chez les Francs. 6 ed. Paris 1893.

— Études germaniques : les Germains avant le Christianisme. 6 ed. Paris 1894.

Pflugk-Harttung, Julius A. G. von.

Die Schriften S. Patricks. Neue Heidelberger Jahrbücher, Bd. III, Heft, 1, 1893.

Plummer, Alfred.

The Churches in Britain before 1000. 2 vols. Lond. 1912.

Pryce, John.

The Ancient British Church. Lond. 1878.

Rhŷs, John.

Lectures on the Origin and Growth of Religion as Illustrated by Celtic Heathendom. Hibbert Lect. 1886, Lond. 1888.

Robinson, F. N.

The Irish Practice of Fasting. Putnam Anniversary Volume, Cedar Rapids, Iowa, 1909, p. 567 f.

Rolffs, Ernst.

Das Indulgenz-Edict des römischen Bischofs Kallist, in Texte u. Untersuchungen zur Gesch. der Althr. Litt. Bd. 11. Leips. 1893.

Rolleston, T. W.

The High Deeds of Finn. Lond. 1910.

Saltet, Louis.

Les Réordinations : étude sur le sacrament de l'ordre. Paris 1907.

Sandys, J. E.

A History of Classical Scholarship, 3 vols. Camb. 1903-1908.

Schmitz, Hermann Joseph.

Columban und das Busswesen im fränkischen Reich, Archiv. f. Kath. Kirchenrecht, Mainz 1883.

— Die Bussbücher und die Bussdisciplin der Kirche. Mainz 1883.

— Die Bussbücher und das Kanonische Bussverfahren nach handschriftlichen Quellen. Düsseldorf 1898.

— Seebass und Hinschius in ihrer Stellung zur Columban Frage, Archiv. f. Katholisches Kirchenrecht, Bd. LXXI, Heft 4. Mainz 1894.

Schrader, O.

Aryan Religion, Art. in Hastings Encyc. of Relig. and Ethics, Vol. II, p. 19.

Seebass, Otto.

Über Columba von Luxeuils Klosterregel und Bussbuch. Dresden, 1883.

— Poenitentiale Columbani. Zeitschrift f. Kirchengesch. Bd. XIV, p. 430 f. Gotha, 1894.

— Über das Regelbuch Beneditkts von Aniane. Zeitschr. für Kg., Bd. 15 (1895) p. 255 f.

— Ein bisher noch nicht veröffentlichtes Poenitential einer bobbienser Handschrift der Ambrosiana, Deutsche Zeitschr. f. Kirchenrecht, Bd. VI, Heft. 1, Freiburg u. Leipzig 1896.

Seebohm, Frederic.

The Tribal System of Wales. Lond. 1895.

Squire, Charles.
The Mythology of the British Islands. Lond. Glasg. and Dublin, 1905.
Stokes, Margaret.
Six Months in the Appennines. Lond. 1892.
— Three Months in the Forests of France. Lond. 1895.
Stokes, Whitley.
Sitting Dharna, Academy, Sept. 12, 1885, p. 169.
Stuffler, John.
Review of A. D'Ales. L'edit de Calliste. Zeitschr. f. cathol. Theol. 1914.
Thrall, Wm. Flint.
Vergil's Æneid and the Irish Imrama ; Zimmer's Theory. Modern Philology, Vol. XV, University of Chicago, Dec. 1917.
Tixeront, J.
Le Sacrament de Pénitence dans l'antiquité chrétienne. Paris, 1914.
Todd, James Henthorn.
St. Patrick Apostle of Ireland. Dublin 1864.
Traube, L.
Peronna Scottorum, ein Beitrag zur uberlieferungsgeschichte und zur Palaeographie des Mittelalters. Sitzungsber. d. Königl. Akad. zu München (philos.-histor.-classe) 1900, p. 469 f.
Ua Clerigh, Arthur.
The History of Ireland to the Coming of Henry II, Vol. I. Lond. 1908.
Ussher, James.
Whole works of the Reverend James Ussher, Lord Bishop of Armagh, 13 vols., ed. Chas. Richard Elrington. Dubl. 1847-1864.
Valroger, L. de.
Les Celtes et la Gaule celtique. Paris, 1879. Cf. Review by D'Arbois de Jubainville. Bibl. de l'école des Chartres, 1879, p. 198.
Vendryes, J.
De Hibernicis vocabulis quae a Latina lingua originem duxerunt, Paris 1902. Review by H. d'Arbois de Jubainville in Journal des Savants 1903, p. 162 f.
Warren, F. E.
Liturgy and Ritual of the Celtic Church. Oxf. 1881.

Walter, Ferdinand.
Das Alte Wales; ein Beitrag zur Völkerrechts und Kirchengeschichte. Bonn 1859.
Watkins, Oscar D.
A History of Penance, 2 vols. Lond. 1920.
Watson, W. J.
The Celtic Church in its Relation to Paganism. Celt. Rev. Vol. X, p. 263.
Williams, Hugh.
Christianity in Early Britain. Oxf. 1912.
Wood-Martin, W. G.
Traces of the Elder Faiths of Ireland, a Folk-lore Sketch. Lond., N. Y., Bombay, 1902.
— Pagan Ireland, an Archaeological Sketch. Lond., 1895.
Zimmer, Heinrich.
Nennius Vindicatus. Berl. 1893.
— Brendans Meerfahrt, Zeitschr. f. deutsches Alterthum Bd. 33. Berl. 1889. pp. 129-330 ; 257-338.
— Ueber die Bedeutung des irischen Elements für die Mittelalterliche Cultur. Preussische Jahrbücher, Bd. 59. (1887) pp. 27-59. tr. Jane L. Edmands, The Irish Element in Mediaeval Culture, N. Y. 1891.
— Pelagius in Irland. Berl. 1901.
— Die Keltische Kirche, article in Realencyclopädie für Protestantische Theologie und Kirche, Bd. 10, 1901. tr. A. Meyer, The Celtic Church in Britain and Ireland. Lond. 1902.
— Ueber direkte Handelsverbindungen Westgalliens mit Irland im Altertum und frühen Mittelalter, Sitzungsber. der. Berl. Acad. 1909, pp. 363-400, 430-476, 543-613, and 1910 pp. 1031-1119. Cf. Review by Krusch, B., Neues Archiv. der Gesellschaft f. ältere deutsche Geschichtskunde. Hanover u. Leipzig. Bd. 35, p. 274.

PRINCIPAL SERIAL PUBLICATIONS.

The Celtic Review, Edin., 1904 f.
Eriu, Journal of the School of Irish Learning, Dubl., 1894 f.
Revue celtique, Paris, 1870 f.
Revue d'histoire ecclésiastique, Louvain, 1900 f.
Revue d'histoire et de la littérature religieuses, Paris 1910 f.
Revue historique, Paris 1876.

Zeitschrift für celtische Philologie, Halle, 1897 f.
Zeitschrift für Kirchengeschichte, Gotha, 1877 f.

GENERAL WORKS OF REFERENCE.

The Catholic Encyclopedia, 16 vols., New York, 1908-1914.

The Dictionary of National Biography, 63 vols., 3 supplementary vols., Lond. 1885-1911.

The Encyclopedia Britannica, Eleventh Edition, 29 vols., Camb. 1911.

The Hastings Encyclopedia of Religion and Ethics, Edin. and New York, 1908 f.

Realencyclopëdie für protestantische Theologie und Kirche, third Edition, 24 vols., Leipz. 1896-1913.

The new Schaff- Herzog Encyclopedia of Religious Knowledge, 12 vols., New York and Lond., 1908-1912.

Smith, Sir W. and Wace H., Dictionary of Christian Biography, Literature, Sects and Doctrines, 4 vols., Lond. and Bost. 1877-1887.

Smith, Sir W. and Cheetham. S, Dictionary of Christian Antiquities. 2 vols, Lond. 1876-1880.

Vacant, A. et Mangenot, E., Dictionnaire de théologie catholique, Paris 1909 f.

CHAPTER I

Survey of the Literary Sources.

The extant penitential writings which emanate from the Celtic churches of Britain and Ireland may be indicated by the following titles. (The order followed in this list is, as will be shown below, at least approximately chronological).

1. — THE EARLIEST IRISH PENITENTIALS.

1) *The Canons of Saint-Patrick.*
2) *The Canones Hibernenses.*

2. — PENITENTIALS OF GILDAS AND FINNIAN.

3) *The Prefatio Gildae de Penitentia.*
4) *The Poenitentiale Vinniai.*

3. — PENITENTIALS CONNECTED WITH SAINT-DAVID.

5) *Excerpta quaedam de libro Davidis.*
6) *Canons of the Sinodus Aquilonalis Britanniae.*
7) *Canons of the Sinodus Luci Victoriae.*

4. — THE POENITENTIALE COLUMBANI

8) *The Poenitentiale Columbani (de poenitentiarum mensura taxanda).*

5. — SEVENTH CENTURY WELSH AND IRISH COLLECTIONS.

9) *The Canones Wallici.*
10) *The Collectio Canonum Hibernensis.*
11) *The Canones Adamnani.*

The Celtic origin of the above-named books and fragments will appear in the ensuing discussion. Notice may conveniently be taken here of a few additional works of the class, which though not produced in any portion of the Celtic church, yet give evidence of use by their authors of Celtic materials.

6. — Related Anglo-Saxon Penitentials.

12) *The Poenitentiale Theodori.*
13) *The Poenitentiale Bedae.*
14) *The Poenitentiale Egberti.*

7. — Related Frankish Penitentials.

15) *The Poenitentiale Cummeani.*
16) *The " Poenitentiale Bigotianum ".*
17) *The Poenitentiale Valicellanum I.*

The secondary list, comprising nos. 12 to 17, is selected from a considerably larger group of penitentials, the basis of selection being that of approximation to the Celtic type. Most of them are accessible to the reader in Wasserschleben[1], and Schmitz[2]. Nos. 12, 13 and 14 are of Anglo-Saxon, while nos. 15, 16 and 17 are of Frankish origin. These lists include all the works to be examined in this chapter. A few other penitentials which exhibit Celtic influence will be referred to in the development of the treatise.

We now proceed to examine these books in the order named, with a view to determine, wherever possible, authorship and date, and to describe the outstanding features of each work.

1. *Die Bussordnungen der abendländischen Kirche.*
2. *Bussbücher und Bussdisciplin der Kirche.*

1. — The Earliest Irish Penitentials.

1) *The Canons of Saint-Patrick.*

The Latin title is *Incipit sinodus episcoporum, id est Patricii, Auxilii, Iserníni.* This collection, consisting of 34 canons, is given by Haddan and Stubbs [1]. The editors argue from internal evidence that these canons are not to be ascribed to Patrick and his associates, but are a product of the eighth century. The evidence for this is, however, far from conclusive. The expression *mos antiquus* in can. 25 is taken as a proof of long-existing Irish church tradition, whereas the context leaves it quite possible that the reference is to a non-Irish antiquity. Again the date is set by Haddan and Stubbs at a time when the British and Irish churches had become estranged, for the reason that can. 33 refuses the privilege of ministry to British clerics in Ireland without letters of recommendation [2]. But is not the implication rather that properly accredited British clerics would be received without objection? The contrary hypothesis makes meaningless the qualification *sine epistola.* On the other hand Bury has shown, from a careful analysis of the references to the contents of this document in the *Collectio canonum Hibernensis* (c. A. D. 700), and from other tests, that the canons were very early accepted as the work of Patrick, and finds nothing to warrant their rejection [3]. Even the traces of a territorial episcopate shown in can. 30, Bury [4] believes to be no anachronism for the time of Patrick. He regards the canons as having been promulgated in a "conclave" of Patrick and his two distinguished lieutenants, probably in Leinster, where Auxilius and Iserninus were then or afterwards bishops. The three leaders would be likely to provide for the issue of instructions to the clergy in accordance

1. Councils and Ecumenical Documents, etc., Vol. II, p. 329 f.

2. *Clericus qui de Britanis ad nos venit sine epistola, etsi habitet in plebe, non licitum ministrare.*

3. Life of St. Patrick, p. 168 and p. 236 f.

4. Ibid., p. 243.

with the decisions arrived at, and the canons may well be simply the contents of a circular issued for this purpose.

The hypothesis that the document is a circular of instructions addressed to the clergy is well borne out by its contents. Seventeen of the thirty-four canons deal with the discipline of the clergy, and most of these are regulative rather than penitential. A number[1] prescribe simple excommunication, with no statement of a period of time. In the case of the major sins of manslaughter, fornication, and ressorting to the soothsayers, a period of penance is set. For each of these offences, which are grouped together as equal in heinousness, the term of penance is only one year. At the close of the year during which apparently the culprit is regarded as excommunicate, he is to bring witnesses and be reconciled by the priest[2]. Only half a year is required for theft[3]; if possible what has been stolen is to be restored.

The historic relations of this document will appear when we come to distinguish between the ecclesiastical and the cultural elements which entered into the penitential system. It is sufficient to note here the absence of some of the characteristics of the penitentials subsequently produced. There is as yet no recognition of the principle of composition, nor is reconciliation private, as later. Indeed the type of penance, so far as can be determined, corresponds more nearly to that employed in the early church than to that which was soon to develop in Ireland[4].

2) *The Canones Hibernenses.*

This is the name given to a group of six short sets of canons, all of which are contained in a Paris MS. together

1. Cans. 1, 6, 19, 21, 22, 26, 27, 32.
2. Can. 14.
3. Can. 15.
4. The thirty-one canons of a second synod attributed to St. Patrick are, on the evidence for their sources adduced by Bury (op. cit. p. 238 f.), compiled from the acts of synods held in Ireland in the seventh century in connection with the Roman reforms then introduced. Can. 3 of the series refers to the power of binding and loosing as vested in the abbot, and recommends mildness where there is evidence of repentance.

with other penitential materials yet to be noted, and in a MS. of Saint-Germain [1]. Of the six sections only the first four are penitential. No. I. bears the double title *de disputatione Hibernensis sinodi S. Gregorii Nasaseni sermo de innumerabilis peccatis incipit*; but contains nothing more than twenty-nine canons of a penitential character. Here the periods of penance assigned are on a much severer scale than in the canons of Saint-Patrick. For parricide the term is fourteen years [2]. For ordinary homicide it is seven or ten years and the authority of an otherwise unknown " Monochema " is cited [3]. The canon reads like an interpolation after the preceding one, where it is simply stated : *Haec est poenitentiae homicidi, vii anni in pane et aqua agitur*. The saint referred to may have given his dictum at a later date than that of the main part of the document. For adultery seven years is again the term prescribed, and seven and a half years is the heavy penalty for drinking blood or urine. For eating horse flesh it is four years [4]. Lighter offences, chiefly in eating and drinking, are given their proportional penalty of from five days to a year. The formula " *in pane et aqua* " is used to describe

1. Cod. Par. 3182, formerly Bigot. 89 ; Cod. Sangerm. 121. Published by Wasserschleben, op. cit., p. 136 f.

2. Can. I.

3. *Poenitentia homicidi vii anni in pane et aqua vel x, ut dicit Monochema*. Can. 3. (No Celtic saint of the name Monochema appears. — Is the reference to Mochumma, Bishop of St. Machay " probably in the fifth, sixth or seventh century ", mentioned by O'Hanlon, Lives of the Irish Saints, Vol. I, p. 580 ?)

4. Rendering *aequii*, as *equi* in can, 13 : Poenitentia esus carnis aequii iiii anni i. p. e. a. For other evidence of the confusion of these two words see Seybolt, R. T., Manuale Scholarium, Camb. 1921, p. 32, n. 7. The language might possibly be taken to refer, though by an awkward interpretation, to the eating of human flesh ; but for cannibalism the penalty seems too light. Among the ancient Saxons those suspected of witchcraft were sometimes eaten ; as appears from the punishment of the practice by Charlemagne with death. Cf. Capitularia De Partibus Saxoniae, VI. — Si quis a diabolo deceptus crediderit, secundum morem paganorum, virum aliquem aut feminam strigam esse homines commedere, & propter hoc ipsam incenderit, vel carnem ejus ad commedendum dederit, vel ipsam ederit, capitis sententia punietur. — Baluzius, Carol. Magn. Capitul., Vol. 6, Col. 251 ; mon. Germ. Hist., Leges, T. II, p. 68.

the penance in all but five of the twenty-nine canons; in most of them it is reduced to the initials *i. p. e. a.* Mention is made of the imposition of the bishop's hands at the close of a season of penance [1]. In this practice we recognize again the memory of the ecclesiastical penance of the fourth century. But in another respect we are startled to discover a new development in the direction of accommodation to national custom. We meet here the use of the word *ancilla* as a unit of payment. Can. 10 reads : *Praetium animae de perditionem filii et mulieris xii ancellae.* Can. 11 gives as a penalty for the same offence *xii anni in pane et aqua.* Thus *xii ancillae* are recognized as equivalent to *xii anni*, or one *ancilla* to one year of bread and water penance. This early instance of composition is of special interest because is not only illustrates the commutation of penance to payment, but gives us the basis of most later schedules of composition, viz., one *ancilla* (Irish *cumhal*, female slave) in lieu of one year [2]. No. II. of the collection is entitled *De arreis incipit. Arreum* is Latin for O. Ir. *arra*, substitute, compensation, or legal equivalent [3]. This section contains twelve canons, which constitute a list of equivalents among the familiar penalties, with the aim of shortening, by intensifying, the exercises of penance. Cans. 3 to 11 consist each of so many equivalents for one year's penance. In can. 3 this period is commuted to three days spent in the sepulchre of a saint, without food, drink, or sleep, singing psalms and praying the *horae*. Can. 4 assigns even more severe ascetic tests, to be performed, however, not in a sepulchre but in a church, during the same three-day period [4]. Genuflections are to accompany the singing and

1. Impositione manus episcopi, — can. 12.

2. Can. 9, which may be an interpretive gloss, states the value of an *ancilla* thus : — *xii altilia vel xiii sicli praetium unuscujusque ancillae.* Du Cange (Glossarium, t. vii, p. 470) says one *siclus* = two silver *denarii*. According to this the price of one *ancilla* would be equivalent to twenty-six silver *denarii*. But Seebohm would read *xii sicli*. See his discussion of the value of the *cumhal*, A. S. Law, p. 101 f.

3. K. Meyer translates the word "equivalent, substitute, commutation". — Rev. Celt., Vol. XV, 1894, p. 486 note.

4. "*sine cibu et potu et somno et vestitu sine sede*"

prayer. Can. 5 gives as the equivalent for a year's ordinary penance *xii dies et noctes super xii bucellos* (Cod. Par. 3182 has *bucellas*) *de tribus panibus, qui efficiuntur de tertia parte coaid siir troscho*[1]. And can. 7 extends the commuted time to one month *in dolore magno, ut dubibus sit de vita.* In other canons it is forty, fifty, or a hundred days.

The section is of the greatest importance as illustrating the principle of equivalents, by which any term of penance could be reduced by heightening the austerities undertaken. This form of composition is quite as prominent in the later history of penance as composition in money. The canons before us illustrate the attempt to follow this principle with no relaxation of actual pains inflicted, such as was of course involved in a money settlement.

The principle of composition is well illustrated by No. III. of the series, *Sinodus Hibernensis decrevit.* Indeed the section as a whole bears the aspect of a state code for criminal offences, and gives us a typical example of how composition operated in national customary law. Yet the canons have reference to ecclesiastical persons, and indicate the great respect in which the latter were held. As in the Brehon Law and in the Anglo-Saxon codes, the punishments are graded according to the rank of the party injured, not of the offender. The insertion, at the end of the set, of a *dictum* of Patrick which is also contained in the *Collectio canonum Hibernensis*[2] indicates that the canons were in all probability used by churchmen, and helps to visualize the adoption by the church of national legal customs. The dictum of Patrick is distinctly penitential, and makes an interesting modification on native law. Can. 1 ascribes to the "*sapientes*" the judgment that he who sheds the blood of a bishop or "excelsus princeps" or "scriba"[3] shall be crucified or render "*vii ancillas*". Can. 4, in the case in which the bishop is assaulted but his blood does not run down to the ground, provides for the amputation of the assailant's

1. I can obtain no explanation of the Old Irish words.
2. Coll. can. Hib., lib. xlviii, c. 5.
3. On the functions of this official see Reeves, Adamnan, p. 365.

hand, or half of the before-mentioned payment. For a priest the amount is half that for a bishop. The dictum of Patrick amends these regulations so as to abolish the penalties of death aud mutilation and substitute a period of penance. The alternative is now stated : *-vii ancillarum pretium reddat aut vii annis peniteat cum episcopo vel scriba.* We observe that here, as in can. 1., one *ancilla* is equivalent to one year's penance.

It would be vain to attempt precision in regard to the date of these canons, but the process which they picture of adaptation and amalgamation of Christian and pre-Christian methods of dealing with crimes, may safely be connected with the fifth century, when Christianity became general in Ireland. Further, the authenticity of the dictum of Patrick is measurably corroborated by its appearance in the *Coll. can. Hib.* where it is introduced by the phrase *Sinodus Hibernensis ait.* It cannot of course be claimed that this amendment was attached to the canons immediately on their compilation. It may have been attached at any time before c. 700, the approximate date of the *Collectio.* (See § 10) of the present chapter). If it is really Patrick's amendment that fact would itself be sufficient evidence of the amalgamation spoken of as taking place before the death of Patrick, c. 461 [1].

No. IV, *De Jectione*, contains only six canons, and deals with the offences of inhospitality and refusal to succour the helpless. For refusing succour to a Bishop, and so causing his death, the payment is *L ancillas.* As we should expect, this is commutable into the same number of years [2].

1. This is the date arrived at by Bury for Patrick's death. — Life of St. Patrick, p. 208. The principle expressed here is one which is very early recognized, as shown by canon I of the section, and it may have been approved by Patrick, or otherwise officially, during his life.

2. No. V, De canibus sinodus sapientium, has no ecclesiastical terminology. It contains only four canons, dealing with restitution to be made for the depradations of dogs, and for the killing of watchdogs. Cf. The Book of Aicill in Anc. Laws of Irel., Vol. III, p. 410 f. — Another section, *Item sinodus sapientia sic de decimis disputant*, deals with tithes.

2. — The Penitentials of Gildas and Finnian.

3) *The Prefatio Gildae de Penitentia.*

This set of regulations, in twenty-seven canons, appears, with nos. 5 and 6 following, in only one MS, the Parisian Codex 3182, which is one of the sources for the *Canones Hibernenses* [1]. There seems no reason to reject Gildas' authorship of the *Prefatio*, especially in view of that authors's known connection with penitential literature [2]. It is quoted in a number of subsequently written penitentials. Its contents, however, render it of comparatively slight value for the evolution of the penitential literature. Schmitz points out [3] that it resembles a monastic rule, and that most of its provisions could be fulfilled only in a cloister. The penalties include the nocturnal singing of psalms [4], and deprivation of the evening meal [5]. The *Prefatio Gildae* contains no provisions for the laity. It has reference however to clerics not under monastic rules [6]. Schmitz observes the lightness of the penalties imposed, in comparison with later Roman usage. One illustration of this will suffice. Can. 11 mentions, as subject to a penance of three forty-day periods, an offence for which from fifteen years to a life sentence is the punishment prescribed in the *Poenitentiale Haltigerii*, can. 54. An examination of the involved question of the dates of Gildas will be necessary when we attempt to determine the authorship of the *Poenitentiale Vinniai*.

1. Maassen has indicated (Gesch. der Quellen und der Literatur des Kanonischen Rechts, p. 786) that this codex, the known history of which goes back to a Norman cloister, is of Irish origin.
2. See below, p. 33 f.
3. Bussbücher, I, p. 495.
4. Can. 22, " *iii noctis horis stanto vigilet..... xxviii aut xxx psalmos canat.*
5. Can. 10, *coena privatur.*
6. Can. 3, *Si vero sine monachi voto presbyter aut diaconus peccaverit, sicut monachus sine gradu sic peniteat.*

4) *The Poenitentiale Vinniai.*

Wassesrchleben has published this weighty document from an eighth century MS (Sangerm. 121), two MSS of the ninth century, and one of the eleventh or twelfth [1]. Let us address ourselves to the question of its authorship.

The name " Vinniaus " appears as " Vennianus " in a letter addressed by Columbanus to Gregory the Great [2]. These forms are apparently variations of the more common " Finnianus " [3], which also take the forms " Finian ", " Finan ", " Fintan ", " Findian ". Two outstanding Irish saints of the sixth century bore this name, St. Finnian of Clonard and St. Finnian of Moville. It is to the former of these that Wasserschleben would ascribe the penitential, while he admits that no direct evidence exists for the identification [4]. Schmitz opposes this view, and uses a twelfth century *Vita S. Fridiani* given by Colgan, to prove that Finnian of Moville brought penitential canons from Rome [5]. The argument of Schmitz is by no neans convincing, however, and is a striking example of that writer's determination to assert a Roman origin for the penitential literature.There is no basis for the identification of Colgan's St. Fridian of Lucca with this or any Finnian, an identification which, suggested by Colgan, is assumed without proof by Schmitz, who simply calls the " Fridianus " of Colgan's text "Finnian ", throughout the paragraph which he professes to quote. Nor are the " canons " which St. Fridian brought from Rome stated in the *Vita* to have been penitential canons. It has been argued, on the cóntrary, that

1. Wasserschl., *op. cit.*, p. 118 f.

2. *Vennianus auctor Gildam de his interrogavit et ellegantissime illi rescripsit.* — *Epistolae Columbani*, éd. Gundlach, Wilh., in *Mon. Ger. Hist., Ep. Merov. et Karol. Aevi*, Tom. I, p. 159.

3. Bolland, *Acta Sanct.*, Tom. VII (Mart. I.), p. 391, *et al.*

4. " Wiewohl wir nicht die geringste Notiz von einem Poenitential dieses Vinniaus haben ". — Wasserschl., *op. cit.*, p. 10.

5. Schmitz, Bussbücher, I, p. 448-449. — Colgan, Acta SS. Hib., p. 642 f.

they may have been copies of the Gospels, to which the name " canon " was sometimes applied [1].

Neither Wasserschleben nor Schmitz, then, has succeeded in establishing any real probability for either Finnian. The case for Finnian of Moville, however, has been given the support of another investigator [2]. Seebass at first tried to solve the question in agreement with Wasserschleben, by resorting to an elder Gildas who d. 512, as the author referred to by Columbanus. He found support for this distinction in Ussher, who in his *Britannicarum Ecclesiarum Antiquitates* broke up the *Vitae S. Gildae* so as to produce a " Gildas Albanius " prior to " Gildas Badonicus " author of the *De Excidio Britanniae* [3]. Seebass, however, subsequently altered this opinion, and identified " Vinniaus " of the penitential with Finnian of Moville, and the Gildas of Columban's letter with " Gildas Badonicus " [4]. The so-called " Gildas Albanius " may be excluded from our discussion, not only because Seebass discarded the idea of his connection with the Finnian of the penitential, but because he is probably to be excluded from history [5]. The " Vennianus " of Columban's letter, may fairly be assumed to be the author of the penitential, since on the one hand, Columban here calls him an " author ", and, on the other hand, the *Poenit. Col.*, in its authentic portions, shows (as we shall see in a later paragraph) a copious use of the *Poenit. Vinn.*

According to Columban this Vennianus asked for and obtained from Gildas a ruling on the question of monks who through exaggerated zeal disobey their abbots and leave the

1. Todd, St. Patrick, Apostle of Ireland, p. 123; Stokes, Tripartite Life, Vol. II, p. 567; Anc. Laws of Ireland. Vol. I, pp. 16, 18.

2. Über Columba von Luxeuils Klosterregel u. Bussbuch, p. 59.

3. Whole Works of the Most Revd. James Ussher, Lord Archbishop of Armagh, Vol. V, p. 506, Vol. VI, p. 520. (The *Antiquitates*, which occupies Vols. V and VI of the edition, was originally published in 1639.) Cf. Boll., Acta SS., Tom. III (Jan 3), p. 567 f.

4. Seebass, Das Poenitentiale Columbani, in Zeitschr. f. Kg., Bd. XIV, (1894) p. 436-437.

5. Bradshaw, Collected Papers, p. 417 f. — Lloyd, History of Wales, Vol. I, p. 134.

monasteries for a hermit life [1]. Seebass finds in Haddan and Stubbs [2] an " epistle " of Gildas, which he believes to be Gildas' reply to the request of Finnian. The editors of this work argue [3] that the collection which includes this letter, having been preserved in Ireland only, must have been written in Ireland, and therefore assign a date during Gildas' conjectured visit there between 565 and 570. Such a date would exclude Finnian of Clonard as the correspondent of Gildas, for this Finnian must have died about 550. Seebass, following Reeves [4], ascribes his death to 549. The Annals of the Four Masters [5] give 548. It is purely by this process of inference, and not on the ground of any historical connection of Finnian of Moville with Gildas or with the penitential literature, that the conclusion is drawn of the latter's authorship [6]. But there are weak links in the chain of inference followed by Seebass. In fact all the links are weak. In the first place, the argument of Haddan and Stubbs that because extant copies of the supposed fragment of Gildas appear in Ireland alone it must have been written in Ireland, falls to the ground when we remember the circumstances. Granting Seebass' assumption that this is the answer of Gildas to the inquiry of Finnian, we have surely as much reason to think that it was written in Britain as in Ireland. It is not the writer but the recipient of a letter for which request had been made, whom we should expect to treasure the instructions it contained and secure its preservation.

While we are without evidence of any acquaintance between Gildas and Finnian of Moville, we are assured of the close

1. Ep. Columb., loc. cit.
2. Councils, etc., Vol. I, p. 110. De monachis qui veniunt de loco viliore ad perfectiorem, etc.
3. *Op. cit.*, p. 103.
4. Adamnan, Appendix to Preface, p. lxxxiii.
5. Apparently used by Schmitz, although he cites instead the Annals of Ulster, — Bussb., I, p. 498.
6. Schmitz, in the passage just cited, seeks to enforce the argument for Finnian of Moville on the ground that he was a bishop while his namesake was not. But other penitential authors, such as Columban, were not bishops.

association of the Welsh saint with Finnian of Clonard. According to the Lismore Life of Finnian of Clonard the latter was associate and pupil of David, Gildas and " Cathmael ", (Cadoc ?) during a thirty-year residence in Britain prior to the founding of Clonard (c. 520 or 530) [1]. Even by a liberal deduction from the period here assigned [2] for his British studies we may safely trust the uniform tradition of his connection with Gildas. The instruction contained in the so-called epistle of Gildas cited by Seebass, may well have been the fruit of this association, and Finnian of Clonard may have received it from his friend and teacher after his return to Ireland and during his active monastic work there. This swings back the possible date from Haddan and Stubbs' 562 to c. 520-550. The death of Finnian of Clonard can hardly have been much before 550. If we are to accept the notice in the *Chronicon Scottorum*, and in the Lismore Life of Finnian, Finnian died of the plague at the close of the visitation of 547-550 [3]. But it is worth mentioning that the Annals of Innisfallen, to which O'Curry gives a high authority [4] place the death of Gildas at 562 and that of Finnian of Clonard at 552.

Again, Seebass assumes dates for both the birth and death of Gildas which are in all probability later than those which a critical account must assign. The date of Gildas' birth is by his own statement involved with that of the Battle of Badon Hill. This event, Gildas tells us [5], took place " in the forty-fourth year ", which was the year of his birth, — *qui et meae nativitatis est*. Now the date usually assigned for this battle,

1. Finnian spends " thirty years studying together with the British elders who were along with him.." On one occasion, though an " unknown youth, " he acts as arbiter in a dispute between David and Gildas.— Stokes, Lives of Saints from the Book of Lismore, p. 223.

2. Colgan. Vita S. Finniani, in Acta SS. Hib., p. 394 makes him thirty years of age on going to Britain and makes him remain there only eight years.

3. " Findian died at Clonard for the sake of the people of the Gael, that they might not all die of the Yellow Plague ". — Stokes, Lives of Saints from the Book of Lismore, p. 229.

4. Lectures on the Materials of Anc. Ir. Hist., p. 75 f.

5. *De Excidio Britanniae*, 26.

viz 516, rests upon the frail evidence of the ninth century *Annales Cambriae*, where it is said that Gildas was born in the year 72, i, e, the seventy-second year from the beginning of the *Annales*, conjecturally 444. (444 + 72 = 516.)

But the associates of Gildas, e. g. David and Cadoc, with whom his name is often linked, as well as Finnian of Clonard, require an earlier date than this for his birth [1]. And Bede, who used a copy of Gildas, in a passage based on the *De Excidio* [2] makes the date forty-four years from the settlement of the Saxons. As Bede's date for this event is 449, this testimony yields the date 493 for the birth of Gildas. M. Arthur de la Borderie has presented a strong argument for this date [3]. The phrase by which Bede determines the date is " *adventus eorum in Britanniam* ". M. de la Borderie regards this phrase as having been simply copied from the text of Gildas which Bede possessed. It has been dropped, he argues, from the extant text, leaving the sense incomplete, but with its restoration the sense is restored. The emendation is both brilliant and reasonable. If it is permitted it settles the date of Gildas' birth on the fairly reliable ground of his own declaration.

The date 516, or any later date, would not only make impossible the relationship of senior and junior on the part of Gildas and Finnian, but would render highly improbable any relation, between the two men. Independently of this consideration, and also apparently of the argument of Borderie, the later date for Gildas has been discarded by such recent writers as Lloyd and Thurneysen [4]. Williams accepts de la Borderie's date, but regards the phrase " adventus etc. " as Bede's own interpretation of the incomplete statement of Gildas [5]. Others

1. Cf. *Vita Davidis*, Boll. A. SS. Tom. VII (Mart. I), p. 38.
2. Hist. eccles., I, 16.
3. Rev. Celt., Vol. VI, 1883, p. I f. — " La date de la naissance de Gildas ".
4. Lloyd History of Wales, Vol. I, p. 136. Thurneysen, R., reviewing Mommsen's edition of Gildas and Nennius, in the M. G. H. — Zeitschr. f. Celt. Phil. Bd. I (1897), p. 147.
5. Cymmrodorion Record Series, No. 3, part I, p. 63. Cf. his Christianity in Early Britain, p. 367.

have advanced a still earlier date. Baring-Gould and Fisher [1] explain Gildas 26 so as to make the forty-four years measure the period between the victory of Ambrosius Aurelianus, mentioned in the previous section, and the Battle of Mount Badon. The dates of two events are given as 476 and 520 respectively, and the birth of Gildas is connected with the *former* date. This can hardly be regarded as the obvious meaning of the passage, and it does not account for Bede's *adventus eorum in Britanniam.* We know nothing directly of the date of the birth of Finnian of Clonard. He may easily have been a few years junior to a man born in 493. While the date 476 for Gildas would make more certain the possibility of his being Finnian's adviser, that of 493 is early enough to satisfy the relationship referred to, and to make possible the advice sent by Gildas to Finnian, which is mentioned by Columbanus [2].

As to Finnian of Moville, there is no reason to connect him either with Gildas or with Columbanus. Of noble or royal Ulster parentage, he was born and labored in Ulster [3]. His more famous namesake of Clonard was like Columban a Leinster man. His fame would certainly be known to Columban. In 550 Columban was a boy about ten years of age. His first teacher was Sinnell, a pupil of Finnian of Clonard [4]. He subsequently became a pupil of Comgall of Bangor, one of Finnian of Clonard's " Twelve Disciples ", and thus became heir to the teaching of this Finnian. Comgall was Dalaradian Pict;

1. Lives of the British Saints, Vol. III, p. 101 f.

2. Either 476 or 493 would agree with the probable date of Gildas' death, which is rather before than after 570. In the Annals of Tigernach, ed. Whitley Stokes in Rev. Celt., Vol 17 (1896), p. 149, under date apparently of 570, is the line

Ite Cluana Credil Gillasque (quierunt)
(Ite of Cluain Credil and Gildas died.)

The corresponding records inserted here by Stokes from the Chronicon Scottorum, the Annals of Innisfallen, and the Four Masters, are respectively 571, 562 and 569. The Bollandists give Gildas' dates as 493-583. — A. SS., Tom. III (Jan. 3), p. 568.

3. Cf. John O'Hanlon, Lives of the Irish Saints, Vol. IX, p. 254.

4. Jonas, Vita Columbani 3, in Krusch, *Mon. Ger. Hist., Scriptores, Rer. Mer.* Tom. IV, p. 69.

in early life he is said to have studied with David and Gildas [1].

These facts render it highly probable that the author we are seeking for the *Poenitentiale Vinniaï* is no other than the " Tutor of the Saints of Ireland ", Finnian of Clonard. His authorship of the penitential explicitly removes all trace of direct and contemporary continental influence on that document, such as would attach to it if it were the work of Finnian of Moville. For the latter is credited with having visited Rome and brought back with him certain writings [2]. But the former is definitely dissociated from Rome in the best source we have for his life. The Lismore life of Findian (as his name is there spelled), states that after spending thirty years in Britain he had a desire to go to Rome, but God's angel came to him and said : " What would be given to thee at Rome will be given to thee here. Go and renew faith and belief in Ireland after Patrick ". So he returned to Ireland according to God's will [3]. Thus the penitential of Finnian is an Irish product, written before the middle of the sixth century by an Irishman under Welsh influence, and with no Roman associations.

We now turn to an examination of the contents of this important penitential. It is in fifty-three canons or paragraphs, and divides itself naturally at the end of can. 34. The first part deals with the offences of clerics, the second with those of the laity. The opening paragraph makes a general statement about the guilt and penance connected with sins ot the heart [4].

At the same time the principle of a mechanical prescription of so much penance for so much sin prevails ; and the differentiation of sins and penalties is more minute than in the documents previously reviewed. In the case of clerics,

1. Williams, Cymmrodorion Record Series, No. 3, part 2, p. 274.

2. Colgan, A. SS. Hib., p. 643, — Cf. Todd, St. Patrick, p. 101 f.

3. Stokes, Lives of Saints, etc., p. 224. — The version of the story in the Cod. Salmanticensis is slightly different. See De Smedt et de Backer, A. SS. Hib., col. 194.

4. *Si quis in corde suo per cogitationem peccaverit et confestim penituerit, percutiat pectus suum et petat a Deo veniam et satisfaciat, ut sanus sit.*

penalties are increased where there is scandal. One year of penance is prescribed for fornication which is kept secret (can. 10); the same crime when publicly known is punished by a six-year term (can. 21). Can. 25 prescribes one year for theft by a cleric, " *et reddat quadruplum proximo suo* ". Penalties for clerics are generally considerably higher than for laymen. Part of the penance consists, in certain instances, of a payment to be made to a priest. A layman who is guilty of fornication and the shedding of blood, when he turns from his evil ways, is required to go unarmed and to be deprived of his wife for three years, during the first year of which his diet is to consist of bread and water. At the end of the three year period he is to give money to the priest before being restored to communion [1], and provide a supper for the " servants " of God ". (can. 35.) Apparently this is what is meant again in can. 36 by " *det helimosinam pro anima sua* ". Considerable emphasis is laid upon sexual sins. " *Puellae Dei* " are specially protected. The permanence of marriage, and continence within the married state, are guarded under penalties.

The value of penance as absolving from guilt is forcibly asserted in can. 47, where by way of comment on the pennance assigned for the neglect of a child by its parents the remark is made : " *quia nullum crimen, quod non potest redimi per penitentiam quamdiu sumus in hoc corpore* ".

Finnian closes his booklet with a paragraph addressed to his " most dear brothers " in which he claims for the work the sanction of scripture and of the opinions of the learned [2]. He is manifestly conscious of formulating rather than of originating a tradition. His penitential probably does little more than codify current usage. His " *doctissimi* " doubtless included some of his notable Welsh and Irish contemporaries. That his principles constituted a total departure both from those of

1. *pecuniam dabit pro redemptione anime sue et fructum poenitentie in manu sacerdotis.*

2. *Haec, amantissimi fratres, secundum sententiam scripturarum vel opinionem quorundam doctissimorum, pauca de penitentiae remediis vestro amore compulsus supra possibilitatem meam potestatemque temptavi scribere.* Can. 53.

the ancient church and from those of earlier and contemporary non-Celtic monasticism, will appear in a later chapter [1].

3. — Penitentials connected with St. David.

5) *Excerpta quaedam de libro Davidis.*
6) *Canons of the Sinodus Aquilonalis Britanniae.*
7) *Canons of the Sinodus Luci Victoriae.*

The documents numbered 5, 6 and 7, of the penitential series given above, form a group of canons of Welsh synods connected with the name of St. David, Patron of Wales. Wasserschleben [2] has adopted the date given by Ussher [3] and by the Bollandists [4] for the death of David, viz., the year 544. Haddan and Stubbs, on the unreliable evidence of the *Annales Cambriae* [5], place the event in the year 601 [6]. J.E. Lloyd inclines toward a date of 588 or 589 [7]. But he does not appear to have seen the argument of Nicholson [8] who brings very strong palaeographical and chronological evidence for a date of 547.

Rhygyfarch, or Ricemarchus, who wrote (c. 1090) the

1. See below, ch. II.
2. Bussordn., p. 9.
3. Works, Vol. V, p. 274.
4. A.SS., Tom. 7 (Mart. I), pp. 40-41.
5. On the character of these annals see Nicholson's discussion in the Zeitschrift f. Celt. Philol., Bd. 8 (1910), p. 121. (" The *Annales Cambriae* and their so-called Exordium. ")
6. Councils, etc., Vol. I, p. 116.
7. Hist. of Wales, Vol. 1, p. 152 f.
8. Zeitschr. f. Celt. Philol., Bd. 6 (1908), p. 541 f. The article (" Remarks on the date of the First Settlement of the Saxons in Britain "), is like that just cited in Bd. 8 of the same publication, directed against the conclusions of A. Anscombe whose long discussion of the date of the Saxon Invasion appeared in the Zeitschrift Bd. 3. (Anscombe's radical revision of dates would give us David's death in 501, a palaeographical restoration for the 601 of the *Ann. Camb.*).

earliest extant account of David [1], makes David the dominating figure at certain Welsh synods [2] and notes concerning the canons of these synods that they were promulgated by David as bishop. The language used [3] is of a piece with the context, in which extravagant assertion is made of the authority of David in the British Church. It is impossible to assign specific dates for the synods in question. Haddan and Stubbs give 569 as the date of the second of the two synods; but this is based on the *Annales Cambriae*, and is excluded on the evidence for an earlier date for the death of David. Ricemarchus admits of a lapse of time, perhaps of years, between the synods [4]. The Bollandist account dates the Synod of Brevi 519, and that of the Grove of Victory 529, and these dates are followed by Schmitz [5]. Ricemarchus, writing at Menevia, is not acquainted with the canons of these synods, and believes them no longer extant. His view of the purpose of the synods is that the were called for the suppression of Pelagianism. But in France, apparently through Breton channels, there have been preserved what purport to be the canons in question, and they give a different aspect to the work of the synods. They indicate that the object in view was not the suppression of heresy, but the reform of the discipline of the Church.

With the canons of the *Sinodus Aquilonalis Britanniae* (conjecturally that called by Ricemarchus "*Brevi*") and those of the *Sinodus Luci Victoriae* (called by Ricemarchus "*Sinodus Victorie*") are connected in the Paris MS 3182 a group of similar canons which may safely be regarded as belonging to the same reform movement, called *Excerpta quaedam de libro Davidis* [6]. The first-mentioned of the group

1. The document is published in Rees, Cambro-British Saints, p. 117 f, with Eng. tr. p. 418 f.
2. *Op. cit.*, p. 139.
3. *Quae ore firmavit solus ipse episcopus sua sancta manu litteris mandavit.*
4. *Succedente temporum serie, op. cit.*, p. 139.
5. Bussbücher, I, p. 490-491.
6. Marteneet Durand, Thesaurus Novus, Tom. IV, col. 9 ; Wasserschl. Bussordn., p. 103 ; Haddan and Stubbs, Councils, etc., Vol. I, p. 118.

consists of seven canons, the second of nine and the third of sixteen. In all three there is little conflict and little repetition; nor on the other hand, is there any evidence of well-planned arrangement. Certain passages suggest that the later of the two synods made somewhat drastic changes in the direction of greater severity, upon the provisions of the earlier synod. *Sin. Aq. Brit.* can. 4, sets a graded scale of penance for theft of food, beginning with the period of a quadragesima for a first offence. *Sin. Luc. Vict.* makes a general rule for theft, and extends to one year the penalty for one offence. A peculiar feature of the *Sin. Luc. Vict.* is the final canon [1] which gives an automatic scale of reduction of penalties for the laity in comparison with those assigned for the clergy.

The *Excerpta* begin with four canons on drunkenness. The quest for the inner motive, which we saw to be characteristic of the *Poenit. Vinn.* appears here even in the case of drunkenness. Can. 2 assigns fifteen days for drunkenness "*per ignorantiam*", forty days where it takes place "*per negligentiam*", and three quadragesimas if "*per contemptum*" [2].

The contact between penitential method and native law appears in the *Excerpta*. Can. 6 requires compensation to the parents of a dishonored virgin or widow, in addition to a year's penance [3]. But, as in the dictum of Patrick attached to the *Canones Hibernenses*, the church can commute this payment to a penance period. "*Si non habuerit dotem iii annos poeniteat*", the canon cited adds. Thus the "dos" for seduction could be commuted into two years of penance.

The nocturnal singing of psalms, as a penitential exercise, is prescribed in canons 8 and 9 of this set. It is to be observed that the form of prescription apparently precludes the act of confession between the offence and the penance [4]. The penance

1. *Totum hoc quod diximus, si post votum perfectionis fecerit homo, si autem ante votum, annus diminuitur de omnibus* (*his tribus*, ad. Martene); *de reliquis vero, ut debet, minuitur, dum non vovit.*

2. Cf. Cans. 8, 9, where the distinction *cum voluntate* and *sine voluntate* is made for pollution during sleep.

3. *Dotem det parentibus ejus, et anno uno peniteat.*

4. e. g., can. 8. *Qui in sompnis cum voluntate pollutus est, surgat canatque*

in this case was evidently not imposed by a confessor, but assumed by the offender; and the canon obviously applies to monks and clerics who might be supposed to know its terms.

An unusual penalty appears in can. 11, where for a group of grave offences the head is to be laid on the earth during one year of penance, the second year on a stone and the third on a board.

4. — The Poenitentiale Columbani.

The *Poenitentiale Columbani* or *Liber S. Columbani abbatis de poenitentiarum mensura taxanda* [1], has been the subject of considerable discussion. Wasserschleben regarded it as written on the Continent and at most only partially the work of. Columban [2]. Schmitz found no evidence to connect it with Columban, but held it to be written in the eighth century by some monk who was a follower of Columban's rule [3]. Columban, Schmitz believed, cannot be credited with the authorship of any penitential. Seebass, however, had no difficulty in demolishing the argument of Schmitz in his particular, and establishing an external probability that Columban wrote a penitential. This he did [4] mainly by reference to the accepted writings of Columban and to the *Vita Columbani* of Jonas of Bobbio [5]. Indeed one need hardly go beyond the *Vita* and the letter of Columbanus to Gregory I. in order to reach this

viii psalmos; et in die illo in pane et aqua vivat. Sin autem, xxx psalmos canat.

1. For the text see Wasserschl. Bussordn, p. 353 f.; Schmitz, Bussbücher I., p. 588 f.; Seebass, Zeitschr. f. Kg., Bd. 14 (1895), p. 441 f., The work was first published in 1667 by Th. Sirinus from the till then unpublished edition of Patrick Fleming made in 1626 from one of the two Bobbio MSS. in which the work is extant. *Patricii Flemingi collectanea sacra seu S. Columbani acta et opuscula*, Lyons, 1667. A copy of this collection is given in Migne, Patr. Lat., Tom. 80, col. 209 f.

2. Bussordn., p. 54.

3. Bussbücher Bd. I, p. 592 f.

4. *Op. cit.*, p. 430 f.

5. Ed. Bruno Krusch, in *M.G.H.*, *Scriptores Rerum Merovingicarum*, Tom. 4, pp. 64-108.

result. In the *Vita* Jonas twice refers to the *poenitentiae medicamenta* employed by Columban. In one reference he informs us of the previous neglect of penance in Gaul [1]. In the other he notes that the people came from all quarters to Columban for penance [2]. The evidence is convincing that Jonas regarded Columban as the restorer of penitential discipline in the Vosges region; even more convincing perhaps than if Jonas mentioned any particular penitential work from his hand, for in that case we might have suspected that the references to the exercise of penance by Columban were suggested by an acquaintance with a book ascribed to Columban. Again the acquaintance of Columban with the work of Gildas and of Vinniaus [3] rests on passages in the letter to Gregory which have to do with questions of discipline. These passages therefore reinforce our assurance that Columban was interested in promoting penance among his followers, and at the same time indicate his respect for Celtic penitential writers of the previous generation.

But if this is the case, it would then be surprising if he were not also the author of a penitential. By the time of his activity, the last decade of the sixth century, the use of penitential books was already an established Celtic custom, as the works ascribed to earlier author's show. We have every reason to think that Columban followed the example of his honored Celtic masters, and compiled some penitential work.

There are certain presuppositions with which we are justified in approaching any document claiming to be a penitential written by him. First we should except to find in it, if it is genuine, some evidence of a use of the models provided by those Celtic masters who are referred to in his correspondence. The failure of the document to exhibit this feature might not be a conclusive argument against its genuineness, but it would at once create a serious doubt. Again, we should not be surprised to find traces of the influence of other Celtic

1. *Vix vel paucis in illis reperiebantur locis. Vita* 11.
2. *Undique ad poenitentiae medicamenta plebes concurrere. Vita* 17.
3. See above, p. 33 f.

writers of penitentials, who had preceded Columban. And furthermore, our assurance of the genuineness of the work would be greatly increased by finding in the document some evidence of the conditions of the time and place of Columban's labors. Let us observe how the *Poenitentiale Columbani* meets these presuppositions.

Let us note, in the first place, the general structure of this work. It consists of 42 canons, which fall into five natural divisions. These five sections are marked off by short explanatory headings, which occur as follows :—

1) Can. 1 consists of a statement of the purpose of a penitential work : *Poenitentia vera est poenitenda non admittere, sed admissa deflere. Sed quia hanc multorum fragilitas, ut non dicam omnium, rumpit, mensurae noscendae sunt poenitentiae, quarum sic ordo a sanctis traditur patribus, ut juxta magnitudinem culparum etiam longitudo statuatur poenitentiarum.*

2) Between can. 8 and can. 9 occur the words : *Haec de causis casualibus ; ceterum de minutis morum inconditorum.*

3) Between can. 12 and can. 13 is inserted an extended paragraph introducing the next section : *Diversitas culparum diversitatem facit poenitentiarum ; nam et corporum medici diversis medicamenta generibus componunt...* So also the spiritual physician should with various kinds of treatment heal the wounds, diseases, pains, sicknesses and infirmities of souls. The regulations to follow are promulgated *juxta seniorum traditiones et juxta nostra ex parte intelligentiam.*

4) Between can. 24 and can. 25, the division is marked by the words : *Sed haec de clericis et monachis mixtim dicta sint ; caeterum de laicis.*

5) Between can. 37 and 38. The section following is headed : *Postremo de minutis monachorum agendum est sanctionibus.*

It becomes evident at once that the principal break in the document occurs at the end of can. 12. The intervening paragraph here is of the nature of an independent introduction, and this suggests that we are dealing not with one continuous work, but with two books in juxtaposition. This will become a more evident fact as we proceed ; but we may here for the sake of convenience anticipate the data that are to follow and adopt the device of the several editors of the penitential, who speak of cans. 1-12 as *Poenit. Col. A* and the remaining portion of the document as *Poenit. Col. B.* 1-30.

The analysis now to be made is intended in the first place to prove Columban's authorship of *Poenit. Col. B* [1], and in the second place to bring some hitherto unnoticed arguments for ascribing *Poenit. Col. A* likewise to his authorship, while probably written at different date from B.

The following order of treatment will place before us the evidence that is necessary :

1) Correspondences and divergences between *Poenit. Col. B* and *Poenit. Vinn.*

2) Correspondences and divergences between *Poenit. Col. B* and the *Pref. Gild.*

3) Correspondences between *Poenit. Col. B* and other Celtic documents.

4) Remarks on the place of origin of *Poenit. Col. B.*

A similar treatment of *Poenit. Col. A*, and a comparison of the contents of A and B will place before us the data for favoring Columban's authorship of *A*.

1) Correspondences and divergences between *Poenit. Col. B* and *Poenit. Vinn.*

Col. B 1 and Vinn. 23. Col. B omits stages and details of ten year penance for homicide given in Vinn. Otherwise provisions are identical.

Col. B 2 and Vinn. 12. As in Col. A 4, Col. B has here *si quis* for *si quis clericus* in Vinn. Col. B omits stages and details of penance.

Col. B 4 and Vinn. 11. Similar and in part identical provisions *re* adultery of clerics.

Col. B 5 and Vinn. 22. Col. omits the remark of Vinn. on

1. With the exception of B 26-30. This portion may simply be left out of our argument. It is entirely monastic, and may be an appended fragment of a monastic rule. Seebass argues for its retention as a part of *B*, by an ingenious use of a parallel with Cassian's *Collatio*, XX. Zeitschr. f. Kg., Bd. 18 (1898), pp. 70-71. It contains no penitential regulations. For the opinion of Seebass that the closing section of the Regula Coenobialis

the difficulty of pardon for perjury, and the special conditions imposed. Both assign a seven year penance, with no more taking of oaths.

Col. B 6 and Vinn. 18-20. Phraseology different, provisions in part identical.

Col. B 7 and Vinn. 25-26. One year's penance for theft by a cleric in both. Vinn. has *et reddat quadruplum proximo suo;* Col. B omits *quadruplum.* For habitual offences both assign three years.

Col. B 8 and Vinn. 27. Seven years penance in both for returning to a mistress after vows. Some phrases identical, others similar.

Col. B 9 and Vinn. 8, 9. Col. B appears to condense the more extended statement of Vinn.

Col. B 11 and Vinn. 7. Col B changes penalty for concupiscence from forty days to one year.

Col. B 13 and Vinn. 35. General structure suggests Col. B modelled in Vinn.

Col. B 16 and Vinn. 36. Both prescribe one year for adultery. Col. B adds permission of marriage *si virgo virgini conjunctus est*, with a year's penance to follow.

Col. B 20 and Vinn. 22. Col. B follows Vinn. roughly in demanding liberation of a slave and liberal alms for perjury.

Col. B 21 and Vinn. 9. Both demand forty days penance with damages for assault. Col. B adds provision for the injured during his convalescence [1].

Col. B 23 and Vinn. 17. Col. B follows Vinn. and differs from Col. B 11 in assigning forty days for concupiscence.

In the above comparison it appears that no less than fourteen out of the twenty-five capitula in the document under consideration show a marked resemblance to passages in the *Poenit. Vinn.* It will readily be admitted that the resemblance, in some cases involving a common phraseology, is not accidental. It is sufficient for our purpose to indicate that the

ascribed to Columban really belongs here, see his Über Columba von Luxeuils Klosterregel und Bussbuch, p. 49, and p. 49 below.

1. This may well be copied from Irish law. Cf. The Ancient Laws of Ireland, Vol. III, pp. 337, 471, 481: Vol. V, pp. 301, 307, 333, etc.

Poenit. Col. B preserves a memory of the *Poenit. Vinn.* But the facts certainly suggest more than a memory. They entirely justify the remark of Seebass, that the author had an exemplar of the *Poenit. Vinn.* before him [1]. At the same time there is no slavish copying of the earlier writer. The differences are marked. Not a single canon is identical in all respects. We are reminded by our comparison of the note in which the author of *Col. B* describes the genesis of the work: *juxta seniorum traditiones et juxta nostram ex parte intelligentiam.* These words indeed form a perfect description both of the indebtedness to Finnian and of the independence and originality which characterise the book. The author's *seniorum traditiones* are manifestly not the usages of remoter church fathers, but those of his own Celtic masters, foremost among whom stands Finnian. Even in his independence he is honoring the spirit of the *Poenit. Vinn.* whose author freely says: "If anyone will propose better rules we will accept and follow them [2]." It is worth remembering that Columban's first teacher was Sinell, a pupil of Finnian of Clonard [3].

2) Correspondences and divergences between *Poenit. Col. B* and *Pref. Gild.*

It is not possible here to show such an array of similar provisions as has just been observed; but there are considerable traces of influence. In *Col. B 12* the offence of vomiting the sacrament, through drunkenness or gluttony (*voracitas*), is made punishable by a term of three *quadragesimae.* In the *Pref. Gild.* 7 the same offence calls for a penalty of "vii superpositiones" [4] and deprivation of supper. Again *Pref. Gild.* 9

1. Über Columba von Luxeuils Klosterregel und Bussbuch, p. 57.
2. *Poenit. Vinn.* Can. 53.
3. Jonas, Vita S. Col. 3rd ed. Krusch, Script. Rer. Merov. (Mon. Germ. Hist.), Vol. IV, p. 69. Margaret Stokes, Three Months in the Appenines, p. 109-110.
4. Seebass, in another connection, thinks *superpositio* equivalent to *superpositio silentii.* Zeitschr. f. Kg. Bd. 18 (1898), p. 65. This seems more probable than *superpositio jejunii* (Cf. Sin. Elvir can XXIII), especially in connection with "*cenam suam non presumat*". Pref. Gild. 8 has *diei superpositione et multa increpatione plectatur*; apparently the culprit was to be subjected to reproaches without permission to reply.

prescribes three *quadragesimae* for losing the tokens of the sacrament through carelessness : for this *Col. B 12* prescribes one year. Thus in each instance where the same offences are treated in both, *Poenit. Col. B* assigns considerably heavier penalties. This is not surprising when we recall the (already noted) lightness of the penalties in the *Prefatio.* These loose parallels suggest, if they do not prove with certainty, that the author of *Col. B* was acquainted with and here seeking to improve upon the *Pref. Gild.*, recalling its regulations from memory, if not using a MS.

3) Correspondences of *Poenit. Col. B* with other Celtic documents.

In Col. B 4 we noted a parallel with Vinn. 11. While the parallel is a real one, the canon as a whole resembles more closely *Excerpta Quaedam* 7, which has iv, vi, vii and xiii years (on a slightly different classification of clerical ranks), for the iii, v, vii and xii years of *Col. B 4*. This looks very much like a slight revision of the terms of the canon in the *Liber Davidis.*

It was the opinion of Seebass [1] that the closing portion (Ch. 10 f.) of the *Regula coenobialis* ascribed to Columban has been detached from the last section of *Poenit. Col. B.* In support of this view it is noteworthy that the section of the Regula referred to is mainly penitential in character. It consists of a list of penalties for offences characteristic of monastic life. It is remarkable for its generous employment of corporal punishment (*percussiones* and *plagae*). Still more prominent is the feature of penitential singing of the psalms, a form of penance employed for all manner of trivial monastic failings [2]. This characteristic places the chapters in question in close relationship with the Welsh penitentials in which, as we saw, the penalty of psalm-singing was employed. If Seebass is right in making this document an integral part of *Poenit. Col. B*, we have in the feature an additional claim for the connec-

1. Über Columba von Luxeuils Klosterregel und Bussbuch, p. 49.
2. See the critical text of the Regula by Seebass in the Zeitschrift f. Kg. Bd. 15 (1895), p. 366 f.

tion of the whole work with the Celtic spiritual fathers of Columban. We have thus ascertained that B was written by some one who was clearly acquainted with Finnian's penitential, and who very probably used also two Welsh documents credited respectively to Gildas and David. *Col. B* manifestly springs from the heart of the Celtic Church, and seems to reflect, in an extraordinary manner, the association of those three Celtic saints of the early sixth century, to whose friendship we had occasion to refer above.

Col. B then answers well to the presuppositions that would suggest themselves for a penitential work from the pen of St. Columban.

4) Remarks on the Place of Origin of Col. B. — From the above considerations we might fairly claim Columban's authorship of this part of the document which bears his name. But an additional argument has been advanced, for which we are mainly indebted to Hauck, who follows up a suggestion of Seebass [1]. Hauck makes it clear that the reference to heathen feasts in *Col. B 24* (mensae demoniorum..... pro cultu demonum aut honore simulachrorum) answers to the stage in religion of the inhabitants of the Luxeuil region in Columban's time. He further proves that the heretical Bonosiaci mentioned in *Col. B 25* appear in the same region about the same time. The argument from the last mentioned paragraph, it must be admitted, is insecure, as the canon contains prescriptions for penance which are not Celtic but characteristically Catholic, including a graded public discipline and reconciliation by a Catholic Bishop [2]. The canon appears to be a rare instance of the survival in Gaul of the ancient discipline, and may perhaps more safely be regarded as an interpolation than as having been accepted by Columban himself. Yet it

1. Seebass, Zeitschr. f. Kg. Bd. 14 (1894), p. 435; Hauck, Kirchengerch. Deutschlands, Bd. I, p. 277.

2. Post manus impositionem Catholici episcopi altario jungatur. From these "phrases which correspond to no practice at Luxeuil, and would there be hardly intelligible" the canon has recently been pronounced "due to some Gaelic source outside Columbanus, whether adopted into the penitential by Columbanus himself or by another". — Oscar D. Watkins, A History of Penance, Vol. II, p. 519.

has the value for our argument of added certainty of time and place; for even if an interpolation it could on Hauck's evidence have been inserted only on the region of Luxeuil and soon after Columban's work there.

Thus the chain of evidence for Columban's authorship of B is complete. It consists in the inherent probability of his writing a penitential; in the use in the book of Celtic authorities, and of just those Celtic writers who are otherwise known to have been favored by Columban; in the use of these authors with just that degree of respect and of independence with which writer of *Poenit. Col. B* claims to have used his authorities; and in references to two elements in the environment of Columban at Luxeuil. We may, therefore, with assurance, ascribe the work to the author whose name it bears.

5) The Authorship of *Poenit. Col. A.*

Let us now proceed to subject to the same process the first part of the combined penitential, *Poenit. Col. A.* The following parallels to *Poenit. Vinn.* are to be noted :

Col. A 2 and Vinn. 1-3. Some phrases are common. Both assign half a year's penance for major sins of the heart.

Col. A 3 and Vinn. 12-13. Both have ten years for homicide. Otherwise the arrangement of the text forbids exact comparison.

Col. A 4 and Vinn. 25. Both assign one year's penance for theft Col. omitting the restriction to clerics and the phrase *reddat quadruplum proximo suo* found in *Vinn.*

Col. A 5 and Vinn. 8. Vinn. has one year, *Col.* three years for striking a brother cleric in a quarrel.

Col. A 12 and Vinn. 28-29. The lists of contraries in each, though divergent in detail, illustrate a common principle.

From these parallels it appears that *Col. A* is as closely connected with *Vinn.* as is *Col. B.* This statement applies, it will be noted, especially to the section A 1-8. Yet the resemblance in A 12 is also noteworthy [1]. To this we shall require to return in a moment.

1. This passage reads : Verbosus vero taciturnitate damnandus est,

The author of *Poenit. Col. A* was therefore a close follower of Vinnian. But the greatest difficulty in the way of Columban's own authorship of A now arises. The booklet is not only independent of B, but shows one or two clear divergences from B. A5 prescribes three years for assault, while B9 has one year. A6 punishes a drunken offence at the sacrament with one quadragesima, while in B12 the term is with three quadragesimas. There is also a variation in the penalty for fornication by monks between A3 and B4, the former requiring a three year penance, the latter five years.

On the other hand it may be noted that A4 agress with B7 in prescribing one year for theft, and that one provision in A6 is identical with one in B12. Furthermore, it cannot be said that the discrepancies which appear between A and B are such as to render a common authorship impossible. They are no greater, for example, than those which appear in the well authenticated canons of Basil the Great [1]. Seebass has noted the probable connection between Col. A1 and Cassian's *Collatio, XX,* 5 [2]. We know that Columbanus read and followed Cassian from his *Instructiones XVII, de octo principalibus vitiis* [3] which is based on Cassian's Collationes V [4]. The trace of Cassian therefore tends to support Columban's authorship of A [5]. But Columban's authorship may be

inquietus mansuetudine, gulosus jejunio, somnolentius vigilia, superbus carcere, destitutor repulsione, unusquisque juxta quod meretur quoaequalia sentiat, ut justus juste vivat. Cf. *Vinn.*, 28 : Haec est poenitentia ejus criminis, ut e contrariis contraria curet et emendet; *Vinn.*, 29 : sed e contrariis ut diximus festinemus curare contraria et vitia mundemus.

1. Cf. Basil, Ad. Amphiloch, VIII and LVII ; IV and L.
2. Zeitschr. f. Kg. Bd. 14, 1894, p. 441 n.
3. Migne, Patr. Lat., Tom. 80, col. 259, 260.
4. *Ibid.*, Tom. 49, col. 611.
5. This argument is weakened but not annulled by the fact that the passage has other parallels in early literature. A 1 reads : Poenitentia vera est poenitenda non admittere, sed admissa deflere. The parallel in Cassian is Poenitentiae..... perfecta definitio est ut peccata..... nequaquam alterius admittamus. Cf. Ambrose, Serm. 9 *de Quadragesima* : Poenitentia est et mala praeterita plangere, et plangenda iterum non admittere. This definition is quoted in Gratian's *Concordia*, the section *De Poenitentia*, III, can. I. (Migne, Patrol. Lat., Tom. 187, col. 1594), and the idea became

supported on other grounds, hitherto overlooked. Allusion was made above to the influence of *Vinn.* 28, 29, on A 12. Now Columban's *Instructiones XVII* shows high probability of influence from the same passage in Vinnian. It contains a detailed statement expounding Vinnian's principle that "contraries are to be cured by contraries [1]". This common use by Columban and by the author of *Col. A* of a principle asserted by Vinnian, adds to those considerations which make for Columban's authorship of A.

Probably the simplest explanation of the matter is to suppose that both parts of the *Poenit. Col.* were written by Columban, but at different times and in different circumstances. When Columban came to the Luxeuil region he had before him a career of quarter of a century, time for considerable development (590-615). It has been supposed that he made visits to Italy prior to his ejection from Luxeuil [2]. In 610 he was ejected by Brunehild and Thierry; he then labored for a time in Neustria, subsequently in Switzerland, and finally founded his monastery of Bobbio in Italy, with which he was connected for three years (612-615). During these changes he may have prepared, or begun, a revised penitential, adapted to the environment in which he found himself and reflecting his ripening experience. It is very likely that *Poenit. Col. A* is a sketch, or fragment, of such a revision.

It must be admitted, however, that other hypotheses are not excluded. It is not impossible that A preceded B, and came with Columban and his twelve disciples into Gaul from Ireland. Columban may have received it, for example, from St. Sinell, his exacting instructor as a youth [3], or from

a commonplace. A similar statement is ascribed to Augustine, but is probably from Gennadius, *De dogmat. eccl.*, 54. See Gratian, *op. cit.*, III, can. iii.

1. Haec igitur omnium origines et causae sunt malorum; quae sic sunt sananda per contraria. Gula triplex vincenda est per abstinentiam jejunii de hora nona in horam nonam. Fornicatio... per castitatem et continentiam... cupiditas vero nihil habendo proprium vincitur... Ira... patientia et mansueta levitate superanda est. Tristitia vero laetitia spirituali... Vana gloria... atque superbia... humilitate... et contritione.

2. M. Stokes, Six Mos. in the Appennines, Preface, p. 11 f.

3. Jonas, *op. cit.*, 9.

Comgall of Bangor, the honored master whom he reverently mentions by the name *Faustus* in his *Instructiones II*, 1 [1]. Both were pupils of Finnian of Clonard, and would be likely to prepare penitential rules.

Nor can I refrain fromsuggesting the consideration of the name of Culumba of Iona, (d. 597). The exercise of penance by Columba is a prominent feature in his career as recorded by Adamnan [2]. He was a pupil of both Finnians [3], and a life-long friend of Comgall [4]. In the debate at the Synod of Whitby (664) Wilfrid spoke of Columba's " regula et praecepta " [5]. It is now shown to be probable that another important document in the series under review emanated from Iona a century after Columba [6]. The close similarity, or identity, of the names of the Iona and the Luxeuil saint might account for the juxtaposition in one codex, as from one author, of productions of the two. Next to the claim of Columban himself, that of Columba seems most capable of defence.

5. — Seventh Century Welsh and Irish Collections.

We may conveniently group nos. (9) (10) and (11) of the titles noted above, each of which contains considerable material not of a penitential character.

9) *The Canones Wallici.*

This document appears in two slightly variant MSS, Saint-Germain 121 (eighth century), and Paris 3182, (eleventh or twelfth century). A collation of these MSS, has been published by Wasserschleben [7]; the later text had previously been published by Martene and Durand [8]. Haddan and Stubbs have edited the work adopting the numerical order of the Saint-

1. Migne, Patrol. Lat., Tom. 80, col. 253. Cf. Reeves, Adamnan p. 220.
2. See e. g. Adamnan lib. II, c. XXIX, XXX, XLI.
3. Stokes, Three Middle Irish Homilies, p. 105.
4. Reeves, Adamnan, p. 220.
5. Bede, Hist. Eccles., lib. III, c. 25.
6. See the discussion of the Collectio canonum Hibernensis below, p. 56.
7. Bussordn., p. 124, f.
8. Thesaurus Novus Anecdotorum, Tom. IV, p. 13 f.

Germain MS [1]. Although the Paris MS. entitles the work " Incipiunt excerpta de libris Romanorum et Francorum " the contents point unmistakably to a Welsh origin. Haddan and Stubbs suggest a date of between 550 and 650 A. D.

The work consists mainly of a scale of fines for crimes and injuries, illustrating the common Celtic features of composition. As Schmitz remarks these provisions cannot be regarded as penitential canons [2]. It is rather to be compared with the mediaeval codes of Welsh Law, such as the Laws of Howel Dda (907-940), and with the Ancient Laws of Ireland. It is manifestly affected by Goidelic customs, as is indicated by the frequent reference to *ancillae* and *servi* as the unit of payment in legal transactions, instead of the usual Brythonic unit of cattle [3]. Payments are also made in *argenti librae*, *stagni librae*, *vaccae*, *solidi*, etc. The evidence points to an origin in southern (Goidelic) Wales [4]. Slavery is an accepted feature of the social order. We shall later briefly revert to the bearing of this work on the relation of the penitentials to native law.

The *Canones Wallici* do not represent the findings ofchurch councils. They are evidently civil and not ecclesiastical in their character. But they give evidence ot the place of the church as protected by the state, and assume the existence ot a church penitential discipline. A layman who has a charge against a cleric is required to bring the case before a bishop [5]. Coming to a priest for confession after committing a fault, is encouraged [6]. Assaults which take place in front of a church are subject to special penalties in the form of " alms " [7]. When a layman beats a cleric he must " redeem his hand ", and come to penance [8]. (Cf. *Can. Hib.* Sect. III, can. 4,

1. Councils, etc., Vol. I, p. 127 f.
2. Bussbücher, Bd. I, p. 501 . . . . enthält Compositions-Bestimmungen welche ebenfalls nicht als Busscanones abgesehen werden können.
3. Seebohm, A. S. Law, pp. 107-108.
4. Ibid.
5. Can. 40.
6. Can. 46.
7. Cans. 52, 53.
8. Can. 65.

manus percutientis abscidatur aut dimidium vii ancillarum reddat). No specific terms of penance are prescribed.

10) *The Collectio Canonum Hibernensis.*

This document is of great importance in the history of the Irish church, but its origin is a matter of uncertainty. It has been carefully edited by Wasserchleben [1], and forms the subject of two interesting discussions by Bradshaw [2]; but it still lacks an adequate introduction. Both the authorities named place the date of the document about A. D. 700 and regard it as the collected canons of a series of Irish synods. The latest author named in the Collectio is Theodore of Tarsus (d. 690) [3]. Bradshaw, in an acute and technical argument, gives reasons for believing that it was preserved in Brittany. He also suggests that the compiler was Cummean, the author of the *Poenit. Cummeani* [4]; but in the uncompleted draft of his paper the proof of this identification is not presented. Bradshaw's conjecture is suggested by the fact that Cummean, though a contemporary writer, does not cite the Hibernensis. The question of the authorship of the *Collectio* has more recently been taken up in an article by E. W. B. Nicholson [5]. By a slight emendation of the O. Ir. colophon in which the scribe of the *Collectio* names himself and the place in which he wrote, Nicholson makes out that it was really compiled at Iona. From the Romanizing tendency of the work, and from the fact that in five MSS. it is followed immediately by the *Canones Adamnani* and that a later exemplar contains one of

1. Die Irische Kanonensammlung, Giessen 1874. 2nd ed. Leipzig 1885. The document was partially given by d'Achéry, Specilegium, Tom. I, p. 492, f. and by Martene, Thes. Nov. Anec., Tom. IV, p. 1 f.

2. Collected Papers of Henry Bradshaw, Camb. 1889, containing " Early Collection of Canons commonly known as the *Hibernensis*, a Letter to Wasserschleben, May 1885 "; Bradshaw, Henry " The Early Collection of Canons known as the *Hibernensis*, Two unfinished papers ", Camb. 1893.

3. Hence Maassen first suggested the now generally accepted date. Gesch. der Quellen des Kanonischen Rechts, Bd. I, pp. 954, 973 f.

4. Unfinished Papers, p. 38.

5. Zeitschr. f. Celt. Phil. Bd. III (1901), p. 99 f.

these canons, Nicholson insists that the compiler was no other than Adamnan himself. The quotation from the *Poenit. Theod.* contained in the *Collectio*, would, he points out, occur very naturally in a Romanizing work of Adamnan, who is known to have returned to Iona in 688 from a visit to the English monasteries.

On the paleographical portion of this argument the present writer can offer no judgment. But the ascription of the work to Adamnan seems historically a very possible solution. The collected *acta* of the Romanizing Irish synods of the seventh century, may well have been thought by Adamnan a valuable instrument for his newly formed purpose of bringing resolute and conservative Iona into the Roman union, and he may have collected them mainly with that object in view. The brilliant conjecture of Nicholson, in the absence of any other plausible account of the origin of the document, may be regarded as the likeliest hypothesis.

The *Hibernensis* is manifestly intended to bring Celtic and and Catholic Christianity together. It represents the process of Romanization in Ireland, but does not thereby repudiate the Celtic tradition. The frequent use of the name of St. Patrick as authority for canons, and the quotation of the "Canons of St. Patrick" [1] indicate the intention of conserving the traditional usages so far as possible [2]. Welsh canons, as well as Irish, are found, and fragments from Gildas are quoted [3]. Names are very frequently wrongly attached to

1. Canons of the (genuine) first Synod of St. Patrick reappear in the *Collectio* as follows :

Collectio	XXVIII,	cap.	10,	from Syn. I	St. Patrick.	can. 14
«	XXIX	«	8	«	«	« 15
«	XXXIII	«	1	«	«	« 1
«	XXXIX	«	10	«	«	« 11
«	XXXIX	«	11	«	«	« 3
«	XLII	«	25,26	«	«	« 1, 3, 4,
«	XLIII	«	4	«	«	« 28
«	LII	«	7	«	«	« 6

2. "Das nationale Kirchenrecht möglichst zu konserviren" Wasserschl., *op. cit.*, p. VI. Cf. 2nd. ed., p. XIII.

3. Lib. XII, can. 5.

the canons quoted, as e. g. when Patrick is credited with passages from the *Poenit. Vinn.* [1]. The mass of the material is not Celtic in origin, however, but from a variety of non-Celtic sources. The prominence of biblical, especially Old Testament, elements, is remarkable. The canons of Nicea, Ancyra, Gangra, Antioch, Laodicea and Chalcedon are utilized. A number of the church Fathers are quoted. Dionysius (Exiguus) is twice mentioned by name [2], but it is doubtful whether the Dionysian Collection has been used, as its use would likely have obviated the frequency of mistaken ascriptions of anthorship [3]. A letter of Leo I. to Rusticus of Narbonne is the only papal document used [4]. The penitential customs of the Celtic church are not greatly modified in the *Collectio*. Specific rules of penance in the document are few, and they tend in the main to confirm the usages which appear in the penitentials. The seven year period for homicide, based on the seven-*ancillae* body-price of Goidelic law, again appear [5]. The dictum of Patrick which is appended to the *Canones Hibernenses* I, and which authorizes commutation in the characteristic formula " vii ancillarum pretium aut vii annis ", is repeated in the *Collectio* [6]. Exile as a penitential duty is prescribed for violation of a bishop's or a martyr's relics [7]. The amputation of a hand or a foot is part of the penalty for theft in a church, but this penalty of mutilation is commuted to penance in an accompanying canon [8]. By scriptural examples the church is made the place of penances [9]. The validity of penance in absolving from sin is asserted without qualification [10]. As between fasting and alms, superior value is laid upon the latter, in a canon ascribed to St. Jerome [11].

1. Lib. LXVI, cap. 32, quoting *Pœnit. Vinn.*, cans. 43, 45.
2. Lib. XXVIII, cap. 5, cap. 10.
3. Wasserschleben, *op. cit.*, p. vii.
4. Maassen, Gesch. d. Quellen, p. 881.
5. Lib. XXVIII, cap. 10.
6. Lib. XLVIII, cap. 5.
7. Lib. XLIV, cap. 8.
8. Lib. XXIX, cap. 1.
9. Lib. XLVII, cap. 13. De loco poenitentiae et orationis.
10. Penitentia aboleri peccata indubitatum credimus. Lib. xlvii, cap. 11.
11. Lib. XIII, cap. 8.

It may here be observed that the attitude of the Scotto-Roman synods of the seventh century, as represented by the *Collectio*, in supporting rather than suppressing the penance of the penitentials, gave to the native penance freedom of developement and expansion which another course taken at this juncture would have denied it.

11) *The Canones Adamnani.*

This set of canons, if a genuine work of Adamnan abbot of Iona (d. 704), must approximately synchronize with the *Collectio canonum Hibernensis*. The document is not of sufficient importance to call for any extended treatment. It consists of twenty canons dealing with the question of clean and unclean meats, making regulations under the sanction of religion which reflect primitive and Old Testament restrictions regarding animals to be eaten, together with some more enlightened sanitary rules. Animals that have been killed without proper bleeding, swine that have fed on carcasses, and birds and beasts of prey, are prohibited. While not strictly a penitential work, these canons are on the border-line between primitive prohibitions (*tabu*) and penitential conceptions. They are included in the Parisian Codex 3182 to which we have frequently referred. Later penitentials like those of Theodore and Cummean contain similar material [1].

6. — Related Anglo Saxon Penitentials.

12) *The Poenitentiale Theodori.*

The importance of this work, emanating from Theodore of Tarsus (Archbishop of Canterbury 668-690) is generally recognized. Perhaps the most original and valuable part of Wasserschleben's essay on the history of the penitentials is that in which he determines the true Penitential of Theodore [2]. The tradition of Theodore's authorship of a penitential of

1. *Poenit. Theod.* Lib. I, vii, cans. 6-12 ; *Poenit. Cumm.* I, cans. 14-38.
2. Bussordn., pp. 14-37.

great influence goes back to the Poenitentiale Egberti (734-766) and to the *Liber Pontificalis* (eighth century). But Bede and other near contemporaries of Theodore offer no corroboration; and the work published by Spelmann from a Cambridge MS. in 1639 as the *Poenitentiale Theodori Archiepiscopi* showed late elements. Joh. Morinus, in his classical history of penitential discipline, rejected the portions of this work authorizing composition, but regarded the remainder as the genuine work of Theodore [1]. The whole document was uncritically accepted by Thorpe and appears in full in his " Ancient Laws and Institutes of England [2]. Meanwhile, in 1677, Jacques Petit published 14 *capitula* of a *Poenitentiale Theodori* from a MS. taken from the library of de Thou, together with a collection of pseudo-Theodorean capitula [3]. Wasserschleben, however, discovered MSS. which led him to adopt as the *Poenit. Theod.* a work in two books, of which the first is a true penitential in fifteen *capitula*, and the second is the fourteen *capitula* of Petit [4]. Haddan and Stubbs working independently of Wasserschleben and using a Cambridge MS. superior to any used by him, reached the same conclusion, and have since published the newly-discovered *Poenit. Theod.* ascribing it to Theodore " with the utmost confidence " [5].

The *Poenit. Theod.* is not, and does not profess to be a direct work of Theodore of Tarsus. It professes to be made up mainly of answers given by the Archbishop to a certain (otherwise unknown) presbyter, Eoda, and compiled by a scribe who hides behind the vague pseudonym of *Discipulus Umbrensium.* This mysterious intermediary, the original editor or compiler of the penitential, is thought by Haddan and Stubbs to have been " either a native of Northumbria who had been a disciple of Theodore, or, more probably, an

1. Commentarius Historicus (1651), lib. x, ch. 17.
2. Vol. II, p. 227 f.
3. Petit's *capitula* will be found reprinted in Migne, P. L., Tom. 99, col. 959 (1851).
4. For details of the MSS. used see Wasserschl. Bussordn., p. 19 f. and Haddan and Stubbs, Councils, etc. Vol. III, p. 174 f.
5. Haddan and Stubbs, *op. cit.*, p. 173.

Englishman of southern birth who had studied under the northern scholars [1]. The corrupt text of the preface of the work is read by Wasserschleben to mean that Eoda had derived some materials also from the study of a certain " libellus scottorum ", the compiler of which was regarded by Theodore as himself an ecclesiastic [2]. Can we identify the " libellus scottorum " or " Irish booklet " which yielded a contribution to the *Poenit. Theod*? We can, and with certainty. It is no other than the *Canones Hibernenses*, or a part of that document. For this we have the evidence of the repetition in the *Poenit. Theod.* of some of these canons. Thus *Theod.* Lib. I, c. IV, can. 3, *Homicida autem x vel vii annos*, is a repetition of *Can. Hib.* I, can. 3. But there appears a more specific proof. *Theod.* lib. I, c. vii can. 5 reads :

> Item *xii* triduana pro anno pensanda, Theodorus laudavit. De egressis (aegris) quaque pretium viri vel ancillae pro anno, vel dimidium omnium quae possidet dare, et si quem frauderet reddere quadruplum, ut Christus judicavit. Ista testimonia sunt de eo quod in prefatione diximus de libello Scottorum.

That is to say Theodore approved *Can. Hib. II, can. 6* (*arreum anni xii triduani*), and, for sick penitents, favored composition in money at the rate of *pretium viri vel ancillae pro anno*, a principle exemplified in the same Irish document section III ; (scriptural forms of restitution are mentioned as alternatives). " These are the proofs ", says Discipulus Umbrensium, " of what we said in the preface about the *libellus Scottorum* ". The evidence is as specific as we could desire.

The compiler, then, makes it quite clear that Theodore himself, and not merely Eoda, responded to the Irish influence. Theodore's recognition of composition and commutation in penance is based upon Irish penitential practice, and taken directly from Irish written sources, not, be it observed, from Anglo-Saxon national custom.

But Theodore's instructions to Eoda also reflected the influence of other Celtic sources. Thus *Theod. lib. I, c. IV.*

1. Haddan and Stubbs, *op. cit.*, p. 173.
2. Wasserschl., *op. cit.*, p. 183.

can. I, which repeats the " *vii vel x annos* " of *Can. Hib.* I, can. 3, adds : " *Si tamen reddere vult propinquis pecuniam aestimationis, levior erit poenitentia, id est dimidio spatii.* " This half-and-half composition, the reduction of a term of penance by a payment, is very similar in effect to *Poenit. Col.* B. 13. A knowledge of *Vinn.* 37 is apparent in *Theod.* lib. I. c. XIV, *can.* 11, and of *Sin. Luc. Vict.*, *can.* 8, in *Theod.* lib. I, c. II, can. 7.

13) *The Poenitentiale Bedae* and 14) *The Poenitentiale Egberti.*

A *Poenitentiale Bedae* given by Wasserschleben is regarded by him as emanating from Beda Venerabilis (d. 735), but as " a compilation of excerpts from the penitentials of Gildas, Vinniaus, the *Sin. Luc. Vict.*, the *Sin. Aquil. Brit.*, the penitential canons of Theodore, and the Ordo Romanus [1] ". Except for the introduction which has been prefixed from the Ordo Romanus, the work consists of poenitential canons in the ordinary form. It is totally lacking in originality, and simply carries on the strain of the Celtic manuals. Schmitz would dissociate it from Bede, and assign a ninth century date ; as also to the related work ascribed to Egbert of York, (d. 766) [2]. The *Poenitentiale Egberti*, while somewhat more independent, bears the same general character as the Poenit. Bed., and is largely indebted to Theodore. The direct influence of Celtic works is apparent, however, and in at least one instance we find agreement with a Celtic authority, in divergence from Theodore [3]. Albers in 1901 published a text boaring the name of Bede which contains much material in common with both these penitentials. Albers shows reason for dating his form of the book within the pontificate of

1. Wasserschleben, Bussordnungen, p. 39. (The earliest reference to the Ordo Romanus is said to be in a letter of Alcuin to Eanbild of York, c. 796. See Haddan and Stubbs, Councils, etc., vol. III, p. 503.)
2. Bussbücher, Bd. I., p. 555.
3. Cap. IX (cans. 8, 9, 10, 11, 12) of the Pœnit. Egberti goes back to Excerpta Quaedam, cans. 3, 9, 10, and imposes psalm-singing for pollution in sleep, on a scale little varied from the original. Cf. Wasserschleben, Bussordn., p. 102 and p. 241.

Gregory II., a. d. 721-731, i. e. in the later period of Bede's activity [1]. In this probably genuine work of Bede the Celtic elements appear not less prominently than in those just noticed. The passage in the Egberti to which reference has been made is identical in Albers text [2].

7. — Related Frankish Penitentials

15) *The Poenitentiale Cummeani.*

The *Poenitentiale Cummeani* presents a problem of authorship which Wasserschleben has treated in an original and fairly conclusive manner [3]. The close relationship in contents between *Poenit. Cumm.* and *Poenit. Theod.*, was formerly accounted for on the ground that Cummean was a predecessor of Theodore, and, (according to Theiner) [4] identical with the well-known abbot of Iona, who died in 601.

Wasserschleben however, from a description of the author which appears in a ninth century St. Gall MS. of the penitential as " *abbas in Scotia ortus* ", argues that the work is that of a Scot who at the time of writing is no longer in his native country, but on the Continent. The work, he points out, while extant in a number of continental MSS. does not appear in England, an indication that it originated on the Continent. Wasserschleben finds among the twenty-one saints of his name mentioned by Colgan one who is stated by Ughellus [5] to have died at Bobbio in the time of King Luitprand (711-744). To this early eighth century writer Wasserschleben would ascribe the penitential.

1. B. Albers, Wann sind die Beda-Egbert'schen Bussbücher verfasst worden, und Wer ist ihr Verfasser? Archiv f. Kathol. Kirchenrecht, Bd. 81, 1901, p. 393 f. Albers bases his argument mainly on the language found near the end of the document, Item ex decreto pape gregorii junioris qui nunc romanam catholicam regit matrem ecclesiam (*Ibid.*, p. 417). In the MS (Codex Barbarinianus XI., 120) « *nuc* » occurs for « *nunc* ».
2. Albers, *op. cit.*, pp. 411-412.
3. Bussordn., p. 61 f. The text is given, p. 460 f.
4. Disquisitiones Criticae, p. 280.
5. Ital. Sacr., Tom. IV, col. 949-960

16) *The Poenitentiale Bigotianum.*

There is a close resemblance between the *Poenit. Cumm.* and the anonymous eighth century *Poenit. Bigotianum* (so called from the Codex Bigot. 89, now known as Paris 3182, in which it appears). Each of these works is prefaced by an introduction in which elaborate scales of commutation of penances to briefer terms, or into money payments, appear. Both are also remarkable for the way in which the mediaeval classification of sins is used in the framework [1].

A recently published penitential in the Old Irish language (unknown, of course, to Wasserschleben) exhibits both these features, and seems closely related to *Poenit. Cumm.* A date " not later than the eighth century " is ascribed to the MS. of this penitential by Kuno Meyer [2] while E. G. Gwynn would date it about 800 [3]. The Irish MS. is therefore earlier than any MS. of *Bigot.* or *Cumm.*, none of the MSS. of which are earlier than the ninth century. It seems probable that the basis of *Poenit. Cumm.* and its near relative *Poenit. Bigot.*, lies in this briefer Irish document; and that the features of the latter were developed under the influence of *Poenit. Theod.* and with due regard to earlier Celtic works. Otherwise we should be obliged to regard the Irish treatise in question as based upon Cummean, although it excludes the features borrowed by Cummean from Theodore, a highly improbable solution.

17) *The Poenitentiale Valicellanum I.*

Schmitz complains [4] that Wasserschleben did nothing to

1. The subject of the " eight principal sins " is treated by Cassian, who is followed by Columban. It is these writers who are used here rather than Gregory the Great. Cassian's complete list of the sins which arise from the eight principal sins is quoted in the introduction to *Poenit. Bigot.*, and the main body of this penitential is entitled, " *De remediis vitiorum capitula octo* ".

2. The Old Irish Treatise " de Arreis ". Rev. Celt. Tom. XV (1894), p. 485.

3. An Irish Penitential, Eriu, Vol. VII. (1914), p. 121.

4. Bussbücher, Bd. I, p. 3.

clarify the question of the " Poenitentiale Romanum ", references to which occur as early as *Poenit. Cumm.* [1]. It is the aim of Schmitz to prove that the original sources of the penitential literature lie in the Roman church. In his twelfth chapter Schmitz reviews the conclusions of Hildenbrand [2], and Wasserschleben. Hildenbrand regarded the term *Poenitentiale Romanum* as applying not to a single work but to all the various penitentials circulating in the Continental Church. Wasserschleben agreed to this [3] and regarded the term as signifying " kein einzelnes Beichtbuch sondern eine bestimmte Qualität der Beichtbücher ", the word " *Romanum* " referring not to an official authorization but to a general one throughout the Roman west. Schmitz argues, on the other hand, for the implication of authority in the word " *Romanum* ". He makes it equivalent to " canonical ", and uses the references to " sinodus Romanum " in the *Collectio canonum Hibernensis* [4]. The document on which Schmitz specially relies, as a representative early Roman penitential, is that called by him *Poenitentiale Valicellanum I.* He publishes this document from a tenth century MS [5]. In his fourteenth chapter he notes a correspondence between the penitential and the ancient *Lex Dei* attributed to Rufinus. Apart from the notorious unpopularity of Rufinus at Rome, it may be replied that the alleged resemblance is by no means close, as the table given by Schmitz clearly shows, and that the appended text of the *Lex Dei* is not analogous to this or any penitential in form or content. It is simply a selection of passages from the Pentateuch, with no penitential exercises prescribed.

The *Poenit. Valicell. I.* is obviously related, however, to the British and Irish documents we have been studying. This

1. *Poenit. Cumm.* vii, can. 11 quotes *Poenit. Theod.* lib. II, c. x, can. 5. as *de Romano poenitentiale.*

2. Untersuchungen über die germanischen Poenitentialbücher, Würzburg 1851.

3. Bussordn. p. 75.

4. The term " sinodus Romanum " in this connection no doubt really refers to pro-Roman Irish synods. See Bury, Life of St. Patrick, p. 239.

5. Cod. Valicell. E 15. Bussbücher, Bd. I, p. 239 f.

relation, which is apparent even on a casual reading, has been shown in a detailed analysis by Hinschius [1]. This analysis indicates the use of *Poenit. Vinn.*, *Sin. Aquil. Brit.*, *Excerpta Quaedam*, *Poenit. Bedae*, *Poenit. Egberti*, and especially of *Poenit. Theod.* As Schmitz himself places the earliest portion of the compilation (the " *leges canonicae* "), in the early part of the eighth century [2], there arises no question of the influence indicated by Hinschius being from this penitential to the sixth and seventh century works referred to, but it is evident that the *Poenit. Valicell. I.* of Schmitz is dominated by Celtic influence [3].

1. Hinschius, F. H. P., System des Katholischen Kirchenrechts, mit besonderer Rücksicht auf Deutschland, Berlin, 1869-1897, Bd. V., p. 92.
2. Bussbücher, Bd. I, pp. 237-238.
3. The language of Schmitz in describing the nature of the Roman influence on the penitentials is not always consistent. In his Bussbücher Bd. II, p. 140 he writes ; " Das Beiwort *Romanum* " bezeichnet, wie wir sahen, die *consuetudo* und Tradition der römischen Kirche in Beobachtung der kanonischen Regel " ; and in the previous page he denies any " authoritative Anerkennung der römischen Kirche für irgend ein Bussbuch ". But authoritative recognition by the Roman church is clearly implied in his Bussbücher Bd. I, pp. 174-175 ; — Die Entstehung eines *Poenitentiale Romanum* welches ja auch zu den Kirchenbüchern gehorte, wird man sich ebenfalls in Rom unter Oberaufsicht und Controle der Papste und de römischen Kirche zu denken haben. . . Das Beiwort " *Romanum* " zu *Poenitentiale* bezeichnet also unmittelbar den Ort der Entstehung, und in abgeleiteten Sinne so viel als " *commune* ", " *gemeinkirchliches* " Bussbuch. (This contradiction has already been observed by Hauck.)

CHAPTER II

The Relation of the Celtic Penitentials to the Penitential Discipline of the Ancient Catholic Church.

1. — Origins of the Welsh and Irish Churches.

In 1851 an investigator of the penitentials remarked : "The earliest history of the ancient British and Irish church is veiled in thickest darkness [1]". Since this statement was written, J.H. Todd [2], E.D. Killen [3], Alphons Bellesheim [4], Heinrich Zimmer [5], J.B. Bury [6], A.R. MacEwen [7], and others have studied the Irish side of the question, while J.W. Willis Bund [8], Hugh Williams [9], and William Hughes [10] have given us books on the Welsh Church, and Dom Louis Gougaud has made use of the growing periodical literature on Celtic origins, in a well-annotated volume covering the ancient churches of Britain, Armorica and Ireland [11]. The researches of a large company of Celtic scholars have illumined problems of race, language, social organization and religion in all parts of the Celtic world, and supplied to the student

1. Wasserschleben, Bussordn., p. 5.
2. St. Patrick, Apostle of Ireland, Dublin, 1864.
3. Ecclesiastical History of Ireland, Dublin, 1875.
4. Geschichte der katholischen Kirche in Irland, Bd. I. Mainz, 1890.
5. Die keltische Kirche (Realencyclopädie, Bd. 10, 1901) tr. A. Meyer, The Celtic Church in Britain and Ireland, Lond., 1902.
6. The Life of St. Patrick, Lond., 1905.
7. A History of the Church in Scotland, Vol. I, Lond., N.Y., Toronto, 1913.
8. The Celtic Church in Wales, Lond., 1897.
9. Christianity in Early Britain, Oxf., 1912.
10. A History of the Church of the Cymry, Lond., 1916.
11. Les Chrétientés celtiques, Paris, 1911.

new means of understanding the conditions in which Christianity functioned in those regions in the early period. The aggressive scholarship of Zimmer, in particular, has promoted fresh consideration of the documents bearing on the beginnings of the Celtic churches, and a large amount of editorial and critical work of value has been done.

Yet the uncertainty lamented by Wasserschleben is by no means entirely dispelled; and in speaking of the origins of British and of Irish Christianity we are still largely in the region of conjecture. When, whence, and through whose efforts, did the Christian religion first come to either island? In both cases it must be said that the answer cannot be given specifically and with perfect assurance. To answer with assurance one is still obliged to resort to statements of a somewhat general character.

1) *The British Church.*

In the absence of trustworthy records old writers accepted materials of the slightest historical value to account for the introduction of Christianity into Britain. When we reach a period of authentic history the British church has already grown to considerable strength, and we are left to conjecture regarding the date and source of the Christian message first preached in the Province. Bede's statement of the matter is entirely misleading [1]. He connects the event with the name of a British King Lucius, who, he tells us, introduced Christianity during the pontificate of Eleuther. But Bede's date, A.D. 156, is fifteen years earlier than the earliest possible date, and twenty-one years earlier than the date generally accepted, of the elevation of Eleuther to the see of Rome; while King Lucius cannot be identified [2]. Valueless as Bede's own story is, his belief as to the date of the beginnings of the British Church is probably not far wrong. It is true that

1. Hist. Eccles. lib. I, ch. 4.
2. A. Plummer traces the Lucius story to the *Catalogus Felicianus*, c. A.D. 530. Churches in Britain before 1000 A.D. Vol. I, pp. 5-7.

Irenaeus writing "against Heresies" about 195 omits Britain from a list of territories into which Christianity has spread; but the list he gives [1] is not otherwise exhaustive. Tertullian writing about 208, speak of haunts of the Britons not reached by the Romans, but subjugated to Christ [2]. This is no very exact statement, but it must signify that the writer had heard of the entrance of Christianity and its progress in the Island, and understood that it had been carried beyond the standards of empire. In view of all the possibilities of the case, it is by no means necessary to exclude this opinion. But we must leap another century before the first definite evidence appears.

Another tradition accepted by Bede and also by Gildas may be regarded as having a basis of fact, — the story of the martyrdom of St. Alban, a British convert, at Verulam, Hertfordshire [3]. This event Bede connects with the persecutions which began under Diocletian and continued for about a decade (303-313). In Britain no general persecution took place, and the death of the martyr at this period may have been due to local conflict, an interpretation not incompatible with the details of Bede's account.

About the time of the edict of Milan by which Constantine freed the church of the Empire (313), the British church emerges on the plain field of history. Three British bishops, from York, London, and either Lincoln or Caerleon-upon-Usk, attended the important Council of Arles in 314 [4]. At the Council of Ariminium in 359 it is probable that a considerably larger number were present, for a contemporary writer informs us that all but three of them refused an allowance for expenses [5]. When St. Patrick, who was born about

1. Contra Haeres, I, 3. Cf. Pryce, John, The Ancient British Church, p. 31.

2. Britannorum inaccessa Romanis loca, Christo vero subdita. Adv. Jud., 7. Williams (Christianity in Early Britain, p. 73), argues for the accuracy of the words.

3. Bede, Hist. Eccles., lib. I, ch. 7; Haddan and Stubbs, Councils, etc., Vol. I, p. 5; Gildas, De Excidio Britanniae, 8.

4. Haddan and Stubbs, Councils, etc. Vol. I, p. 7.

5. The three who accepted did so "*inopia proprii*". Sulpicius Severus,

389, asserts that his father, grandfather, and, according to one MS., his great-grandfather, were in holy offices [1], it is implied that the faith had reached the region of his birth, probably Glamorganshire, Wales [2], as early as the opening of the fourth century. Contemporary references to the British Church in the fourth century [3] indicate that it had a name for orthodoxy. But by the beginning of the fifth century it had nursed up the arch-heretic, Pelagius, who gave his name to that heresy which the Church has found the most difficult of all to repress [4]. Associated with him was the able Irish disputant, Celestius. The spread of heresy in Britain occasioned the mission to Britain of Germanus and Lupus, Gallic bishops, who discomfited the Pelagians at Verulam, 429 [5]. Germanus, the hero of the story, was a Celt of Armorica. He was in Britain again about 448. Bede, following the late fifth century account by Constantius, presbyter of Lyons [6], gives heresy again as the reason: a likely guess, however, is that a pagan reaction had set in [7].

The efforts made to restore the Church of the Britons were only partially successful. The testimony of Gildas, of Bede, and of the writings of St. Patrick, all alike indicate the low condition of British Christianity in the fifth century. The

Historia Sacra, lib. II, c. 41. Migne, Patrol. Lat. T. 20, col. 152. (What is implied as to the total number from Britain present is doubtful; these three may possibly have been all.)

1. Patrick, Confessio, 1.

2. Bury, Life of St. Patrick, p. 322 f.

3. Bright cities a number of these. Chapters on Early English Church History, p. 12 f.

4. The view that Pelagius was an Irishman (Zimmer, Pelagius in Irland, p. 18) has been conclusively refuted by Williams, "Zimmer on the History of the Celtic Church", in Zeitschr. f. Celt. Phil., Bd. IV, p. 531 f. Bury (Life of St. Patrick, p. 43) thinks he belonged to a Scottic tribe settled in Wales. Bury also holds that Celestius was not Irish, but a native of Campania. See Lawlor's note on "Coelestius" in G.T. Stokes, Ireland and the Celtic Church, sixth edition, p. 363. I adopt the view of Stokes and Williams.

5. According to Bede, Hist. Eccles., lib. I, ch. 17.

6. Bede, *op. cit*, I., 20: Constantius, Vita Germani, I, 28.

7. Bund, Celtic Church in Wales, p. 109.

Anglo-Saxon invasions wrought the ruin of the church in the territories conquered. By the end of the century the surviving Britons had been either reduced to subjection or forced within the territories which, approximately, their descendants still occupy, Wales, Cornwall and Strathclyde. Not until c. 493, when the invaders were signally defeated at Mons Badonicus [1], were the Britons able to arrest the progress of their hitherto triumphant foe.

The ancient Church of the British Province was now represented by the Church of Wales, which reached a high stage of organization and produced some notable saints in the course of the sixth century. The Welsh church was largely isolated from non-Celtic influences, but maintained constant communication with the churches of Armorica and Ireland. In all probability the greater number of its leaders were natives of one or other of these regions, or of Strathclyde [2]. This foreign, yet Celtic, influence is an important factor in the Welsh Church, but does not wholly eliminate the strain of the more ancient British Christianity. Llandaff, in a Goidelic section of Wales, laid claim to a sort of primacy among the Welsh bishoprics; Menevia in the extreme south-west and at the point of intercourse with Ireland, became the more influential in the time of St. David. Newell has indicated that the five Welsh bishoprics of the sixth century corresponded in some degree to older political divisions [3]. The life of the church was largely in the monasteries, which were located in all the episcopal centres and scattered throughout Wales, especially in the southern coastal region, where they

1. The date has been discussed with reference to the birth of Gildas. See above, p. 35 f.

2. Bund explains the frequency of illegitimacy of birth in the lives of the Welsh saints on this basis. As foreigners they had no tribal rights, and so were represented as illegitimate by the hagiographers. See Bund, Celtic Church in Wales, p. 433. The close relations existing between the Welsh, Irish and Armorican churches are abundantly attested quite independently of Bund's theory. Cf. the story of St. Padarn being followed from Armorica to Britain by 847 monks — Rees, Cambro-British Saints, p. 190.

3. A. J. Newell, The Ancient British Church (Lond. and N.Y., 1895), p. 41.

occupied remote and solitary places. It is highly probable that these monasteries sprang from the Gallic monastic movement under St. Martin of Tours. St. Ninian a British missionary to the Picts of Galloway, dedicated his stone church at Candida Casa to Martin about 397, the probable date of Martin's death [1].

It is not improbable that peculiar direction was given to penance in British Christianity prior to the penitential writings of Gildas and David. The mention in Gildas, *Prefatio* 5, of "*antiqui patres*" is explained by Williams to refer exclusively to the fathers of the British Church [2]. This judgment seems equally applicable to the expression "*antiqui sancti*" in the *Excerpta Quaedam* 10. These writers seem conscious of a traditional penitential practice peculiar to their own church. What this practice was we can only guess from what appears in the later documents.

2) *The Irish Church.*

It was in the year 432 that St. Patrick came to Ireland as a missionary of the Christian religion. Investigation has made it increasingly clear that Christianity had already obtained some acceptance in Ireland before the mission of Patrick. Among well-known early Irish Christians are Mansuetus who became bishop of Toul c. 330 [3], and Celestius the ablest propagandist of Pelagianism [4], who was renowned over Europe twenty years before the beginning of Patrick's work. The lives of certain Irish saints (e.g. Kieran, Ibar, Abban) represent these shadowy persons as older contemporaries of the Apostle of Ireland. And there is in the Chronicle of Prosper of Aquitaine a slender but trustworthy record of the existence of Christianity in Leinster by the year 431. Under that date

1. Bede, Hist. Eccles., III, 4; For the twelfth century life of Ninian see A.P. Forbes, Lives of S. Ninian and S. Kentigern, Edin, 1874.

2. Gildae de Excidio, etc., in Cymmrod. Rec. Ser. No. 3, pt. II, p. 279.

3. K. Meyer, Learning in Ireland in the Fifth Century, p. 23, and note 17.

4. See above, p. 70, n. 4.

Prosper states that one Palladins was ordained by Pope Celestine and sent, as their first bishop, to the Scots who were believers in Christ [1]. Irish sources connect with the ministry of Palladius the foundation of a least three churches near Wicklow [2]. The theory of Zimmer that the work of Patrick was comparatively insignificant as Christianity had been widely accepted before him, is based in part upon the identification, previously suggested by Loofs, of Patrick with this Palladius [3]. The argument of Zimmer has met with little acceptance, and has been ably answered by Bury [4], Gwynn [5] and Williams [6].

Efforts have been made with more success to show the probability of the entrance of Christianity at an early stage by establishing proof of traffic between Ireland and the Continent in pre-Christian and early Christian times. George Coffey was among the first to observe the evidence for this, and after earlier studies, showed in 1910, with some fulness, the archaeological indications for direct intercourse with Gaul before the first century of the Christian Era [7]. Zimmer's elaborate study of the subject appeared in the transactions of the Berlin Academy for 1909-1910 [8]. Alice Stopford Green

1. Ad Scottos in Christum credentes ordinatur a papa Coelestino Palladius, et primus episcopus mittitur. — Migne, Patrol. Lat., T. 51, col. 595.

2. See Shearman, Loca Patriciana, p. 25 f.; Annals of the Four Masters for the year 430.

3. Loofs, Friedrich, Antiquae Britonum Scottorumque Ecclesiae quales fuerint mores, etc. Leips, 1882, p. 44; Zimmer, Celtic Church, p. 18 f.

4. Life of St. Patrick. App., 21, p. 384.

5. Gwynn, in his edition of the Book of Armagh, pp. xcvii to c, uses Tirechán's seventh century Life of St. Patrick to refute Zimmer's view.

6. Article in Zeitschr. f. Celt. Phil., Bd. IV, p. 531 f. cited above, note 22.

7. Archalological Evidence for the Intercourse of Gaul with Ireland before the First Century. — Proc. of Roy. Ir. Acad., Vol. XXVIII, sec. C., 1910, pp. 96-106.

8. Ueber direkte Handelsverbindungen Westgalliens mit Irland im Altertum und frühen Mittelalter — Sitzungsber. d. Königl. preuss. Akad. (hist.-phil. Classe) 1909, pp. 363-400; 430-470; 543-613; 1910, pp. 1031-1119. Cf. Review by B. Krusch, in Neues Archiv. Bd. XXV, p. 374, and reply by F. Haverfield, "Ancient Rome and Ireland", in Engl. Hist. Rev., Jan. 1913.

has some valuable material illustrating the early trade routes in her book "The Old Irish World" (1912). And Kuno Meyer has noted the proofs that certain Gauls were in Ireland during the second half of the third century [1]. Zimmer's description of this Gallic-Irish trade as "lebhafter Handel" [2] is perhaps an exaggeration, but the evidence of some knowledge, intercourse and trade, is overwhelming. Through this channel of common intercourse Zimmer believed the Irish received Christianity from Gaul. Martin of Tours planted some monasteries in West Gaul from which in course of time Irish monasticism arose [3]. Thus Martin is to be connected with Irish as well as with Welsh monasticism.

In some papers of Zimmer posthumously published in an unfinished state, we find what appears to be conclusive evidence of a profound Gallic influence on Ireland about the middle of the fifth century [4]. Here Zimmer uses an early scribal note on a statement of Virgilius Maro Grammaticus, hitherto overlooked. The note explains that fifth-century author's reference to the invasions of Huns, Vandals, Goths and Alans, as follows:

"Owing to whose devastation all the learned men on this side of the sea fled away, and in transmarine parts, i.e. in *Hiberia* [5] and wherever they betook themselves, brought about a very great advance of learning to the inhabitants of those regions."

Zimmer thought this note was written in West Gaul in the sixth century. The statement is believed to supply the key to that phenomenal development of Irish scholarship which made Ireland almost the only home of classical learning in

1. "Gauls in Ireland". Eriu, Vol. IV (1910), p. 208.
2. Sitzungsber. der Kgl. preuss. Akad. 1909, p. 365.
3. *Op. cit.*, p. 558.
4. K. Meyer. "Aus dem Nachlass Heinrich Zimmers" in Zeitschr. f. Celtische Philologie, Bd. 9 (1913), p. 117 f.
5. For this form cf. Patrick, Confessio 16, "Hiberione", and Epistola, 16 "Indignum est illis Hiberia nati sumus". (N.J.D. White has edited the Latin writings of St. Patrick with a translation. "Libri Sancti Patricii" in Proc. of Roy. Ir. Acad., Vol. XXV (Dub., 1902) Sec. C., p. 201 f.)

the Dark Ages. The scholars of the Continent found asylum, and willing pupils, in Ireland, and the race of Irish scholars that arose in the following century, returned with interest the debt to Europe [1].

This migration of scholars took place mainly during the labors of St. Patrick (432-461). Patrick calls himself, not without reason, "*rusticissimus*", and is sincerely aware of his defective education [2]. It does not appear that he obtained, or indeed sought, aid from the scholars. There is one significant reference in his *Confession* to certain "*Dominicati rhethorici*" "lordly rhetoricians" who have criticized his ignorance [3].

A knowledge of Martin of Tours in Ireland is well attested. Ninian's institution of *Candida Casa* dedicated to Martin (c. 397) was frequented by Irish monks in the sixth century [4]. An early attempt was made to connect Patrick with Martin, as nephew and pupil [5], and a version of Sulpicius Severus' life of Martin was incorporated in the Book of Armagh [6]. It is not unlikely that this represents a vague memory of Martin's influence on Irish Christianity before Patrick.

Columban's letters reveal the consciousness of a distinct Irish church tradition reaching back to earlier generations. It is perhaps more accurate to speak of this as a *Celtic* church tradition, since he refers to Gildas as an authority [7]. The language employed by Columban in his letter to Gregory the Great shows his loyalty to a succession of Celtic teachers, and comparative indifference to the teachers of the Catholic Church [8].

1. Cf. K. Meyer, Learning in Ireland, *passim*.
2. Patrick, Confessio, I, 13, *et. al.*
3. The expression is otherwise read "*Domini ignari rhethorici*," but there is no reason to think they were not professed Christians. Patrick Confessio, 13.
4. Haddan and Stubbs, Councils, etc., Vol. I, p. 120.
5. Stokes, Tripartite Life, Vol. I, p. 25.
6. Gwynn, Book of Armagh, p. CCLIX.
7. See above, p. 32 f.
8. The calculations of Victorius were unacceptable to "nostris magistris

At the Council of Whitby in 664 the Scottic abbot of Lindisfarne, Colman, in debate with Wilfrid, showed how fundamental were the distinctions between Roman and Celtic Christianity. These distinctions lay not merely in differences of custom regarding Easter and the tonsure, which during a long period of virtual isolation from continental ecclesiasticism had become fixed tradition among the Celts. They lay also in deep-seated loyalties. Wilfrid asserts that Rome, France, Africa, Asia, Egypt and Greece are in agreement, "a few men in the corner of the remotest island" stubbornly adhere to an outworn practice. Though worsted in his endeavor to show the catholicity of the Celtic practices in question, Colman could not deny the tradition hallowed by the lives his Scottic saints : "Their life, customs, and discipline", said he, "I never cease to follow [1]".

2. — General Character of Penance in the Ancient Church.

We have seen that the earliest penitential documents of the Celtic churches take us back to the life-time of Patrick, whose mission in Ireland covers the period 432-461. What, if any, church penitential practices existed prior to this period, either in Wales or in Ireland, we have no means of finding out. The beginning of Patrick's work synchronizes approximately with the death of Augustine (430) and with the Council of Ephesus (431) which condemned Nestorius and Celestius. The Council of Chalcedon, which settled the principal doctrinal questions of the period, followed in 451. Patrick's mission brings Ireland definitely into the range of Church history. It also takes place at a period of importance for the formulation of the results of the first four hundred years of Christianity. Our question is to what extent the penitential

et Hibernensis antiquis philosophis et sapientibus". M.G.H., Epistolae Merov. Ævi. Tom. I. Ep. Columbani, I, p. 157.

1. Bede, Hist. Eccles., IV, 25.

practice of those four centuries (c. A. D. 50-450) determined that of the Celtic penitentials. Before an answer to this question can be given it will be necessary to understand something of the penitential discipline of the early church, to the end of this period. In this age of " social " Christianity it may be necessary to recall the fact that the Christian religion was always interpreted in early times primarily as a means of escape from sin and its spiritual penalties. This being so, there were two motives which led to the insistence on penitence which appears in the New Testament writers, in Tertullian, in Chrysostom and in Augustine. One was the desire to maintain the church as a body of people of unpolluted holiness. This ecclesiastical interest led to suspension of privileges and excommunication in the case of those whose lives violated the moral standards of the church. The other was the unwillingness to cast off such persons permanently. Both ecclesiastical and fraternal considerations were opposed to the permanent loss of members; the latter especially since this meant resigning the unfortunate offenders to the devil for eternal punishment. This led to the encouragement of penitent sinners, and to the assigning of works or ceremonies as conditions of their restoration to full membership. These are the main principles of the early penitential discipline which appear in the Pauline letters [1]. These fundamental motives can be observed throughout the early period, and are, indeed, inherent in all penitential systems.

Within the period we are now considering, the penitential discipline passed through certain evolutions. During that era there grew up a set of customs in the treatment of penitents which acquired the sanction of influential fathers of the church and of church councils, and so were regarded as fixed and authoritive. When we compare this early penance with that of late Roman Catholicism, we are struck by the contrast which at once appears, between the late mediaeval secrecy of confession and the ancient practice of the public confession of sins.

1. E. g. 1 Cor. 5 : 2-5 ; 2 Cor. 2 : 6-7.

The evidence is clear and indisputable for the public character of first century penance. The " wicked man " of 1 Cor. 5 is to be temporarily delivered over to Satan by the church " gathered together ". This action is taken in order that " the spirit (of the offender) may be saved ", and also that the " old leaven " may be purged out before it corrupts the whole mass. The punishment was inflicted " by the many " [1], and apparently involved ascetic acts of a severe character (" the destruction of the flesh "). The publicity of the penalty was regarded as an addition to its severity [2].

Sins requiring discipline naturally divided themselves into those which were public and scandalous, and those which were secret and unobserved. The open confession of sins was not precluded by the fact of their being already matter of common report; on the other hand a contrite acknowledgement of them was the beginning of discipline for scandalous sinners. But secret sins, too, were frequently subjected to public confession, at least by the second century. Thus the Didache gives the command; " In church thou shalt confess thy transgressions and shalt not betake thyself to prayer with an evil conscience " [3]. This confession was a part of the Sunday service, in which it preceded the eucharist. " And every Lord's day gather yourselves together and give thanks, first confessing your transgressions [4], that your sacrifice may be pure ", says the same work.

The Greek word ἐξομολόγησις, used for this public confession, was taken over into the Latin literature. It was very early extended to include the whole process of penance. Irenaeus speaks of an Asiatic deacon's wife who had been victimized " in mind and in body " by the magician Marcus, and who, after her conversion, " spent her whole time in the exercise of public confession (ἐξομολόγησις) weeping over and

1. 2 Cor. 2, 6.
2. 2 Cor. 2, 7.
3. ἐν ἐκκλησίᾳ ἐξομολογήσῃ τὰ παραπτώματά σου, καὶ ὀυ προσελέυσῃ ἐπὶ προσευχήν σου ἐν συνειδήσει πονηρᾷ. Did. IV, 14.
4. καὶ εὐχαριστήσατε προεξομολογησάμενοι τὰ παραπτώματα υμῶν, Did. XIV, 1.

lamenting the defilment which she had received from this magician " [1]. Tertullian in his work " On Repentance " asserts (following Hermas) that only one repentance after baptism is possible. But as restoring is a greater thing than giving, this second repentance is a greater privilege involving " laborious " conditions [2]. These conditions are stated in a later chapter. In Tertullian's view *exomologesis* becomes " discipline for man's prostration and humiliation, enjoining a demeanor calculated to move mercy ". It involves adopting the habit of mourning, fasting, groans, prayers and outcries to God, besides which the penitent is " to bow before the feet of the presbyters and to kneel to God's dear ones; to enjoin all the brethren to be his ambassadors to bear his deprecatory supplication " (before God) [3].

In further proof that Tertullian's conception of exomologesis was of a public confession and penance, we may note his lament [4] that most men shun or postpone it as being a public exposure of themselves (*publicationem sui*). " Is it better ", he asks, " to be damned in secret than to absolved in public ? " (*An melius est damnatum latere quam palam absolvi* ?)

One effect of the Novatian Schism was to stimulate the development of the penance system. Gradually the technique of the system was extended as penalties were officially and authoritatively provided for an increasing number of offences. In the fourth century the so-called " stations " of penitents were in full vogue [5]. By this arrangement penitents were divided into four classes, and to each was assigned a special position at the church meetings. The Council of Nice [6] mentions three of

1. Contra Haereses. I, 13, 5.

2. De Penitentia, 7.

3. Presbyteris advolvi, et c(h)aris Dei adgeniculari, omnibus fratribus legationes deprecationis suae injungere. *Ibid.*, 9.

4. *Ibid.*, 10.

5. The word " station " is used as early as Hermas. " As I was fasting and seated on a certain mountain and giving thanks unto the Lord for all that he had done unto me, I see the Shepherd seated by me and saying : " Why hast thou come hither in the early morn ? " " Because sir ", said I, " I keep a station " (ὅτι, φημί, κύριε, στατίωνα ἔχω) " What ", saith he, " is a station ? " " I am fasting, sir ", said I. Hermas, Simil. 5, 1.

6. Can, 11.

these four classes. The one omitted is that of the συγκλαίοντες, *flentes*, or " weepers ", who were in the first or lowest stage of penance, and whose station was outside the door of the church [1]. The other three stations were within the building. The ἀκροώμενοι, *audientes*, or " hearers " were placed in the vestibule (ἐν τῷ νάρθηκι); they were dismissed after the lesson and sermon and before the eucharist [2]. The ὑποπίπτοντες, *substrati* or " kneelers ", were stationed further forward, yet in the rear of the congregation. When others stood during prayer these were required to kneel. They came to church clothed in sack-cloth and with ashes on their heads [3]. Finally the συνιστάμενοι, *consistentes* or " co-standers ", were mingled with the congregation although they were not yet permitted to communicate [4].

This brief description makes it clear that the typical penance of the church was public in all its stages. No concession was made to the sensitiveness of the offender. There was a considered attempt to make of penance a public humiliation, the endurance of which would form a safe guarantee of sincere repentance [5].

The development of the penance system was no doubt considerably influenced by civil law. Morinus notes that after Augustine's time penitential rules were extended to include " all crimes which the civil law punished with death, exile or other grave corporal penalty " [6]. There was also a marked tendency to increase the periods assigned for penance, after the middle of the third century [7]. It would appear that the church then made a vigorous effort to maintain discipline against the lax tendencies which were incidental to the " long

1. Greg. Thaum., Canonical Epistle, Can., 11. The 25th canon of th Council of Ancyra calls this class the χειμαζόμενοι or *hiemantes*, since they were exposed to the weather as they stood without to implore the prayers of the faithful.
2. Greg. Thaum., *loc. cit.*
3. Jerome, Ep. 30.
4. Greg. Thaum., *loc. cit.*
5. Cf. Ambrose, De Penitentia, lib. II, c. 10.
6. Commentarius Historicus, lib. V, c. 5.
7. *Ibid*, lib. IV, c. 9.

peace " of the church before Diocletian and its full toleration after the Edict of Milan. Hitherto severity in discipline had been rare, and had consisted mainly of outright and permanent expulsion for incorrigible offenders. Now, increasingly, sins of all degrees of gravity were assigned their appropriate terms of penance. This tendency is already present in the canons of the Synod of Elvira (305), which assign, for instance, a five year penance for adultery [1]. The decrees of Ancyra (314) set a five year term for involuntary homicide [2]. This term is doubled (c. 375) by Basil the Great [3]. Not infrequently the canons state that discretion is allowed to bishops in the extension or mitigation of the canonical terms [4].

A most typical document of the era is the series of canonical letters written by Basil of Caesarea to Amphilochius [5]. Basil here supplies us with what is partly a codification of traditional custom, and partly a statement of his own opinion, on most of the cases arising in penitential discipline. His canons are not without inconsistencies and discrepancies in the duration of the penances prescribed [6]. The personal distinction of their author gave an authority to these canons which sustained them in high esteem through the centuries following. They are referred to with great respect by the Council of Trullo (692); although this council ventures to modify their terms [7] it nevertheless regards them in the light of established church law [8]. They may then be regarded as evidence for the penance of the fourth century that is typical and reliable.

1. Sin. Elvr. Can., 69; Mansi, Concil, T. II, col. 17.
2. Sin. Ancyr. Can., 23; *op. cit.*, col. 11.
3. Ad Amphil., 57 ; Migne, Patrol. Græca, T. 32, col. 798.
4. E. g., Concil. Nic. can., 12 ; Mansi, Concil., T. II, col. 674 ; Basil, Ad Amphil. can., 54, 74.
5. These three letters are numbered cxcix, ccxvii, and clxxxviii in the epistles of Basil which may he found in Migne, Patrol. Græca, T. 32. They were written c. 374-376. The canons contained in them are numbered continuously through the three letters.
6. E. g. Cans. 8 and 57 ; cans. 4 and 50.
7. Concil. Quinsextum, Can. 40.
8. *Ibid.*, can. 87; Migne, *op. cit.*, col. 979.

These canons refer throughout to the system of graded public penance outlined above, and regularly subdivide the longer terms of penance into periods to be spent in each of the *stations*. The word "exomolegesis" is used to include both confession and penance [1], which are parts of the same process of public humiliation. There is no suggestion that any other kind of penance is in existence. This representative document of Ancient Church penance corroborates the otherwise abundant evidence that the typical and normal penance of the period was essentially a public discipline [2].

3. — Was Private Penance Practiced in the Ancient Church?

The evidence for public confession and penance in the Ancient Church is abundant. But the question may still be raised wheter anything corresponding to the private penance of the later period was also in use. This matter has received attention from a number of writers. The claim of most Roman Catholic writers is that the private exercise of penance was sacramental even during the ancient period. This claim has been denied by Lagarde [3], who finds no trace of the Roman confessional down to the period of Gregory the Great. His position coincides mainly with that of Lea [4]. It has been combatted by Tixeront [5], who, following the older work of Frank [6] attempts to show the existence of the Catholic system of sacramental private confession from the early centuries. With the aid of these and some other writers, we shall briefly examine the facts.

Much space is devoted by Frank to the difficult ques-

1. Can. 74; *op. cit.*, col. 804.
2. Cf. Morinus, Commentarius, lib. V, c. 21.
3. "Saint Augustin a-t-il connu la confession?" with similar studies of Chrysostom and Gregory the Great, *Revue d'histoire et de la littérature religieuses*, 1913-1914.
4. History of Auricular Confession and Indulgences.
5. Le sacrement de pénitence dans l'antiquité chrétienne.
6. Die Bussdisciplin der Kirche (Mainz, 1867).

tion of the Presbyters of Penance, and their abolition by the Patriarch Nectarius of Constantinople (c. 391) [1]. This Frank supposes to be a proof of his contention for private penance. But an unbiased examination of the sources will hardly be found to support such a conclusion. The only information we have of the incident is found in the histories of Socrates and of Sozomen [2]. Socrates is the superior authority. He has his information from Eudaemon, who claimed to have given the advice on which Nectarius acted. He states that the office was created at the time of the Decian persecution and Novatian heresy, and that those who had sinned after baptism (apparently *lapsi*, in the original stage) were to confess their sins to the presbyters of penance. The scandalous incident on account of which it was decided to abolish the office, is stated differently by the two historians. Sozomen's account is that an assault was committed by a deacon on a penitent matron in the church. In the more credible statement of Socrates the woman's confession inculpated both herself and the deacon, and the offence took place elsewhere. In both narratives it is made explicit that the scandal arose from the woman's confession. The assumption that this confession, made to the presbyter of penance, was secret, leaves the fact of the scandal unexplained. Nor does either account, on this basis, justify the action taken against the office of Presbyter of Penance. No charge against this official is made or implied.

The whole matter, however, becomes explicable if we suppose that the guilty deacon was present at a session in wich the woman's manner of life was exposed by her own confession. He probably served, as deacon, on a tribunal presided over by the presbyter, whose duty it was, says Sozomen " to preside over the imposition of penance ". If the deacon made the woman's confession the basis of his advances, his act would constitute a despicable breach of honor, and bring the penitentiary office into disrepute. We

1. Frank, *op. cit.*, p. 412 f.

2. Socrates, Eccles. Hist. lib. V, c. 19 ; Migne, Patrol. Græca, T. 61. col. 614. Sozomen, Eccles. Hist. lib. vii, c. 16 ; *op. cit.* ; t. 67, col. 1479.

have good evidence that deacons elsewhere had part in the assigning of penance [1].

The Presbyter of Penance, then, was an official of the church, not a father-confessor. No doubt the multitude of cases of penance incidental to the persecutions, had made it necessary to appoint a special official to take charge of the matter, which had formerly been a function of the whole church represented by the Presbyterium. The object aimed at was not secrecy, but efficiency.

Nor is it necessary to suppose that the public were excluded from the sessions at which the presbyter " presided "; although the cases were no longer brought into the assembly of the whole congregation.

That the drastic action of Nectarius in suppressing the office at Constantinople was regarded by many as a mistake, is evident. Both writers point out that a great decline of penance and discipline was the result. But Sozomen contrasts this decline in the East with the continuation of *public* penance in the West, especially at Rome. We have convincing evidence of the existence of penitentiary priests at Rome in the fourth and fifth centuries. Under their administration penance was public, with reconciliation at the Easter season [2]. About 470 Pope Simplicius appointed a week during which the priests should be present in the three Roman churches of St. Peter, St. Paul and St. Laurence, in order to receive penitents and administer baptism [3]. But probably this arrangement was mainly devised to promote efficiency and save time. There is no proof of actual secrecy, and the interviews may have been preparatory to the usual public confession.

In order to establish a continuity between ancient and mediaeval penance, certain writers have professed to discover sacramental views of penance in the early period. Tixeront indeed asserts that " sacramental public penance is one of

1. Cyprian, Ep. 12, Migne, Patrol. Lat., T. 4, col. 265; Sin. Elvir. Can. 32; Mansii Concil. T. II, col. 11.

2. Schmitz, Bussbücher, Bd. I, p. 56; Bd. II, pp. 67, 68.

3. Lea, Hist. of Auric. Confess. and Indulg. Vol. I, p. 183.

those myths which ought to disappear from history " [1]. He holds, however, that a sacramental character attached to private penance, and that confession was " always and in principle secret ", although absolution was public till the eighth or ninth century [2]. Frank labors to show that the Fathers held confession to a priest to be a " *mysterium* " [3] while Boudhinon connects the sacramental phase of penance with the public discipline and reconciliation of the lenten season, known as " solemn " penance [4].

These variant viewpoints illustrate the difficulty of such writers in finding any thread of continuity for the two periods. The few references they are able to cite in the early literature by no means establish the conception of a sacramental penance. The sacramental conception of penance really became general only in the thirteenth century, and is mainly to be attributed to Peter Lombard (d. 1164) whose " Sentences " included penance among the " seven " sacraments [5]. Yet the writers who favor the view just noted are able to refer to certain instances of private consultation in connection with penance to which some consideration must be given.

It is observed, for example, that Origen recommends seeking out a skilled physician of souls, to whom to confide one's sins ; if advised by him confession to the whole congregation should follow [6]. There is no identification of this expert with priest or bishop or other church functionary. In another context the same authorspeaks of confession only as public [7]. A passage in Chrysostom in which he is alleged to have rejected public for private confession, turns out, on being read in full,

1. Tixeront, *op. cit.*, p. 35.
2. *Op. cit.*, p. 62.
3. Frank, *op. cit.*, p. 399 f.
4. Sur l'histoire de la pénitence, à propos d'un ouvrage récent (referring o Lea's History of Auricular Confession). *Rev. d'hist. et de la litt. relig.*, T. II (1897), p. 306, f. p. 497 f.
5. See Lagarde, Latin Church, p. 32 f. ; Lea, Hist. of Auricular Confess. and Indulg. vol. I, p. 496 f.
6. Origen, Homil. II on Ps. XXXVII, c. 6. — Migne, Patrol. Graeca, T. 12, col. 1586.
7. Homil II, on Leviticus, *op. cit.*, T. 12, col. 412.

to have an entirely different meaning. " Let us not " says Chrysostom, " call ourselves sinners, but also count over our sins, going over them each by each. I do not say to thee, Make a parade of thyself before others; but, Be persuaded by the prophet when he says: Reveal thy way unto the Lord [1]. This does not specifically reject public confession, nor does it in any way recommend private confession to a priest. Indeed it really excludes the latter. Ambrose urges public confession on the part of those who, it would appear, have already confessed their sins to " a man "; and prays for charity that in receiving the confession of a sinner he may able to weep and lament with him [2]. To interpret these exceptional instances as representing a universal practice would be manifestly unfair. But even if the practice of consulting a spiritual adviser before coming to public confession could be shown to be a general one, the instances cited lend no support to the assumption that it was practiced as a substitute for the ordinary public confession. It seems to have had no formal recognition in the church. In Origen it is regarded only as a desirable habit from the standpoint of the individual, not as a substitute, but as a preparation, for public confession. There is no implication that the " skilled physician " of souls has any official rank or even that he is a cleric. Ambrose urges those who have privately confided their sins to another, not to shrink from confessing them openly. Lagarde seems to be fully justified in his opinion that such private penance as can be discovered in the Ancient Church was " independent of ecclesiastical supervision " [3].

M. Tixeront alleges, as an instance of private confession and penance under ecclesiastical supervision a passage from the liturgy of the (heretical) Armenian church of the fifth century [4]. What the *Rituale Armenorum* published by Conybeare [5],

1. Chrysostom, Homil. ad Hebraeos, XXXI., 3 Migne, Patrol. Græca, T. 63, col. 214 (Cf. Homil., XX, 1, which refers to the " weepers ".)

2. Ambrose, De Penitentia, lib. II, c. x; Migne, Patrol. Lat., T. 16, col. 540; *ibid*, c. VIII, *loc. cit.*, col. 536.

3. Latin Church, p. 53.

4. Tixeront, *op. cit.*, pp. 19-20.

5. F. C. Conybeare, Rituale Armenorum, Oxf. 1905, p. 190, f.

which Tixeront cites, really contains in regard to penance, is an elaborate formula for the reception of penitents. The penitents are received at the door of the church by the priest, and enter while the deacon proclaims : " All ye that come unto repentance " [1]. According to one MS, quoted in a footnote [2], " the priest grants remission publicly that the others may be encouraged unto the love and fear of God ". While the sacramental element may be recognized in this, the private element is lacking. In any case Rome did not recognize the church using this ritual, and its penitential usages cannot have been in any way the parent of Western mediaeval penance.

Those who try to construct an early history for private penance in the mediaeval sense, are greatly embarrassed by the silence of St. Augustine on the subject. Augustine addresses his *Confessiones* throughout to God ; but he publishes it to the world. The work is, indeed, a great *exomologesis*, freely exposing private as well as public affairs. Neither in this autobiographical work nor elsewhere does the author advocate private confession or suggest that he himself at any stage resorted to a priest to unburden his heart of sin. The passages in Augustine bearing on the conduct of penance have been carefully analyzed by Lagarde [3]. Lagarde concludes his study by outlining Augustine's teaching on the subject as follows :

1. Augustine distinguishes two kinds of sins, light and grave. Grave sins are those of which one is enough to debar from the Kingdom of Heaven.

2. Light sins are daily remitted through prayer, alms and fasting.

3. Prayer, alms and fasting will efface the grave sins, on condition that the sinner turns from them.

4. Grave sins are hidden or public. Hidden sins are to be repented of with "conversion" (N.B. not confession) in private. Open and scandalous sins are to be confessed openly. For scandalous sins the offender might be excommunicated

1. *Ibid.*, p. 190-191.
2. *Ibid.*, p. 195.
3. Rev. d'hist. et de la litt. relig., 1913.

by means of the power of the keys, but the latter could be employed only for sins of this class.

There is no room in this classification for secret confession. The fact is surely of great significance that Augustine, who comes at the close of the ancient period, takes no cognizance of secret penance. A typical statement of his general position is found in his Sermon CCCXCII, 3, where he lays down the precept : Let us do penance as it is done in the church, that the church may pray for us [1].

But the origin of private penance has been connected with the great pope of the fifth century, whose death took place in the same year as that of St. Patrick, 461. A letter written by Leo the Great in 459, *ad universos episcopos per Companiam, Samnium et Picenum* [2], condemns the practice of forcing penitents to read publicly a *libellus* containing a detailed written confession of their sins. The practice has, he says, no apostolic authority ; and he recommends as sufficient revealing the state of the conscience in a secret confession to the priests. He is solicitous lest many should shrink from penance in fear of much humiliation, *ne multi a poenitentiae remediis arceantur*.

Lea gives considerable importance to this letter, and suggests that Leo here inaugurated the practice of "private penance for private sins [3]". Tixeront uses it to support his contention that confession was previously always secret [4]. In reply to these statements two facts are to be noted. One of these is later stated by Lea himself when he observes that "centuries were to elapse" before any general change in penance can be distinguished [5]; and the other is that Leo is rejecting a special innovation in public penance — the reading of a prepared list of sins committed — and is not pronouncing

1. Agite poenitentiam qualis agitur in ecclesia ut oret pro nobis ecclesia. Migne, Patrol. Lat., T. 39, Col. 1711. For similar expressions see his Ps. XXIII, serm., II, 11.

2. Leo I, Epistolae, CLXVII, 2, in Migne, Patr. Lat., Tom. 54, col. 1217.

3. Hist. of Auric. Confess., Vol. I, p. 183.

4. Tixeront, *op. cit.*, pp. 37, 62.

5. Lea, *op. cit.*, Vol. II, p. 73. Lea notes not only that the typical penance remained public but that *libelli* were approved even by popes.

on the practice of public confession in general. No act of any pope ever prohibited public confession, even of secret sins. Morinus truly states that the *confessio peccatorum occultorum publica* was never forbidden [1]. The church, as we shall see, fought in vain to retain it, against the inroads of the Celtic practice of private penance.

In the political confusion and social disintegration of the fifth and sixth centuries there was a general decline of church *morale*, and the discipline was poorly enforced [2]. The period of Columban's activity in Gaul covers the pontificate ot Gregory the Great (590-604). While Columban was promulgating his Celtic rules of penance, Gregory was urging a reform along the old lines. His references to penance reinforce the view that private penance had no recognized place in the Imperial Church. The penance which Gregory seeks to revive is public penance preceded by public confession. He takes the command " Lazarus, come forth ! ", allegorically, as a summons to confession of sin [3]. Repentance takes place " when the resolute mind begins to let loose against itself words of abhorrence which aforetime from a feeling of shame it kept to itself through weakness [4] ". The great virtue of confession is humility [5], which is testified to in the act of public penance. He speake of public confession of secret sins as a salutary exercise [6]. Gregory seems totally unaware of the type of penitential discipline which by this time was familiar in the Celtic churches. He holds to the principles of the ancient discipline. It is true that he allows himself freedon from the fourth century canons — if he knew them. He has no hard and fast code. His instructions to Augustine of Canterbury condition penalties on the motives of the offender, and set no terms of ascetic privation. "Charity" says Gregory " dictates the measure of the punishment [7] ".

1. Morinus, *op. cit.*, lib. II, c. x.
2. Lagarde, Latin Church., p. 55.
3. Greg. Mag., Moral, XXII, 31, Migne, Patrol. Lat., T. 76, col. 231.
4. *Ibid.*, IX, 66, *op. cit.*, T. 75, col. 896.
5. *Ibid.*, XXII, 33-34, *op. cit.*, T. 76, col. 232.
6. *Ibid.*, XXV, 13, *op. cit.*, T. 76, col. 326.
7. Bede, Hist. Eccles., I, 27.

4. — The Penance of the Early Monasteries.

Allusion has been made in Ch. I above to the bearing on the origins of Irish Christianity, of intercourse in the early centuries between Gaul and Ireland, and to the probable influence of St. Martin of Tours on the origins both of Welsh and of Irish monasticism. It has been argued by Warren from a study of ritual usages, that the Celtic churches felt a powerful influence, through the medium of Gaul, from the church of the East [1]; and the subject has been treated in a broader way by G.T. Stokes [2], who gives many instances of intercourse, on the part of merchants and scholars, between Ireland and the East (especially Syria). These facts make it necessary for us to test the hypothesis that Celtic penance is traceable to the Eastern monasteries, — an hypothesis which is favored by Lagarde [3].

The intense pursuit of salvation from sin which characterized early monasticism, fostered an anxious introspection, and led to habitual confession to those more experienced, for the sake of securing advice and help. Pachomius appears to have given the practice a place in his rule, and it thus became an essential part of cenobite discipline [4]. One of the earliest and fullest writers on the monks of Tabenna is John Cassian — a favorite author, as we saw, of the Irish

1. F.E. Warren, Liturgy and Ritual of the Celtic Church, Oxf., 1881, p. 47 f.

2. Ireland and the Celtic Church, 6th ed. (1907), p. 166 f.

3. "Confession was established about the middle of the fourth century by Pacomius, the founder of cenobitic life. It produced good results. Monks told their temptations and their falls to other monks, who were often not priests, but who had a reputation for sanctity... During the fifth century the institution of Pacomius, under the patronage of Cassian, Palladius and others, emigrated from Egypt to the monasteries of the West, even so far as to the Christian Celtic monks." Latin Church, p. 55.

4. No genuine rule of Pachomius is extant. The so-called Regula S. Pachomii does not enjoin private confession. Cf. Lea, Hist. of Auric. Confession and Indulg., Vol. I, p. 184.

saints. Cassian in describing this monastic confession tells us that the juniors were to lay bare any disquieting thoughts to the seniors, and " not to conceal thoughts in their hearts ". There was, of course, nothing of the nature of sacramental absolution connected with this. It is not indicated that the senior monks themselves were expected to make confessions. The data given would suggest that the practice was regarded as a consultation for spiritual advice; not exclusively a confession of sins but an unburdening of troubled thoughts. So far this corresponds largely to features we shall find in Celtic penance. But there is one great gap between this custom and Celtic penance. It is not suggested either that any penitential schedules were followed, or that penances were even assigned [1]. One looks in vain for evidence of this in Cassian's writings. The references to the subject in the " Conferences " do not support the assumption that it was customary to assign penances. Abbot Moses tells, indeed, of a confession of theft where the contrite confession itself was regarded as sufficient amends [2]. Abbot Pinufius leaves the test of true penitence and pardon to the conscience [3], and elsewhere regards as sufficient confession of sin to God alone [4].

While it is not impossible that some effect on Celtic penance followed from contact in Gaul with this early Egyptian monasticism, it is certainly not justifiable to regard the former as simply an extension to the laity of the latter, as is the opinion both of Lagarde [5] and of Hauck [6]. The evolution from this half-regulated spiritual consultation of a senior monk by a junior, to the codified lay and clerical penance of the penitentials, is assumed but not proven; and between the two there is a vast difference.

Nor can Celtic penance be derived, so far as the sources

1. Cassian, Institutes, lib. IV, c. 9, Migne, Patrol. Lat., T. 49, col. 161.
2. Cassian, Collationes, II, c. 9, *op. cit.*, T. 49, col. 537.
3. *Ibid.*, XX, c. 5, *op. cit.*, T. 59, col. 1154.
4. *Ibid.*, c. 8, *op. cit.*, T. 49, col. 1159.
5. Lagarde, *loc. cit.*
6. Was man anderwärts vornehmlich bei den Mönchen fand, wurde hier (i.e. in Ireland) von den Glaübigen überhaupt geübt. Hauck, Kirchengesh. Deutschlands, Vol. I, p. 273.

indicate, from the practice of Martin of Tours. (St. Martin was a Latin, born in Pannonia. The origin of his monasticism is purely a matter of conjecture [1]). M. Babut has sifted from the largely plagiarized *Vita Martini* of Sulpicius Severus, what can be historically ascertained about that monastic founder [2]. The rigid discipline of Marmoutier consisted mainly in an extreme course of fasting. There is no hint of the practice of confession [3] The monastic rules of Basil the Great made little if any advance on those of the Pachomian monks in respect to confession. The *Regulae Fusius Tractatae* enjoin opening the secrets of the heart to the superior (τῷ προεστῶτι) [4]. Sins are not to be concealed from the brethren [5]. Offences against the rule, such as failure to appear at prayers, are to be confessed [6]. Basil's so-called "shorter rules" the *Regulae Brevius Tractatae* [7] contain some similar precepts. But, in both rules the prescriptions for confession are of a general character, and there is an entire absence of evidence for a developed system of secret penance [8].

In discussing early instances of private confession Lea remarks that "St. Jerome refers to it several times and a canon of the first council of Toledo in 398 shows that in Spain it was becoming a recognized function of the priest at least for virgins under vows [9]". In support of the first of these statements Lea cites Hieron. Ep. XLI, 3, and his *Comment. in Eccles. cap. 10.* The letter is written "to Mar-

1. Babut suggests that he had met Eastern ascetics at Rome, or followed Julian into Mesopotamia and visited the *laurae* of Syria, E. C. Babut, Saint Martin de Tours.

2. *Ibid.*,

3. Ibid., p. 241 f.

4. Basil, Reg. Fus. Tract. Interrogatio, XXVI, in Migne Patr. Graec., Tom. 31, Col. 986.

5. *Ibid.*, Interr., XLVI.

6. *Ibid.*, Interr., XXXIX.

7. Migne, *op. cit.*, col. 1051 f. See e.g. Interrogationes 4 to 13.

8. "The inferiors are bidden to confess their sins to the Superior or else to those who are charged with the pastoral care of weak souls. The monks in question are not necessarily priests but the possessors of the necessary charismatic gifts". Clarke, St. Basil the Great, p. 95.

9. Hist. of Auric. Confess and Indulg., Vol. I, p. 179.

cella against the Montanists [1]". It contains no explicit evidence beyond the assumption that confession and penance are in the charge of priests. In the Commentary Jerome is explaining *si momorderit serpens in silentio* (Eccl. 10.11) with reference to the unrevealed sin which is a wound of the devil, and ought to be confessed to one's *frater et magister* [2]. The emphasis is laid on the act of revealing one's sins. A private interview with a spiritual adviser seems to be suggested, and the passage is on a par with that cited above from Origen. It is not necessary to suppose that such confession was intended to replace the usual public form of confession. This one reference to private confession is, I believe, the only genuine instance in the voluminous work of Jerome, in which there are many references to penance and confession [3].

In the Council of Toledo referred to by Lea we find a prohibition of familiarity between a "puella Dei" and her confessor [4]. This can hardly be said to prove Lea's statement that in Spain private confession "was becoming a recognized function of the priest", even for nuns. It is more probable that the practice referred to was analogous to that of the Eastern and Egyptian monasteries; and if so the confessors selected by the nuns would not necessarily be priests, but persons skilled in the ascetic life, especially senior monks. This interpretation would accord with the regulations of St. Basil, which provided that nuns should make confession to the superior of the monastery, but always in the presence of a senior nun [5].

The monastic practice in the matter of private confession

1. Ep. XLI of the "old edition" is no. 27 of the Benedictine edition.

2. si tacuerit... et non egerit poenitentiam, nec vulnus suum fratri et magistro voluerit confiteri, etc. Migne, Patr. Lat., Tom. 23, col. 1152.

3. See e.g. Comment. in Daniel. cap. 9 (Migne, 25, 541); Comment. in Osee lib. III, cap. 14 (Migne, 25, 942); Comment. in Evangel. Matt. lib. III, cap. 16 (Migne, 26, 122).

4. Item neque puella Dei aut familiaritatem habeat cum confessore aut cum quolibet laico, sibi sanguinis alieni, etc. Concil. Tolet. I, can. 6. Mansi, Concilia, Tom. III, col. 999.

5. St. Basil, Regul. Brev. Tract. 109, 110; Migne, Patrol. Graeca, T. 49, col. 455; col. 1158; Morison, St. Basil and his Rule, p. 100; Clarke, St. Basil the Great, p. 97.

is fixed by St. Benedict in a way which makes no important change from the Eastern rules. Private confession is not commanded, but is recommended as an exercise in humility. Insidious sins are to be revealed to the abbot or one of the senior monks [1]. Priests, as such, have nothing to do with such confession; it is merely a useful means of promoting humility and purity among the monks. Benedict comes no nearer than Pachomius or Basil to the Celtic type of penance which his contemporaries Gildas and Finnian represent.

5. — Celtic Penance compared with that of the Ancient Church.

Even a casual reading of the Celtic penitentials is sufficient to indicate that they represent a system of penance widely different from that of any representative document of the Ancient Church, e.g. the Canonical Letters of Basil. And a careful comparison only serves to reinforce this opinion. Some of the prominent characteristics of the penitentials will later be observed in their relation to the social customs of the Celts [2]. Here we will content ourselves with indicating the fundamental difference regarding secret and public penance.

We have seen that the typical penance of the Ancient Church, to times contemporary with the introduction of the Celtic penitentials, was a public discipline, and that neither ecclesiastical nor monastic institutions exhibit prototypes of the private penance of late mediaeval times. On the other hand the Celtic penance was characteristically private; confession was made to one only, and religiously kept secret, and public reconciliation was not in use.

In our references to secret confession and private penance the suggestion is not intended that the exercise of penance

1. Regula S. Bened., cap. 7, 45, 46. Cf. the special restrictions placed on priests, cap. 60, 62.

2. Chapters III and IV following.

was always and in all stages unknown to any but the confessor and the penitent. In the nature of the case that would be impossible. Many of the penalties employed made the penitent conspicuous in their performance. What is meant by private penance is rather penance dissociated from the congregation, imposed by the confessor on secret confession, and either not involving excommunication or else concluded with a private and not a public reconciliation. This is the character of Celtic penance, and it became the character, in general, of the penance of the mediaeval and modern Catholic Church.

The only evidences for public features ot penance in the Celtic penitential documents, are in those of the time of St. Patrick. The Canons of St. Patrick make a faint attempt to give a public character to reconciliation. The penitent, on completing his term, is to come with witnesses to be received back into the church [1]. The framers of this document were not Irish. Patrick was a Briton trained in Gaul; his two associates were Gauls. They attempted to give a semblance of Catholic practice to the institution of penance in Ireland. That their regulation is so far from that of the ancient practice is probably due to the fact that the native church was already proving recalcitrant against attempts to bring in the public discipline. One other instance can be cited. In the *Canones Hibernenses* there is one mention of public confession of sins *coram sacerdote et plebe post votum* [2]. But it is relegated to the place of an *arreum*, or substitute for other penance, and confined to those who have taken vows.

Warren his mistakenly supposed that public confession was usual in the Celtic churches. He cites a number of instances of what he regards as public confession [3]. But the instances given are mere outbursts of emotion, and manifestly not typical. Neither are they in any ecclesiastical sense public. They are merely cases in which the penitent in his eagerness

1. Impleto cum testibus veniat anno poenitentiae. Sin. Patric. Auxil. et Isern. Can. 14.

2. Can. Hib. II, can. 4.

3. Ritual and Liturgy, p. 148 f.

does not take advantage of the "seal of confession", or wait for a private interview with his confessor.

The term just used, "seal of confession," is of course, as a phrase, an anachronism when applied to the Celtic Church. It was a subject of discussion among the Schoolmen [1]. But it signifies a fact which was familiar and normal, and over which there was no discussion, in Celtic Christianity. Secrecy of confession was guarded by the heaviest spiritual penalties. To disclose the information given by a penitent to his *Anmchara* (confessor), was one of the four sins for which penance itself was of no avail [2]. The early attempts to give a public character to penance left no traces in the typical penance of the Celtic churches. None of the purely Celtic codes supplies references to the ancient penitential authorities. This is probably not due to total ignorance of the latter. There are indications that Basil was known to the sixth century Irish monks. In the Elegy on St. Columba [3] by his survivor Dallan Forgaill occurs the statement "He expounded Basil's judgments". An ancient commentator explains this by saying that Baithne (Columba's successor) quoted a text from Basil for the subduing of (Columba's) pride, at the Assembly of Drumceatt [4]. It is not surprising to find a knowledge of Basil at this stage in Celtic church history, when we remind ourselves of the Greek studies that flourished in the Irish monasteries [5]. But there is nothing to indicate that Gildas, David, Finnian or Columban used Basil's or any other ancient penitential code as a basis for their penitential regulations. It is not till we reach Theodore of Tarsus that the influence of Basil appears.

It must be remembered that Theodore was a native of

1. Lea. Hist. of Auric. Confess. and Indulg., Vol. I, p. 412 f.

2. Martyrology of Œngus. Ed. Stokes, p. 223, note 5; Stokes, Trip. Life Vol. I, p. CLXIV.

3. The *Amra Cholumb Cille* of Dallan Forgaill, ed. J. O'Beirne Crowe, Dublin, 1871, p. 39.

4. Williams, Gildae de Excidio, etc., pt. 2, p. 191.

5. Kuno Meyer, Learning in Ireland, G.T. Stokes, Ireland and the Celtic Church, *loc. cit.*; D'Arbois de Jubainville, Cours de litt. Celt., Tom. 7, p. 112.

Tarsus in Cilicia, that he was sixty years old when he first came to the west, and sixty-six when he became Archbishop of Canterbury. It would therefore be very surprising if we found no references in his penitential to the most famous Eastern code.

The *Poenit. Theod.* has the following references to the canonical letters of Basil :

1. Poenit. Theod., I, II, 7, refers to Basil. *ad Amphil.* 58, 62, 63 (with the phrase *ut Basilius dicit*).

2. Poenit. Theod., I, VIII, 14, refers to Basil *ad Amphil.* 18, 19 (Basilius judicavit).

3. Poenit. Theod., I, XVI, 3, refers to Basil *ad Amphil.* 4 (Basilius hoc judicavit).

4. Poenit. Theod., II, VII, 3, refers to Basil (ut Basilius judicavit).

5. Poenit. Theod., II, VII, 6, refers to Basil *ad Amphil.* 9, 29 (Basilius hoc judicavit).

With the exception of No. 4, which appears to be only mistakenly connected with Basil, Theodore in each case simply uses Basil as a guide to the period of time to be assigned. He entirely omits Basil's references, in the canons used, to the graded public penance of the fourth century. The influence of Basil then, even in the case of Theodore's work, is negligible as a factor in determining the character of the penance of the penitentials.

The typical Celtic penitentials give no statements regarding their divergence from the penance of the Ancient Church. This fact is easily explicable on the ground that no question of the validity of private penance was raised in the environment in which they were written, and their writers, whether or not they were aware of the early practice of the Church, had no occasion to explain their own by contrast with it. But Theodore, with his Eastern training, must have found the form of penance in use in Britain and Ireland unfamiliar and surprising, We have seen that he studied and utilized Irish documents [1]. Either because he was persuaded of the supe-

1. See above, p. 61.

riority of the Celtic usage, or because the latter had already, through the Scottic missionaries, obtained recognition in the English church, he was brought to a conscious departure from the older penance to that of the Celts. This appears not only in his approval of commutations and compositions, to which our attention was called in Chapter I. It appears also in his adoption of private, and formal rejection of public penance. "Public reconciliation" says Theodore "is not authorized in this province, since there is no public penance" (Reconciliatio ideo in hac provincia publice statuta non est, quia et publica poenitentia non est) [1].

It has been suggested that Theodore drew his view of private penance from the penitential which goes by the name of John the Faster [2]. This work is referred to by Morinus as typical of Eastern penance c. A.D. 600 [3], but is really of very doubtful date and authorship. It testifies to a reaction against the public discipline of the Eastern church, but Ermoni has shown its comparative unimportance for the history of Eastern penance [4]. Public penance was retained in the East to the fall of Constantinople [5]. It is not certain that John the Faster's penitential, so-called, was in existence in Theodore's time, and, in view of his other Celtic borrowings, hardly probable that he went to this Eastern work for a custom that flourished in Britain and Ireland before him.

1. Poenit. Theod. lib. I, XIII, 4.
2. Walter Hook, Lives of the Archbishops of Canterbury, Vol. I, p. 168.
3. Morinus, Commentarius, lib. VI, c. XXIII. Morinus published this penitential in an Appendix to his work. It also appears in Migne, Patr. Graec., Tom. 88, col. 1890 f.
4. V. Ermoni, La pénitence dans l'histoire, à propos d'un ouvrage récent. Rev. des questions historiques, Jan. 1900, p. 1 f., especially p. 40.
5. *Ibid.*

CHAPTER III

The Relation of Celtic Penance to Pre-Christian Celtic Customs.

1. — Survival of Paganism in Goidelic Christianity.

It was a remark of Giraldus Cambrensis that Ireland had no martyrs [1]. The process of Christianization in Ireland affords a marked contrast to that which took place in Gaul. When the new religion overspread Gaul the Celtic inhabitants of that province had already been obliged through the operation of Roman edicts, to relinquish much that was distinctive of their native religion. In Gaul Druidism, suppressed by Tiberius and Claudius, had lost its power and largely ceased to function [2]. Ireland lay beyond the range of Roman edicts. She likewise escaped the later ravages of the Teutonic invasion from which the Celts of Britain largely suffered. It was not to imperialism nor to barbarism that the native religion of the Goidel was to make its surrender. Until the coming of Christianity the Irish civilization flourished in unimpaired vitality. It need not therefore surprise us to discover that the church in Ireland made an amicable compromise with the religious practices which preceded it, and that the habits and customs of the nation were little disturbed by the change.

Christianity in Ireland was quietly and gradually imposed upon the native civilization with less of violent and radical transformation than was generally the case elsewhere. The

1. Gir. Camb., *Topog. Hib.*, Distinct. III, ch. XXVII, ch. XXXII.

2. The suppression of the druids by the Emperors was probably due in a great degree to fact that the legal practices of the druids were incompatible with Roman law. — D'Arbois de Jubainville, Cours de Litt. Celt., Tom. VII, p. 172 f.

" kings " as the Irish chieftains were called, were among the first to fall under the influence of the faith; and even when they did not profess belief in it, as in the instance of the High King Loeghaire Mac Niall, they did not subject its apostles to any serious persecution. Irish monks and clergy, on their part, habitually evinced a loyalty to the native culture of which they were heirs. They befriended the bards, and were themselves the agents of the preservation of the national literature [1]. The early Irish Christian literature abounds in evidences of the survival of paganism. Numerous traces of pre-Christian religious custom confront us in almost every document [2]. The Hymn of St. Patrick, regarded by scholars as a genuine product of fifth century Irish Christianity [3], while execrating the druids, seems closely allied in style and character to druidical formulas [4].

When saints come into conflict with druids the former are successful only by a resort to the methods of their adversaries. They may perform greater miracles than the druids, but they are miracles of the same kind; they may surpass the druids in the effectiveness of their maledictions, but the religions conceptions involved are essentially the same on both sides. The birth of Connal Cernach from

1. Plummer, Vitae SS. Hib., Vol. I, Introd., p. cxxx f.

2. Cf. O'Curry, Lectures on the Manuscript Materials, etc., *passim*; Meyer and Nutt, Voyage of Bran, Vol. II, p. 101-102; Plummer, Vitae SS. Hib., Vol. I, Introd. p. cvi, f.; Watson, Celtic Church in its Relation to Paganism, Celt. Rev., Vol. X, p. 263 f.; Wood-Martin, Traces of the Elder Faiths in Ireland; Fowler, Adamnan, Introd., p. xxiii, etc., etc.

3. Lorica of St. Patrick, in Bernard and Atkinson, The Irish *Liber Hymnorum* (Henry Bradshaw Society), Vol. II, p. 49 f. For the date see Vol. II, p. lviii and p. 209. The legendary story of the origin of the Hymn is given in Stokes, Trip. Life, Vol. I, p. 45, f. It is employed by Patrick at the close of a contest between the saint and certain druids.

4. Its character will be sufficiently indicated by the following lines:

I invoke therefore all these forces to intervene between me and every fierce merciless force that can come upon my body and soul:

Against incantations of false prophets
Against black laws of pagans.....
Against spells of women, priests and druids,
Against all knowledge that is forbidden the human soul.

a barren woman is brought about through the magical agency of a druid [1]. In similar circumstances and by similar means St. Finnian brings about the birth of Aed Slane [2]. The tales refer to the magical activities of druids in connection with tribal warfare. The conflict between the druids of Cormac Mac Art and those of the Munster men may be cited [3]. Cormac's druids dry up the rivers; the King of Munster finally secures the most famous of all the druids, who on promise of reward, produces a spring of water where his arrow falls. Similarly Columba prays against Finnian of Moville for the victory of his tribe. In this praying contest Columba addresses Christ as " mo drui... mac De " — " my druid... the Son of God [4] ".

Nothing is more prominent in the fragmentary evidence we have of pre-Christian Ireland, than the power of malediction exercised by the druids. Even the High King Cormac is cursed by his druids for " worshipping the God of Heaven ", and as a result he soon afterwards dies [5]. The same magical accomplishment attaches to the saints of Ireland. The giant St. Ruadan enters into a prolonged cursing contest with King Diarmit of Meath [6]. This feature likewise appears in Columba's conflict with Broichan, King Brude's wizard, a Pictish druid. Here the parties to the struggle use magic on the forces of nature — the wind and the sea — in true druidic fashion [7]. Magic is met by counter-magic. A number of similar instances are found in the sources for the life of St. Patrick. For example, in the Tripartite Life [8], Patrick is

1. Nutt, Voyage of Bran, Vol. II, p. 74-75, from the Coir Anmann, Irische Texte ed. Stokes and Windisch, Bd. III, Heft 2 (1897), p. 393 f.
2. Nutt, *op. cit.*, p. 82 f. Cf. de Smedt and de Backer, Acta SS. Hib., De Sancto Aido, Sect. 18, col. 343.
3. O'Curry, Manuscript Materials, p. 271; Keating, Geoffrey, Hist. of Irel. (Irish Text Soc.), Vol. II, p. 320.
4. Chron. Scot. (Rolls Series), p. 52; Fowler, Adamnan, p. lxiii, Reeves. Adamnan, p. 74.
5. Rolleston. High Deeds of Finn., p. 202.
6. Bolland Acta SS. Tom. 11 (Apr. 2) Vita S. Rodani Cap. II, p. 381.
7. Reeves, Adamnan, lib. II, cap. xxxiii, xxxiv, xxxv, p. 146 f.
8. Tripartite Life, Vol. II, p. 325-326.

attacked by Recrad and nine other druids who intend to kill him. Patrick raises his left hand and curses the druid (magum) who falls dead in the midst of his band. Divination from waves is common to both [1]. Even where the miracles are beneficent they can sometimes be duplicated from the stories of druids. This is the case in reference to Columba's miraculous reconciliation of a wife to her husband [2], an act of magic also recorded of druids [3]. In the Rennes Dindsenchas [4] St. Brigid is herself called a poetess and druidess (*ban-fili* and *ban-drui*).

One of the distinctions early noted between Celtic and other monastics was in the manner of the tonsure. The Celts shaved the front of the head *ab aure usque ad aurem* [5]. This frontal tonsure was thought by the Romanizing opponents of the Celtic churchmen in the seventh century, to have been derived from Simon Magus [6]. But in all probability it was really a copy of the druidical tonsure, referred to in various early documents [7]. *Magus* was the word by which "druid" was expressed in Latin [8]. Hence probably the fancied connection with Simon. In the Forbais Droma Damhghaire the druid who comes to the aid of the King of Munster is said to have studied in the school of Simon Magus [9].

It has even been argued that the monasteries (which it is generally agreed were tribal in organization)[10] were a Christian con-

1. For examples see Watson, Celtic Church in its Relation to Paganism, Celt. Rev., Vol. X (1914-16), p. 277-278.
2. Adamnan, lib. II, c. xli.
3. Joyce, Social Hist., Vol. I, p. 228.
4. Rev. Celt., Tom. XVI (1895), p. 277 (cf., *ibid.* p. 34).
5. Catalogue of the Saints of Ireland, Ussher, Works, Vol. VI, p. 477-479.
6. Fowler, Adamnan, Introd., p. xlii; Gildas, Fragmenta xi, in Williams, Gildae excidio, etc., Cymmrodorion Record Ser. No 3, pt. II, p. 271 Cf. Aldhelm's letter to the King and Bishops of Damnonia, in Mon. Ger. Hist., Epist. Tom. III, col. 231-235; Bede Hist. Eccles, V, 41.
7. Joyce, Social History, Vol. I, p. 233; Rhŷs, Celtic Heathendom, p. 213; Gougaud, Les Chrétientés Celtiques, p. 198.
8. Colgan, Acta SS. Hib. col. 149. Adamnan lib. I, c. 1, c.xxxvii; lib. II, c.xxxiii, c.xxxiv.
9. O'Curry, *loc. cit.*
10. Gougaud, Les Chrétientés Celtiques, pp. 73-74.

tinuation of pre-Christian druidical communities [1]. While the weight of opinion among Celtic scholars is opposed to this [2], yet it is generally admitted that the Irish druids possessed some sort of organization. This may not have been so complete as the organization described by Caesar with regard to the druids of Gaul [3]. But undoubtedly the druids and their pupils associated in considerable numbers. Cathbad the druid, in the *Taín Bó Cúalnge*, has a school of one hundred pupils [4]. The daughters of King Loeghaire were brought up at the court of the king of Connaught, under the instruction of two druids [5]. St. Columba as a lad was put under the instruction of the bard Gemman [6]. To become a *brehon*, or judge, one was required to hold the " degree " of *Ollamh*, for which twelve years of study were requisite [7]. In view of such protracted studies considerable numbers of students must have been simultaneously engaged in the work. If it is not possible to trace definitely an evolution from the druidical to the monastic schools, it is at least a justifiable supposition that the latter would never have flourished as they did without the preparation afforded by the former.

In their social position and political influence the saints were the successors of the druids. Cathbad the druid, has precedence over Conchobar King of Ulster [8]. St. Finnian of Clonard is welcomed on his arrival from Britain by being

1. A. Bertrand, La religion des Gaulois, p. 280 f.

2. D'Arbois de Jubainville, Cours, Tom. VI, p. 106 f.; Dottin, La religion des Celtes, pp. 54-58; MacCullough, Religion of the Ancient Celts, p. 305.

3. *De Bello Gallico*, lib. VI, Ch. XIII, XIV.

4. The Taín Bó Cúalnge, tr. L. Winifred Farraday, p. 26.

5. The story, which comes from Tírechán (7th century) is found in the Trip. Life. Vol. I, p. 99 f.

5. " Probably a Christian bard ", says Reeves, Adamnan, p. 137, note. Columba, himself a poet, may be regarded as a Christian *fili*.

7. O'Curry, Lectures on the Manuscript materials, etc., p. 240. Healy, Insula Sanctorum et Doctorum, ch. II (Irish scholars before St. Patrick). In another instance Cormac musters " all his most learned druids ". *Ibid.*, p. 240. — Cf. O'Curry's remarks on the schools founded by Cormac MacArt (third century). — Manners and Customs. Vol. II, p. 58.

8. D'Arbois de Jubainville, *Cours*. Tom. I, p. 190.

carried on the back of Muirdach, King of Leinster [1]. " Each king appears to have had a druid at his side ", says M. d'Arbois de Jubainville [2]. Columba becomes to Aidan King of Dalriada such an adviser as were Cathbad and Lochru to the kings they served [3]. Plummer believes that the Church took over druidical lands, and Watson argues (from place-names to the same effect [4]).

That the compromise between Irish custom and Christian ethics was early observed, appears in a gloss on the poem attributed to Dubthach, the poet and brehon of Loeghaire, at the opening of the Senchus Mór :

" What is understood by the above decision which God revealed to Dubthach is that it was a middle course between forgiveness and retaliation : for retaliation prevailed in Erin, before Patrick, and Patrick brought forgiveness with him [5] ".

The Christianization of Ireland, while nominally accomplished in the fifth century, was really a very gradual process which never fully eliminated the ancient religious customs and concepts. Pagan practices in marriage were peculiarly prevalent among the Celts both of Ireland and of Wales in mediaeval times [6]. St. Bernard, describing the Ireland of his day, regards it as nominally Christian but really pagan [7].

A penetrating student of the ancient church of Wales attributes the pagan usages which he recognizes in it partly to the close relations existing between Irish and Welsh

1. Stokes, Lives of Saints from the Book of Lismore, p. 224.
2. Cours, Tom. VI, p. 107.
3. Reeves, Adamnan, p. 198-330 ; Trip. Life, Vol. II, p. 273-4.
4. Plummer, Vitae SS. Hib. Vol. I, Introd., p. ciii, Watson, *op. cit.*, p. 270.
5. Ancient Laws of Ireland, Vol. I, p. 15. Dubthach is made to state (*ibid.*, p. 9) that the adoption of Christianity is " the strengthening of paganism ".
6. J. L. Gerigg, Hastings Encyc. of Relig. and Eth., Art. " Ethics, Celtic ".
7. Vita S. Malachiae, in Migne, P. L., Tom. 182, col. 1075, col. 1086, Malachias noster, ortus Hibernia de populo barbaro..... pro mansuetudine Christiana saeva subintroducta barbaries, immo paganismus quidam inductus sub nomine Christiano.

Christianity in the early period [1]. The Goidels of Ireland were represented by a large and dominant population in South Wales. " The Brython " says the same author, " tried to treat Christianity as a system opposed to any existing system. The Goidel regarded it as something to be assimilated into the existing system [2] ". Bund's statement of the case is scarcely exaggerated when he says " Apostolic usage was about the last thing that was considered in either church ", and " In all probability there was a great preponderance of pagan (over Christian) customs [3] ".

2. — Penance in the Aryan World.

It is to these Irish and Welsh churches, with their surviving paganism and their comparative indifference to " apostolic usage ", that we owe the penitential books. It would therefore be very surprising, not to say incomprehensible, if the books in question should fail to exhibit marked traces or the pre-Christian civilization.

It will be of advantage to bear in mind, in connection with the ensuing study, the fact that penance is by no means a product of Christianity. It appears in various forms both in the Semitic and in the Aryan religions of antiquity. A class of priests in ancient Babylon administered penance, using in confession a list of interrogatives to elicit the required information, which strikes Semitic scholars as resembling Christian penitential manuals [4]. After penance this functionary absolves his confessant — a king, in the instance cited — with the prayer,

" O Chamach, regard with pity this sin [5]. "

When we come to examine the earliest laws of Aryan antiquity we find the subject of penance given great prominence.

1. Bund, the Celtic Church in Wales, p. 23.
2. *Ibid.*, p. 366.
3. *Ibid.*, pp. 24-25.
4. Lagrange, Études sur les religions sémitiques, Paris, 1905, p. 225.
5. *Ibid.*, p. 236-237; and see whole of Ch. VI.

A comparison of the early Brahman codes with the codes of Ireland and of Wales, as well as with the penitentials, affords parallels far too close to be accidental. Recent discussions of the Senchus Mór, the ancient Irish code purporting to come from the time of King Loeghaire (c. 440), have tended to support its claims to antiquity [1]. Sir Henry Maine notes the fact that this important code is a store of primitive customs. " In no sense (are these laws) a legislative construction. They are an authentic monument of a very ancient group of Aryan institutions ; they are a collection of rules which have been gradually developed in a way highly favorable to the preservation of archaic peculiarities [2] ". Elsewhere he remarks : " The Brehons are in fact as nearly as possible the Brahmans of India with many of their characteristics altered, and indeed their whole sacerdotal authority abstracted by the influence of Christianity [3] ". It has been observed by several writers that whereas the Christian teachers supplanted the druids in their religious functions, they did not supplant the *fili*, who, as *brehons* (judges), flourished till the sixteenth century [4]. Caesar, in a passage soon to be quoted, ascribes all legal functions to the druids in Celtic Gaul. In Ireland however, legal affairs lay largely with the poet-legists ; the brehons are sometimes distinguished from the *fili* [5], and sometimes both terms are used of the same person (as

1. D'Arbois de Jubainville, Études sur le Senchus Mor, No 2, in Nouvelle Revue historique du droit, 1880, p. 513 f., pp. 533-534. Cf. Zimmer's attempt to identify Russ mac Tricim mentioned in the account of the origin of the Senchus Mór, with the Norse name Trygvason, which would bring the compilation down to the ninth century. (Zeitschr. f. deutsches Alterthums, Bd. 53). This is replied to by A. Nutt, Waifs and Strays of Celtic Tradition, Argyleshire Series, No. IV, Lond. 1891, Introd.

2. Early History of Institutions, p. 11. Comparing the Brehon and Brahman codes he here remarks : " It is not wonderful that the Brehon law, growing together without legislation upon an original body of Aryan custom, should present some very strong analogies to another set of derivative Aryan usages which was similarly developed "

3. Early Law and Custom, p. 162.

4. D'Arbois de Jubainville, Cours. Tom. 7, p. 331 ; Tom. 1, p. 129. Adamnan, Introd., p. vi.

5. Rolleston, High Deeds, p. 186. King Cormac was to have a brehon, a druid, and a bard, with others ministers.

in the case of the poet Dubthach) who is among the reputed compilers of the Senchus Mór [1]. The judicial function has passed from the druids to the *fili*, who are now also known as brehons [2]. Whatever the previous evolution of the brehon class may have been, the Brehon Laws assuredly preserve to us much that pertained to remote Aryan custom, and bear a strong resemblance to the Brahman codes.

The primitive Aryan, like other primitive races, devised a technique for undoing the harm wrought by violation of *tabu*. In course of evolution this gave birth to a complicated religious ceremonial included in which were the elements of a penitential system. In the Brahman codes the conception of defilement as requiring penance is met with more frequently than are more ethical ideas of penance. Remnants of this primitive conception remain in our penitentials and in the Brehon laws. The church in framing the penitentials did not eliminate, while it did considerably modify, pre-Christian views of sin and its guilt and expiation. The penitentials exhibit many of the common elements of this primitive and sub-primitive technique. A list of quotations showing parallels and near-parallels between them and the Brahman codes would fill a considerable volume. The correspondences are not merely in the penitential regulations in themselves, however, but extend to the racial institutions of which both are products. On the Celtic side these are reflected in the early literature generally, and particularly in the Brehon Laws and in the Welsh Laws. For us the advantage of the use of the earlier codes lies in the fact that there is very little that is certainly pre-Christian in the Celtic sources. References to penance in the Brehon or Welsh Laws, or even in the Irish tales, might be taken purely as a product of Christian influence. If we can show in the earlier Aryan sources materials closely analogous to the contents of the penitentials, this will reinforce our supposition that there existed in Celtic culture in the pre-Christian era elements that

1. Ancient Laws of Ireland, Vol. I, p. 5.

2. This is d'Arbois de Jubainville's view — Cours, Tom. I, p. 129. The precise relation of the Brehons to the druids in Ireland is not very clear, but the question is immaterial for our purpose.

made for the rise of the penitential literature and gave to it some of its prominent features.

The difficulty of discovering pre-Christian Celtic confession and penance is enhanced by what is an apparently intentional removal of evidence from the sources. " Nearly all passages (in the Irish texts) relating to cult or ritual, seem to have been deliberatly suppressed [1] ". Such evidence as is left to us is scarcely sufficient to give certainty. We do find instances strongly suggestive of penance in the tales, particularly the *Imrama* and the *Longesa*. To some of these reference will be made below. In one of the earliest of the Welsh tales, Riannon is compelled by doctors and wise men to undergo a seven year penance for the (supposed) murder of her child [2]. The *Túatha dé Danann* in an Irish tale hold a council over an adulterous woman who is banished from the " Land of Promise [3] ". Similar instances could be enumerated in considerable numbers, and some others will have to be referred to below. It is, however, in most instances of this sort, difficult to make sure of the absence of Christian influence in the documents from which the of are taken. The result of the enumeration of a large number of such parallels would create an impression of probability only. By taking a larger view of our subject we may give to our conclusions virtual certainty.

Some initial evidence will be given to show that the functions connected with the penitentials of hearing confession, assigning penance, and reconciling the penitent were exercised in the Aryan world, and in its Celtic portion.

The uniformity of the regulations regarding penance in the Brahman codes indicates their lack of originality in this respect, and their dependence on more remote custom. Their common teaching on the subject of penance may well be expressed by reference to a passage from the Laws of Manu : " By confession, by repentance, by austerity, and by reciting

1. MacCullough, Religion of the Ancient Celts, p. 311.

2. In the story of Pwyll, Prince of Dyved. Loth, Les Mabinogion, Tom. I, p. 108.

3. R. I. Best, " The Adventures of Art son of Conn " in Eriu, Vol. III (1907) p. 151.

the Veda, a sinner is freed from guilt, and in case no other course is possible, by liberality [1] ". With the change of " Veda " to " Psalms " this description of early Aryan penance would faithfully express the principles of the penitential books.

Take another statement from Apastamba's Dharmasutra (Aphorisms of the Sacred Law);

" The spiritual guide (*acharya*) shall order those who whilst participating in the rights of their caste have gone astray through the weakness of their senses, to perform penances proportionate to their sins, according to the precepts of the *smriti* (tradition) [2] ".

The death of a *kshatriya* is expiated by a heavy fine followed by twelve years spent as an *abhisasta*, (criminal) who dwells in a hut in the forest, occasionally begging in the village.

" After having performed this penance for twelve years he must perform the ceremony known by custom, by which he is admitted to the society of the good [3] ". The " ceremony known by custom " can only refer to some priestly act in which the excommunicated person is again received to fellowship. The form of this reconciliation, elsewhere alluded to, varies greatly, and may be secret or public. There is no need to multiply these general references, in which the laws are replete. Let us turn rather to the scantier Celtic material.

" In Caesar's account of the druids " says Sir Henry Maine " there is not a word which does not appear to me perfectly credible [4] ".

Sir Henry has special reference to the legal functions which the druids exercised, and not to the mythology which Caesar ascribes to the Gauls. The passage in Caesar descriptive of the administration of justice by the druids is as follows:

1. Laws of Manu, xi, 228. (The references to the Brahman codes can easily be verified in the volumes of the " Sacred Books of the East " ed. Max Müller, noted in the foregoing Bibliography.)
2. Apast. II, 5, 10, 12.
3. Apast. I, 9, 24, 28 : virtually indentical with Gautama xxii.
4. Early Institutions, p. 28.

" For they judge in almost all controversies, public and private, and if any crime has been committed, or slaying done, or if there is a controversy over inheritance or boundaries, they determine rewards and adjudge penalties. Whoever, whether a private person or a (tribe of) people, does not recognize the award, they interdict from the sacrifices. This penalty is, with them, most grave. Those who come under this interdict are looked upon as in the number of the impious and the criminal; these all persons shun, avoiding their touch or speech, lest they should be hurt by the contagion. Nor to these is justice given if they seek it, nor is any honor shared with them [1] ". According to Caesar, then, the druids exercised justice in both criminal and civil cases, but mingled their judicial with their religious powers, excommunicating and outlawing those who refused to acquiesce in their decisions. The priestly and judicial functions were not merely combined; they were in some degree identical, and law was enforced by an appeal to religious sanctions.

In the Senchus Mór we find evidence of the same conception. In the law of distraint the plaintive fasts at the defendant's door. On this custom the Senchus Mór states : " He who will not give a pledge to fasting is an evader of all; he who disregards all things shall not be paid by God or man [2] ". Thus Ireland was familiar with penal excommunication and outlawry before the Christian religion came. " A ces procedes " says one of the foremost students of Celtic law, " par lesquels ils s'attribuaient une science surnaturelle, les *fili* irlandais joignaient un autre moyen d'influence, c'était de

1. Nam fere de omnibus contreversiis publicis privatisque constituunt, et, si quod est admissum facinus, si caedes facta, si de haereditate, de finibus controversia est, idem decernunt praemia poenasque constituunt, si qui aut privatus aut populus eorum decreto non stetit, sacrificiis interdicunt. Haec poena apud eos est gravissima. Quibus ita est interdictum, hi numero impiorum et sceleratorum habentur, hi omnes decedunt, additum sermonemque defugiunt, ne quid ex contagione incommodi accipiant, neque his petentibus jus redditur neque honos ullus communicatur. — Caesar, De Bello Gallico, lib. VI, c. XIII.

2. Ancient Laws, of Ireland, Vol. I, p. 113.

lancer une sorte d'excommunication contre ceux qui refusaient d'obéir à leurs sentences [1] ".

In any state of society in which religious institutions play a large part and religious leaders function also as civil judges, excommunication will tend to involve all the pains of deprivation of membership in the community ; it will become, in Caesar's words, a *gravissima poena*. And this is precisely what happened in the pre-Christian Celtic world [2]. In Welsh law the outcast was known as a 'kin-wrecked' man [3]. For certain offences, such as the murder of a chief or of one's near kinsman, the offender was not given the option of a fine, as in the usual procedure, but was condemned to " execration and ignominious exile " [4]. When a chief was murdered it was " required of every one of every sex and age within hearing of the horn to follow that exile and to keep up the barking of dogs to the time of his putting to sea, until he shall have passed three score hours out of sight [5] ". These wandering outcasts (" *exules damnatosque* ") seem to have become so numerous in Gaul that they were recruited as fighting contingents to oppose Caesar [6]. In Ireland one who refused to obey the brehon's decision was called *élutach*, a fugitive, and his act of refusal was called *élud*, flight [7].

The Irish language was provided with words to express other phases of penance. The word *aithrige*, penance or penitence, is not a Latin borrowing [8]. It is true that forms of the Lat. *penitentia* appear in many texts [9] ; but the Irish word is much more frequently met with, and cannot but indicate a fact in pre-Christian Irish life. It survived through the period of the ancient Irish church and is used to the

1. D'Arbois de Jubainville, Cours. Tom. 7, p. 329.
2. See T. R. Holmes, Ancient Britain, p. 244, p. 297.
3. See Seebohm, Tribal System of Wales, p. 58.
4. Seebohm, Anglo-Saxon Law, p. 42.
5. Ancient Laws and Institutes of Wales, Vol. II, p. 478.
6. Caesar, De Bello Gallico, lib. V, c. 55, lib. viii, c. 30.
7. D'Arbois de Jubainville, *loc. cit.* : Ancient Laws of Ireland, Vol. I, pp. 112, 215, 236, 258, 264 ; Vol. II, pp. 14, 98, 228, 382.
8. Ancient Laws of Ireland, Vol. III, p. 35, p. 108 ; Vol. V, p. 205.
9. *Op. cit.* Vol. III, p. 107. The gloss on " aithrige " is " *peinde* ".

almost total exclusion of Latin forms in the Homilies from the Leabhar Breac, usually accompanied by *denum* in the sense of " to do or perform penance [1] ". The form *aithrighe* is regularly used for penance (63 times) in a modern Irish work, Donlevy's Catechism (1642) [2].

According to MacCullough the Irish word *geasa*, usually translated *tabu*, meant something more advanced than primitive tabu. It meant not only something which must be avoided for fear of disastrous consequences, but also " an obligation to do something commanded by another [3] ". Thus " Cuchulainn's father put *geasa* upon him that he should not rest till he had found out the cause of the exile of the sons of Doel [4] ". This conception of a religious obligation to fulfill some commission is analagous to the practice of penance. The attempt was made to conceal evidences of the survival of tabu. Plummer notes that an undoubted reference to a violation of sex tabu in an early manuscript of the life of St. Maedoc, is changed in a later MS. so as to refer to an entirely different offence [5]. Old Irish too has a number of words for sin, such as *cin* (*cean*, *cion*) and *fine*. *Fine* is glossed as *pectha* (< *peccata*) in Sanctain's Hymn. Stokes believed the word cognate with Lat. *vitium* [6].

3. — The Function of the Confessor.

Penance was not confined to those under vows, as both the Ancient Laws [7] and the penitentials clearly demonstrate. Confession and penance were generally practiced. St. Brigid is reported as saying, in words that became proverbial : " Anyone without a soul-friend (*anmchara*) is like a body without a

1. See Glossary to Homilies from the Leabhear Breac, p. 536.
2. Archiv f. keltische Lexikographie, Bd. II, p. 7.
3. Religion of the Ancient Celts, p. 252 ; cf. Joyce, Social History, Vol. I, p. 311.
4. *Ibid.*, p. 254.
5. Vitae SS. Hib. Introd., Vol. I, p. XXIX.
6. Cf. Henderson, Survivals, p. 298; Thes. Palaeol., Vol. II, p. 351.
7. Anc. Laws of Ireland, Vol. IV p. 366 ; vol. V, p. 448.

head." [1] If there was any exception to the rule of universal confession, it was due to unusual neglect of custom, or to the refusal of strict confessors to admit certain sinners to conference. Some of the Irish confessors were scrupulous, or arbitrary, in this respect. Columba is said to have given an unqualified refusal to St. Donnan of Eig [2]. St. Mailruan of Tallaght never heard confession of anyone who did not support himself by labor [3]. Ordinarily one desiring to confess, on being refused could no doubt obtain another confessor. Columba when invited to become the confessor of Domnall declines to go himself, but sends Cummian the Tall in his place [4]. The assumption behind such facts is that the practice of seeking a confessor when guilty of any offence, was virtually universal. Its early prevalence in Ireland is striking. In a country peculiarly tenacious of pre-Christian religious practices, we find the early generations of Christians devoted to this custom, while practicing penance in a way considerably different from that in which it appeared in the non-Celtic churches.

In Irish texts, the word used for a confessor, *anmchara*, is of somewhat uncertain etymology. The obvious resemblance to "*anachoreta*" has led to the suggestion that it is only an Irish popular corruption of this Latinized Greek form, and meant originally a hermit. This is the etymology given, e. g., by Vendryes [5]. Evidence of Irish modification of Church Latin is abundant, as the treatise of M. Vendryes shows. Also it is well known that there were hermits in Ireland, and Irish hermits outside of Ireland. But this easy interpretation fails before the evidence that the Irish hermits were *not*, ordinarily, confessors at all. This seems at least the necessary infe-

1. Stokes, Martyrol. of Œngus, pp. 65, 183 ; Plummer, Vitae SS. Hib., Vol. I, Introd., p. CXVI. (The saying is also ascribed to Comgall of Bangor. — O'Hanlon, Lives of the Irish Saints, Vol. IV, p. 48.)

2. Reeves, Adamnan, p. 305.

3. O'Grady, Silva Gadelica, Vol. II, p. 40.

4. Preface to the Hymn of St. Cummian the Tall, Irish Liber Hymnorum, Vol. II, p. 10.

5. J. Vendryes, De Hibernensis vocabulis quæ a Latina lingua originem duxerint, Paris, 1902.

rence from the description given by Marianus Scotus of Ratisbon (late eleventh century) [1]. These were of the same type as the enclosed anchorites of Syria, who had a minimum of intercourse with their kind [2]. Gregory of Tours tells of a Breton saint of this type, named Vennoc (Vennocus Brito), and of Antholius of Bordeaux who lived alone in his cell for eight years, and then became insane and tore down the stone walls that enclosed him [3]. Margaret Stokes finds evidence that cave-dwelling anchorites existed in Italy by the second century [4]. There is no evidence in these cases of the anchorite performing the function of a confessor. His whole manner of life precluded the possibility of this. He was so enclosed that conversation with anyone outside was scarcely possible. It has been pointed out, moreover, that the word *anachoreta* itself was in use, as applied to Irish recluses whom no one might approach [5]. The Irish Canons contain a passage that makes this point clear :

« De variis generis monachorum... Tertium genus est anachoretarum, qui coenobiale conversatione perfecti, semetispsos includunt in cellulis procul a conspectu hominum remoti, nemini ad se prebentes accessum [6] ».

For the word *anmchara* de Jubainville would give a Celtic and not a Latin parentage. According to this scholar the stem "*animon*" in Celtic belief originally meant the link (*lien*) between the mortal body and the immortal body which would be assumed when the dead passed to the western Elysion. The Celtic language had its own word for soul, and did not adopt the Latin *anima* [7]. Whether de Jubainville's explanation

1. Quoted in Zimmer, Irish Element in Mediaeval Culture, p. 88 f.
2. Stokes, G. T., Ireland and the Celtic Church, p. 177 f.
3. Greg. Tur., Hist. Franc. lib. VIII, c. 34. — Poupardin's Edition, p. 332.
4. Six Months in the Appennines, p. 13.
5. D'Arbois de Jubainville, Journal des Savants, 1903, pp. 162, 163.
6. Coll. Can. Hib. lib. xxxix, ch. 3.
7. " Quand un homme expire, la vie s'en va avec le dernier souffle. Ce dernier souffle, identique avec le principe vital, est ce que les Grecs appellent ψυχή, les Latins *anima*..., les Celtes *animu*, au genitif *animonos*. ". M. de Jubainville further shows that many other Celtic words approach as close-

of *anmchara* is regarded as conclusive or not, the rejection of a derivation from *anachoreta* seems justified, and all proof of its consisting of a combination of Latin *anima cara* is wanting. There is, therefore, good reason to suspect that it is of Celtic origin and represents a functionary in pre-Christian Irish life. When we turn to the Welsh language there is no such lack of certainty. The Welsh word for confessor, *beriglour* (*beryglour*, *periglour*, *periglauer*) is regularly used in the Welsh codes [1].

Our interest lies, however, not so much in discovering words for confessor in the Celtic vocabularies, as in determinine whether the function of a confessor was exercised in the pre-Christian Celtic world.

The function represented by *anmchara* has been described by d'Arbois de Jubainville in the phrase " director of conscience " [2]. It is the task of spiritual direction. The abstract noun *anmchairde* is rendered " spiritual guidance" by Kuno Meyer [3]. Whitley Stokes gives " spiritual direction " for the variant form *anmchairdine* [4]. The Welsh word is so used as to indicate that it possesses exactly the same meaning. The content of both terms then is virtually identical with that expressed by the phrase with which Bühler translates *acharya* in the Brahman codes, viz. " spiritual guide ". In both civilizations this functionary appears as the director of the moral life, with special control over the means of escaping from the effects of sin. He is the counsellor and " friend of the soul ". " Created beings ", says Manu, " must be instructed in what concerns their welfare without giving them pain, and gentle speech will be used by the *acharya* who desires to abide by the sacred law [5] ".

ly to Latin which are certainly not borrowed. — La civilisation des Celtes p. 215.

1. Ancient Laws and Institutes of Wales, vol. I, p, 28, p. 85, p. 134. Cf. Wae-Evans, Welsh Mediaeval Law, p. 129, p. 272. The modern Welsh form *periglor* = *curate, priest*.

2. " *Anmchara* signifie ' directeur de conscience ', littéralement, ' ami de l'âme du client '. "

3. The Triads of Ireland, Todd Lect. Ser., in Roy. Ir. Acad. Publ., Dubl., 1906, p. 3; Cf. Eriu, Vol. I, p. 38.

4. Lives of Saints from the Book of Lismore, p. 374.

5. Laws of Manu, II, 159.

In both he possesses in addition, however, unquestioned authority to command to penance, and the legal and penal aspect of his duties is emphasized. While both are provided in the course of development with a code of rules (viz. the penitential regulations of the Brahman Codes and the Celtic penitentials) yet it is plain that their power antedates these codifications and is independent of them. If anyone refuses to abide by their decisions, according to the Brahman codes he is haled before the king, whose domestic priest (*purohita*) examines the case and compels him to undergo the proper penance; if he is not a Brahman he may forfeit his life [1]. For great offences, indeed, self-immolation is a not infrequent penalty [2]. It was a sort of expiatory sacrifice, and is comparable to the primitive practice of human sacrifice which among the Celts was usually of criminals [3]. An old Irish story, found in the Book of Lismore, records a remarkable instance of what is at once penitential and sacrificial self-immolation. King Ailill Banna's people had been defeated in battle, through the king's pride. While in flight from the field Ailill " made swift repentance " (*athirgi*) and commanded his charioteer to turn about that he might die for his people, whereupon he was slain by the enemy, and his people were saved [4]. Among the British Celts, " the death of criminals who surrendered themselves voluntarily was considered sacrificial, inasmuch as they did thereby all in their power to compensate for their crimes [5] ".

For common offences, however, the administrator of penance appoints a period of austerities for purgation. It is a more developed form of early methods of escaping the results of broken *tabu*. The advice given is to be followed without question, as in the Brahman codes so in the Celtic sources. Saint

1. Apast. II, 5, 10, 13.
2. e. g. for killing a Brahmana. Vasishtha XX, 24. It took a variety of forms, e. g. lying on a hot iron bed, or self-mutilation after which the penitent walks till he falls dead. Gautama XXiii, 8 ; 10.
3. Cf. Henderson. Survivals, p. 302 f. As a remnant of early Celtic beliefs Henderson quotes evidence of the superstitious regard for the skull of a suicide who was thought of as a criminal and a sacrificed victim.
4. Stokes, Lives of Saints from the Book of Lismore, p. 307.
5. Hughes, Church of the Cymry, p. 3.

Columban confessed his youthful temptations to a woman, and despite his mother's urgent entreaties, accepted her advice to leave his home [1]. The Senchus Mor itself consists of a compilation of judgments (in hypothetical cases) rendered by Irish *file* or *brehons*. Of Sencha, to whom the earliest part of the collection is traditionally traced, it is remarked by d'Arbois de Jubainville that while the judgments ascribed to him take an imperative form, yet his rôle is that of a simple adviser [2]. Yet " the *file* enjoyed among the masses a respect which, without their possession of force, gave their decisions the value of law [3]". The necessity of treating their judgments with respect is apparent : the alternative was anarchy. Yet it is probable that obedience was not due to deliberate consideration of this reason, but largely to religious feelings. Sir Henry Maine traces the Brehon Code to a system enforced by supernatural sanctions [4]. The clergy adapted to Christian uses the institution of advisory but authoritative arbitration and judgment. As the judgments of the *file* were codified, so were those of the *anmchara* and the *beriglour* ; the penitentials are such codifications, whether we think of those which emanate from national synods or those which claim only a personal authority.

We have already noted instances indicative of the close relation of druids and kings. Every king, we saw, had a druid at his court, and the druid is given precedence over the king [5]. In this respect the Christian saint is plainly the druid's successor. In the *Leabhar na h-uidre* Loeghaire becomes a Christian and accepts " *anmchairdine* " of Patrick [6]. Columba is *anmchara* to Aidan King of Dalriada [7], Adamnan to Finnsnechta Fledach, King of Ireland [8]. In Welsh law the bishop had cer-

1. Jonas. Vita Columbani, 8.
2. Cours, Tom. I, p. 310.
3. Ibid. p. 331.
4. Early Institutions, p. 41.
5. Cf. the close association of king and *acharya* in Gautama XI 1-16, and the Brahman's precedence over the king, *Ibid.*, XI, 1.
6. Trip. Life, Vol. II, p. 564.
7. Reeves, Adamnan, Introd., p. lxxvi.
8. *Ibid.*, p. xliii, p. cl.

tain immunities, not by virtue of the fact that he was bishop only, but because he was also the king's confessor. In the Venedotian Code the chief groom " receives nothing from the bishop, because he (the bishop) is the king's confessor (*beryglour*) to whom the king is to rise, and to sit down after him, and to hold his sleeve while he shall wash himself " [1]. To quote the statement of W. J. Watson, who uses other evidence than that just cited, " the cleric supplants the druid as the king's chief adviser, under the title of *anmchara*, soul-friend [2]".

The teaching function of the *anmchara* or *beriglour* should not be overlooked. Sir Henry Maine's statement that " the Brahons are the Brehmans " quoted above (p. 106) strictly applies rather to the *acharya* than to the Brahmans as a class. The *acharya* was primarily one who attended to the *acara* or conduct of his clients: hence his penitential function. But secondly he was a teacher, and the word is commonly translated " teacher, " or " spiritual teacher ", in the codes. He was chosen by his pupils and normally, but not always, he was a Brahman [3]. There is an old Irish " rule ", ascribed in one MS. to Comgall, which enjoins resorting to " a devout sage to guide thee" [4]. The Welsh laws command that children " go under the hand of a confessor " at the age of seven years [5]. Similarly Colman, son of Luachan goes to a confessor at seven [6]. The confessor in these instances is apparently an instructor as well.

Maine has indicated that both the Brehons and the Hindu

1. Ancient Laws and Instit. of Wales, Vol. I, p. 28.

2. Watson, *op. cit.*, p. 273.

3. It is declared in the *smritis* that a Brahmana alone should be chosen at teacher (*acharya*). In times of distress a Brahman may study under a *Kshatriya* or a *Vaisya*; and during his pupilship he must walk behind such a teacher. — Apastamba, II, 2, 4, 25, -26.

4. Strachan, J., in Eriu, Vol. 1 (1904-5), p. 191 f. §§ 14-15.

5. " Therefore both man and woman are to give *briduw* from a child of the age of seven years which shall go under the hand of a confessor (*periglaur*) " — Anc. Laws and Instit. of Wales, Vol. I, p. 134. — At seven years old " he shall come under the hand of his confessor (*beryglaur*) and shall take duties upon himself ". — *Ibid.*, p. 202.

6. Life of Colman, ed. Kuno Meyer, in Proceedings of Royal Ir. Acad. (Todd Lect. Series), 1906, p. 19.

lawyers were the heads of a spiritual family. The theory of the latter was that the pupil on receiving instruction was born again. " He causes his pupil to be born a second time by imparting to him sacred learning. The second birth is best", says Apastamba [1]. In these codes the initiated are habitually called " twice born men " They reach this stage only after twelve years spent in study of the Vedas, in the *acharya's* house. " We should say " says Maine, of such a graduate, " that he had received his degree » [2]. This happens to be the same period required to qualify for the " degree " of *Ollamh*, through study of the verses of the *file* [3]. In both cases there exists spiritually the relation of father and sons. It is similar with the father-confessors. The explanation offered by Olden for the frank way in which the " sixteen sons " of the vowed virgin saint Darercas are spoken of, is that the sons were sons spiritual, she being their teacher [4]. Similarly in the *Vita prima S. Brendani* we are informed of St. Ita of Cluain Credil : *Hoc enim virgo multos sanctorum Hibernie ab infantia nutruit* [5]. To this celebrated teacher Brendan goes for confession [6]. The more distinguished teachers like Brigid, Finnian, Comgale and Columba, were also distinguished confessors. The relationship at the first is spontaneous and not ecclesiastically regulated, as the instances of confession to women show. The tendency of the penitentials was to take away this freedom and sponta neity, and to connect the function solely with the priesthood. Even Columban, who had confessed to a woman in his youth, writes *confiteatur culpam suam sacerdoti* [7]. The penitential of Theodore shows that going to women for confession was not unknown in England, where Irish influence had been dominant [8].

1. Apastamba I, I, I. 15-16.
2. *Op. cit.*, p. 332.
3. O'Curry, Manuscript Materials, p. 240.
4. T. Olden, On the Consortia of the first Order of Irish Saints. Proceedings of Roy. Ir. Acad., Third Series, Vol. III, 1895, p. 415 f.
5. Vita prima S. Brendani, vi, in Plummer Vitæ SS. Hib., Vol. I, p. 99.
6. *Ibid.*, Sect. lxxxxii, p. 137.
7. Poenit. Col. B. 23.
8. Poenit. Theod. II, vii §, 2.

CHAPTER IV

Special Features of the Celtic Penitentials, as affected by Pre-Christian Customs.

1. — Composition and Commutation.

The statement is made by historians of dogma that composition in penance is originally derived from Germanic law [1]. Two outstanding facts have been observed by such writers, viz., that Germanic law was characterized by the *wergelt* principle, and that this principle appears in the penitentials. But the conclusion they have drawn fails to account for two other equally assured facts. These are that Celtic law not less than Germanic exemplifies this principle, and that the penitential literature was Celtic and not Germanic in origin. The Irish and Welsh documents already discussed are sufficient to show that the system of composition in penance was in full force before any Germanic population was brought under the discipline of the penitentials. The earliest known penitential work to appear on Germanic soil is the *Penitentiale Columbani*, which is undoubtedly the work of an Irishman and true to the Celtic type. In respect to composition it is not even adapted to Frankish legal customs, but closely follows Finnian [2]. The earliest document in the Anglo-Saxon Church is the *Poenit. Theodori*, written a century after Columban's time. Its

1. Harnack, Hist. of Dogma, Vol. V, p. 329.

2. Poenit. Col. B 1, permits a return to one's country after a year's exile undergoing penance; with the return "satisfaciat parentibus ejus, quem occidit vicem filii redens et dicens, Quaecunque vultis faciam vobis". This is evidently modelled on Poenit Vinn. 23 : recipiatur in patria sua et satisfaciat amicis ejus quem occiderat, et vicem pietatis et obedientiae reddat patri aut matri ejus.... et dicat, Ecce ego pro filio vestro quaecunque dixeritis mihi faciam.

authorization of the commutation of penance and of composition in money consists merely in repeating with approval clauses from the *Canones Hibernenses* [1], a document which antedates the *Poenit. Theodori* by considerably more than a century. There is no special reason why composition in penance might not have originated on Frankish or Anglo-Saxon soil, since the principle of composition already prevailed there in native law; but the simple historical fact is that it did not so originate. These nations received the institution, so far as it relates to penance, from Celtic sources. The character of their own pre-Christian customs made its adoption easy and natural; but its origin is none the less foreign to them.

We have seen that no element of composition appears in the penance system of the Imperial Church. That system was no doubt silently conditioned by the conception of crime in the Imperial State. By the Christian era Roman law had reached a far more advanced stage than that of the Celts, whose legal institutions remained comparatively primitive. The penal law of ancient communities is not the law of crimes (*crimina*) but of torts (*delicta*) [2]. The laws of the Twelve Tables preserve some indications of this stage in the Roman legal development [3]. But later Roman law regarded offences like homicide as crimes against the Emperor and the State [4]. Similarly the church of the Roman Empire regarded sins as offences against God and the Church. The customary law of the Celts (as of the Germans) regarded acts classed as crimes by Roman Law only as wrongs (torts) committed

1. Can. Hib. II, 6 : arreum anni XII triduani. Poen. Theod. I, VII, 5 : Item XII triduana pro anno pensanda Theodorus laudavit. De egressis (aegris) quoque pretium viri vel ancillae pro anno, vel dimidium omnium quae possidet dare, et si quem frauderet reddere quadruplum ut Christus judicavit. Ista testimonia sunt de eo quod in praefatione diximus de libello Scottorum. (Cf. above, p. 61).

2. Jeudwine, Tort. Crime and Police in Mediaeval Britain, pt. I, *passim*.

3. Sir Henry Maine, Ancient Law, p. 379 f. The suppression of composition for murder is traditionally ascribed to Numa. D'Arbois de Jubainville, Cours, Tom. 7, p. 77.

4. Hadley, Introd. to Roman Law, p. 14.

against persons, both the sufferer and his immediate kindred. Accordingly crimes which under Roman law would have insolved death, could be expiated under Brehon or Salic law by satisfaction to the person injured or his surviving relatives. This satisfaction took the form of a pecuniary fine called "*éric*" in Irish, "*galanas*" in Welsh, "*wergelt*" in Anglo-Saxon law.

Composition in these codes has special reference to homicide, but applies likewise to all forms of injury to the body, to seduction and theft. The murderer in general had the choice between the payment of the prescribed composition and exile [1]. "At this time" says the Senchus Mor "no one is put to death for his intentional crimes so long as *éric* is obtained [2]". The payment had to be made by the relatives of the offender; failing this they were obliged to surrender him if he had not taken flight [3]. It has been supposed that the early Christian missionaries endeavored to introduce capital punishment, following on a judicial process, for murder [4]. If so the effort was soon proved unsuccessful, and the old custom prevailed.

The *éric*-fine consisted of two distinct parts. These were the *coirp-dîre* or body-fine, which, for all classes was reckoned as seven cumhals (*ancillae*, female slaves) [5] or twenty-one cows, and the (*enech-lann*) (face-price) or honor-price, payable for insult. The *enech-lann* was a payment, according to the rank of the person injured [6]. The body-price is referred to by

1. D'Arbois de Jubainville, Cours, Tom. 7, p. 83.
2. Ancient Laws of Ireland, Vol. I, p. 15.
3. "He is to be given up for it with his cattle and land", *ibid.* Vol. III, p. 69.
4. Joyce, Social History, Vol. I, p. 211.
5. Ancient Laws of Ireland, Vol. III, p. 70.
6. Arthur ua Clerigh. Hist. of Irel., Vol. I, p. 223 f. D'Arbois de Jubainville, Cours, Tom. 7, p. 89. The honor-price was paid together with the body price in homicide. Seebohm says that in this case the honor-price was graded according to the rank of the slayer. It is stated in the Senchus Mor : "Wherever honor price is paid it shall be paid according to the rank of the person to whom it is paid." Ancient Laws of Irel.. Vol. III, p. 99. This may be regarded as the general rule.

St. Patrick as an understood measure of value. He declares that he has distributed an amount of money equivalent to the price of fifteen men [1]. The price of fifteen men would be the price of $15 \times 7 = 105$ slave-women, or 315 cows.

In Welsh law the system was the same in principle while considerably different in detail. Originally the body-price was called *dirwy*. In course of time under the influence of Roman law this fine came to be paid to the king and his officers and corresponded to the Latin *mulcta*. On the departure of the Romans from Britain the native custom was restored; but a new word was used for the body-price, the word for "murder", *galanas*. The *galanas* however was not like the *coirp-dîre*, invariable, but varied with the rank of the victim [2]. It was not all paid to the family of the slain man, but one-third of it went to the king and his officers. The system of payment was enormously detailed, since part of the burden was distributed over the family to fifth cousins, and part of it was paid by the tribe [3]. When those held responsible failed to make the payments on time, the murderer was open to the revenge of his victim's family.

Corresponding to the Irish *enech-lann* was the Welsh *saraad* (or *sarhad*, literally insult, injury), also graded by the rank of the sufferer. Since murder could not be accomplished without insult to the person, the payment of *saraad* always accompanied that of *galanas* [4]. It is worth observing that here also the correspondence with the Brahman codes is close. "He

1. Censeo enim non nimius quam pretuim quindecim hominum distribui illis. Patrick, Confessio. Tírechán changes *hominum* to *animarum hominum*, but D'Arbois de Jubainville translates *animarum* "*de vies*". — Cours, Tom. 7, p. 89.

2. D'Arbois de Jubainville, Cours, Tom. 7, p, 93-97.

3. The payments were presented in fortnightly installments. Seebohm, AS. Law, p. 42. Cf. *Canones Wallici*, Can. 12.

4. Wade-Evans, Welsh mediaeval Law, p. 339. The Venedotian code says "No one is killed without being first subjected to saraad". Anc. Laws & Inst. of Wales, Vol. I, p. 23. For full details of the payment of Composition see this work, Vol. I, p 747; p. 875; *De variis injuriis*, Vol. II, p. 20 f.; and Walter, Das Alte Wales, p. 447. Seebohm, A.S. Law, p. 297 f. shows in detail the use of composition in Scotland. The word there used for *galanas* was *galnes*.

who has killed a *kshatriya* shall give a thousand cows for the expiation of his sin. He shall give a hundred cows for a *Vaisya*, ten for a *Sudra* ", etc. [1]. In these codes composition is placed in the sections dealing with penance, just as we find it in the penitentials.

There are two aspects of the employment of composition in the penitentials, which we may treat separately. The first is the manner of grading the payments according to rank; the second is the tendency to commute penances to fines, which later becomes a serious cause of the decay of discipline.

In regard to the gradation of payments a double scale is applied to ecclesiastics. One who attacks or slays an ecclesiastic of high rank is obliged to pay more heavily than where the victim is a monk or deacon. At the same time a bishop or a presbyter who is guilty of a crime is obliged to pay more heavily than a monk or deacon.

The church succeeded in securing for its leaders a high degree of protection, by making the payments for attacking them as heavy as possible. The *Canones Hibernenses* offer the same protection to the bishop, or the *scriba*, as to the *princeps excelsus*. The last named apparently refers to the ruler of a *túath* or small province, whose honor-price was that here stated viz., *seven cumhals* [2]. These early canons, then, attempted to protect ecclesiastics by a simple application of the principle of honor-price [3]. But in another portion of the same document, we find that a much higher degree of protection is secured against the death of a bishop. The payment for having through inhospitality caused the death of a bishop is stated as *L ancillas reddet, id est VII ancillas unus quisque gradus, vel L annis peniteat*. The amount is made up of a mul-

1. Bühler annotates this passage (Apast. I, 9, 24) thus : " I recognize in this fine a remnant of the law permitting composition for murder which was in force in ancient Greece and among the Teutonic nations. " Sacred Books of the East, Vol. II, p. 78.

2. D'Arbois de Jubainville, Études sur le Senchus Mor, Revue hist. de Droit, Tom. 5 (1881), p. 6. (In the Ancient Laws, Vol. IV, p. 346, this regulation is ascribed to Cormac Mac Art.)

3. The same provision occurs in the law known as the *Crith Gablach*. Ancient Laws of Irel., Vol. IV, p. 363.

tiplication of the body-price for an ordinary man by the number of the rank of the bishop in ecclesiastical orders (7×7) [1]. The principles of Irish law would, without modification, have produced merely the amount of the normal body-price, seven cumhals, plus that of the honor-price which for one of the bishop's rank would be seven cumhals, or fourteen cumhals in all. Whether the change is directly due to Welsh influence or not it would probably be impossible to determine; but this manner of estimating composition is identical with that of Welsh law, which, as we saw, had a variable body-price. Whether on account of this conflict of Irish authorities, or for other reasons, Theodore leaves the penance for a bishop's or a presbyter's murder in the judgment of the king [2].

The second point we noted in regard to the gradation of payments was that the higher clergy were more heavily penalized for a given offence than those of the lower grades. Here however composition largely disappears, the payment being commuted to a period of penance. As the clergy, theoretically as least, possessed no property, they could not be expected to pay; and it does not appear in the penitential literature that the church was obliged to make composition in money for crimes

Composition is not wholly omitted, however, in the case of homicide by the clergy. Both *Poenit. Vinn.* and *Poenit. Col.* prescribe it in modified form. The clerical culprit is first to spend ten years in exile; on his return he is to render satisfaction to the relatives of his victim, by offering them his life-long service in the place of a son [3]. This is heavier than the penance assigned for a lay murderer, in respect only to the number of years in exile; in the case of a layman the term is three years [4]. Manifestly the variation is intended to

1. Canon. Hibern. IV, can. 2. " The bishop, being in the seventh grade of rank in the ecclesiastical hierarchy is to be paid for sevenfold. " Seebohm, A.S. Law, p. 104.

2. Qui autem episcopum vel presbyterum occiderit, regis judicium est de eo. *Poenit. Theod.* I, IV, 5.

3. Poenit. Vinn., can. 23; Poenit. Col. B, 1.

4. *Ibid.*, B. 13

place greater restraint upon clerics. At the same time the old law of composition is by no means lost sight of. The Senchus Mor seems to imply the provision that the relatives, in case no composition is paid and the murderer does not go into exile, may either exact vengeance by death or compel the offender to become their servant for life [1]. To follow the evidence for greater severity toward clerical than toward lay offenders we should require also to observe the Welsh sources. It would take us out of the field of composition proper, to a comparative study of the duration of penance. It is sufficient to note here that while a penance of three years is enjoined for murder by a layman [2], a monk must serve four years, a deacon six, a presbyter seven, and a bishop thirteen, for this crime [3].

While the clergy were thus specially penalized when they were guilty of crimes, the church on the whole obtained very favorable conditions by means of the modifications of the composition system employed in the penitential codes. The bishops enjoyed special privileges, and while in Ireland free laymen obtained *coirp-dîre* on a basis of equality, the bishop's body-price was greatly augmented by being graded according to his rank [4].

Undoubtedly the mutual influence of British and Irish elements in the Celtic church tended to prevent any distinct conflict in the matter of composition between penitentials emanating from Wales and those from Ireland. It is noticeable that the *Canones Wallici* give a definite proof of the tendency to merge Goidelic and Brythonic elements. This document shows Goidelic influence in the fact that it frequently refers to payments of composition in *ancillae*. The value of a female slave was the unit of value for payments in Irish law. (In Welsh law as in the Brahman codes, the

1. Ancient Laws of Irel. Vol. III, p. 69. Cf. the Story of Libran in Adamnan, lib. II, c. XXXIX.

2. *Sin. Luc. Vict.* can. 3.

3. *Excerpta quaedam*, can. 7. (Followed with slight variation in *Poenit. Cumm.* VI, can. 16.)

4. Seebohm, A.S. Law, p. 113.

payments are made in cattle.) This influence may be traceable to the Goidelic population of South Wales, where Goidels were dominant till the conquest by Maelgwyn (d. 447) [1].

There is another feature of composition which calls for a brief reference, viz. the *dos* or payment to the parents for violation of a virgin. It was a Celtic custom in marriage for the bride-groom to pay a sum of money to the bride's parents. The *Leabbar na h-uidre* contains a story of the sons of Milesius who on asking a band of Hebrew women to become their wives were told that they could not obtain their request unless they paid a dowry (*tinscra*) [2]. "It is from these circumstances," the story-teller explains, "that it is the men that purchase wives in Eriu forever; whilst it is the husbands that are purchased by the wives throughout the world besides." The custom existed also in Britanny and Wales. The more common word used in Irish is *Tinol*, in Welsh *agueddy* [3]. The penitentials require the payment of the *dos* in cases of seduction or rape of a virgin or widow. "*Qui autem cum virgine vel vidua necdum disponsata peccaverit, dotem det parentibus ejus, et anno uno peniteat* [4]. The *Poenit. Theod.* omits reference to the dos [5], as does also the *Poenit. Bedae* [6]. The *Poenit. Vinn.* for *dotem* substitutes *helemosinam pro anima sua* [7]. But the *Poenit. Col.* distinctly says the payment is to be made to the parents, as in Celtic custom [8].

(In certain instances a doubling of composition-payments

1. Seebohm, A.S. Law, p. 107-8.
2. O'Curry, Manuscript Materials, p. 501.
3. D'Arbois de Jubainville, Cours. Tom. 7, p. 234. Cf. 'The Courtship of Bec Fola' by B. O'Looney, in Proc. R.I.A., Ms. Ser. Vol. I, pt. I, p. 174, 175. In Brahman law the suitor pays money for his bride. Apast. II, 5, 12, 1.
4. Excerpta Quaedam, can 7.
5. Poenit. Theod. I, II, can 1. "Si quis fornicaverit cum virgine I anno poeniteat."
6. Poenit. Bed. III, can. 1. Adulescens si cum virgine peccaverit, annum I peniteat.
7. Poenit. Vinn., can. 36.
8. Poenit. Col. B. 16 : "si cum puella, duobus annis, reddito tamen humiliatonis ejus pretio parentibus ejus , poeniteat. Can. 14 refers to *pretium pudicitae* paid to the husband whose wife had been violated.

is required. Thus it is a general principle that fines are doubled by malice aforethought [1]. The tendency of the penitentials to require a double or quadruple restitution for theft or other damage [2] has been by some regarded as an evidence of the influence of Roman law. But as this form of settlement is Biblical [3] it seems unnecessary to attribute it to such a source.)

The redemption of penance by money payments is historically traceable to Celtic influence, through the penitential books. The transition from Goidelic law to penitential usage is rendered tolerably simple for the student by reference to the *Canones Hibernenses*. These canons provide for a twelve-year penance period for an offence which is also capable of being expiated by a payment of twelve *ancillae* [4]. For the alternative of crucifixion or a payment of seven *ancillae* stated in the canons, the dictum of Patrick quoted substitutes " the value of seven ancillae or seven years penance [5] ". The collectio Canonum Hibernensis assigns *septem annorum poenitentiam* for homicide [6]. These are but examples of the general rule stated by d'Arbois de Jubainville thus : Le droit canonique irlandais admettait l'équivalence d'une femme esclave et d'une année de pénitence [7]. The steps taken appear to have been first the enactment of a legal death-penalty as an alternative for the Celtic practice of composition or exile, and secondly, perhaps on the failure to enforce this, the replacing of the death penalty by a seven year term of penance. When once the equivalence of an *ancilla* to a year's penance is established, confessors are provided with a ready-reckoner for commutations from penances into payments, which they appear to have used with great freedom.

1. Anc. Laws of Irel., Vol. III, p. 98.
2. Poenit. Vinn. 25 ; Coll. Can. Hibern., lib. XXIX.
3. Ex. 22, 4.
4. Can. Hib. I, cans. 10, 11.
5. *Ibid.*, III, 1, and " Patricius dicit ".
6. Collectio lib. XXXVIII, c. 10.
7. Rev. Celt., Tom. 8, p. 160. Cf. Haddan and Stubbs, Councils, etc., Vol. II, p. 311.

The commutation of penance terms to shorter terms [1] is closely connected with the commutation of penances to fines. The canons *de arreis* (of equivalents), discussed in our survey of the *Canones Hibernenses* in Chapter I, were widely influential in this. We there referred to another treatise *de arreis* of similar character but more detailed, in Old Irish, dating, according to Kuno Meyer [2] not later than the eighth century, perhaps earlier, and according to E.J. Gwynn [3] about A.D. 800. Among the varied austerities by which a given period of bread and water penance may be substituted for, appears that of flagellation (No. 9). Here we have an instance of an Irish practice which was, like so many others connected with penance, subsequently taken up by the Continental church. Morinus found flagellation as a substitute for money payments appearing only about 960 [4]. He had not, of course, seen this document.

The resemblance between commutations in penance and the "estimations" in Lev. 27 has been observed by Fournier [5], and biblical influence is not improbable. Commutation of penance is a feature of early religion, and appears also in the Brahman Codes, where a variety of equivalent penances frequently appears [6]. The parallel with Leviticus is however very remote, the biblical passages can hardly have originated the principle, while they may have been held to sanction it [7].

While commutations thus took innumerable forms, the most important effects on penance came from commutations into money payments. The whole composition practice of both Celtic and Germanic peoples favored this development, and it soon begins to occupy a prominent place in the pages of penitential books, and in the general history of penance.

1. *Can. Hib.*, II (De Arreis).
2. "The Old Irish Treatise *De Arreis*" Rev. Celt., Tom. XV (1894), p. 485 f.
3. "An Irish Penitential" Eriu, Vol. VII, p. 121 f. See above.
4. Commentarius, lib. VII, cap. XIV, p. 471.
5. "Le liber ex lege Moysi", Rev. Celt., Tom. 30, p. 233.
6. e.g. Apastamba I, 9, 27.
7. Fournier, *op. cit.*

In practice it probably outran the sanction of written authorities. The *Canones Wallici* authorize a payment of three *ancillae* plus three *servi* for homicide [1]. But the Liber Llandavensis records that Artmail king of Gwent is forced to do penance in the form of a grant of land to the church, for fratricide [2]. The church had good economic reasons for promoting this form of commutation. Even where the written regulations were not exceeded "the church accepted the old heathen penalty for murder and the proceeds went to form part of the endowment of the church [3]". The protection which the native law gave to the relatives of the murdered man, which, we may say, constituted a primitive form of life insurance, was removed, and the Church became the recipient of the fines. The application of composition by the Church was such as to defeat the purpose of the system in native law, and was, moreover, as we shall see, in its ultimate effects, highly injurious to the discipline of the Church itself.

2. — Fasting in the Penitentials and in Celtic Custom.

Primitive Celtic civilization was familiar with the custom of fasting. A notable phase of this is the frequently mentioned practice of fasting in distraint. The evidence that fasting in distraint was a pre- Christian Irish custom, is unquestionable [4]. The antiquity of the practice is attested by its appearance in many countries, particularly in India. The Brahman codes refer to it as an established custom [5], of the Irish practice Sir

1. Cf. Seebohm's remarks on the Goidelic influence in these canons. A.S. Law, *loc. cit.* This canon (1) seems to regard body-price as fixed, according to Irish custom.
2. Liber Llandav, p. 237.
3. Bund, Celtic Church of Wales, p. 367.
4. Robinson "The Irish Practice of Fasting" in Putnam anniversary Volume 1909, p. 567 f.; Hancock, Preface to Ancient Laws of Ireland, Vol. I, p. xlvi f. Joyce, Social History, Vol. I, p. 206-207 ; D'Arbois de Jubainville, Cours de la littérature Celtique, Tom. 8, p. 220. "Procédure du Jeûne en Irlande", Rev. Celt., Tom. 7 (1886), p. 245 f.
5. Apast. I. 6, 19, 1.

Henry Maine remarks : "The institution is no doubt identical with one largely diffused throughout the East, which is called by the Hindoos 'sitting Dharna'". It was expected that the party being "fasted against" would respond by fasting in turn, until he came to the frame of mind in which he would surrender the amount due. It is denied by Stokes that a religious sanction lay behind the custom [2]. But in his brief note on the subject he fails to account for the extreme rigour of the practice, which seems to suggest a religious motive. Maine, on the other hand, believes that the constraint was religious. "The druid may well have taught that penal consequences in another world would follow the creditor's death by starvation, and there is perhaps a pale reflection of the doctrine in the language of the Senchus Mor: "He who does not give a pledge to fasting is an evader of all; he who disregardes all things shall not be paid by God or man'" [3]. Robinson shows that the principle of fasting was of far more general application in Ireland than appears in the law of distraint. In fact the instances of fasting to obtain some boon are so various as to make it appear to the present writer that fasting in distraint was but a special application of fasting to obtain favors or revenge. In a number of cases the fast is directed against supernatural beings. Thus the sons of Lughaidh Menn fasted on the Túatha de Danann for a gift of lands, and obtained wives and a domnion and great gifts [4]. Connal the Red and his wife fast against the devil to obtain a child [5]. In the Martyrology of Œngus a dumb poet fasts against a nun to obtain speech [6]. In instances where the parties fasted against fail to respond, divine intervention is the rule. In the Tripartitic Life, Patrick fasts against Trían Mac Fiacc on behalf of the latter's

1. Early Institutions, pp. 39, 40.
2. Whitley Stokes, "Sitting Dharna", Academy Sept. 12, 1885 "Primeval sanction was not divine displeasure but suicide by starvation".
3. *Op. cit.*, p. 40.
4. Irische Texte Bd. IV. Pt. I, p. 11 f.
5. Stokes, Voyage of the Hui Corra, Rev. Celt., Tom. 14 (1893), p. 27, f.
6. Stokes, Martyrology of Œngus, p. 167.

abused slaves, and on his refusal to respond the saint curses him and his offspring. Trían is soon afterwards drowned [1]. Germanus of Auxerre fasts against Vortigern, and celestial vengeance falls upon the unyielding defendant [2]. Germanus and Patrick fast against the city of Auxerre (which in the absence of Germanus has become heretical) for three days and nights. Failing to repent, the city is swallowed up in the earth [3].

There exists an old Irish "Saltair" or hymnal, known as the "Saltair na Rann". Its author retells in Irish the Latin "Lives of Adam and Eve" which is itself a reproduction of an early Egyptian document known in ecclesiastical literature as the "Book of Adam and Eve". S.C. Malan hastranslated this book from the Ethiopic, with valuable introduction and notes [4]. He regards it as the work of some pious and orthodox Egyptian of the fifth or sixth century, written in Arabic in Egypt and later translated into Ethiopic [5]. It passed into Ireland, probably in Latin, and reappears in the *Saltair na Rann*, with a notable feature inserted. The Irish story contains an account, entirely wanting in the Book of Adam and Eve, of the forgiveness of Adam being procured by fasting upon God. Standing neck-deep in the Jordan, he induces the river with its tributaries and creatures to fast with him upon God, till he obtains forgiveness [6]. The confusion between the Church fast and the native fasting process which appears in this and similar stories is observed by Robinson who remarks: "Either an instance of fasting for distraint has been brought into close association with devotional fasting, or an incident

1. Stokes, Trip. Life, Vol. I, p. 219.
2. In the Leabhar na h' Uidre, Todd Lect. Ser. (Roy. Ir. Acad.), Vol. VI, p. 14.
3. Stokes, Trip. Life, Vol. II, p. 419 (Note the difference between this and Jonah 3-4.)
4. Malan, The Book of Adam and Eve, Lond. 1882.
5. *Op. cit.*, introd., p. v.
6. Stokes, The *Saltair na Rann*, in Anecdota Oxoniensia, 1892, lines 1629 f. For a free translation see: Eleanor Hull, The Poem-Book of the Gael., p. 37. (F. N. Robinson in a note on the Sources of the Old Saxon Genesis, Mod. Phil., Vol IV (1907) p. 389 f, has traced the influence of the apocryphal Book of Adam and Eve in another sphere.)

originally of the latter type has been interpreted by the Irish in terms of fasting for distraint" [1].

We have seen, from the incidents above cited, that the Irish mind was familiar with the idea of obtaining boons from the supernatural beings by means of fasting. With the emphasis on sin incidental to Christian teaching, forgiveness was one of the most desirable boons to be obtained. The penitential fast of the early church was based on the remotely similar idea that God would be moved to mercy by the practice of austerities. That the Irish mind habitually looked upon the penitential fast as a fast " upon " or "against" God in the full sense in which this idea was contained in the fast for distraint, would probably be too sweeping a statement. But it is inconceivable that so familiar a custom should not have had some affect on the development of the outwardly similar practice of church penance. It would enable even those most unfamiliar with ecclesiastical ideas to conceive of the penitential fast as a valid and effective means of obtaining forgiveness — a doctrine enforced without reservation in the Penitential of Finnan [2]. Undoubtedly the idea of antagonism and compulsion enters into the conception of fasting in the Irich Church. Of this we have a striking example in the story entitled " Tidings of the three Young Clerics" [3]. The " three young clerics" going on a pilgrimage put to sea without provisions, and are miraculously provided with food. They agree to sing daily, one the "three fifties" (or the one hundred and fifty Psalms), the second three times fifty prayers, and the third the hymn of St. Hilary a hundred times over. In course of time the first and second clerics die, and the third is under obligation to fulfil the tasks they had undertaken in addition to his own. He is burdened with the weight of this duty and believes that God has discriminated against him. In anger over his lot, he fasts against God ; but an angel comes to reprove him for this " unlawful fasting ". Robinson points out that

1. Robinson, *op. cit.*, p. 577.
2. *Poenit. Vinn.*, can. 2, can. 47.
3. Stokes, Lives of Saints from the Book of Lismore, pp. vii-x.

the term for "unlawful fasting" is almost identical with that used in the Ancient Laws [1].

3.— Exile in the Penitentials and in Celtic Custom.

The sentence of exile for the greater offences, especially for homicides, is characteristic of the Irish penitentials [2]. The heroic tales of Ireland illustrate the employment of exile as a penalty. A class of tales is known as the *Longesa* or voyages "undertaken involuntarily, as in the case of a banishment or a flight [3]." Such a flight might have a political aspect; but the legal punishment of exile is well authenticated both in Ireland and in Wales. References to *elud* ('flight' in the legal sense) and to the *élutach* (exiled person) are numerous in the Senchus Mor [4]. Failing the payment of composition the criminal must either become an exile or perish. In Wales the murderer of a chief, or of a near kinsman, was sent into exile with execrations. D'Arbois de Jubainville quotes the first century writer, Nicholas of Damascus, who used the word φυγή to denote exile among the Celts, and who remarks on the Celtic custom by which the murderer of a fellow citizen could flee from the community [5]. Caesar's reference to the interdicts of the druids has already been mentioned.

In the lives of saints frequent instances of exile indicate how this feature was merged with excommunication and penance. There are two distinct accounts of the departure of St. Columba from Ireland. According to one of these action against him was taken, by a synod which met at Teltown, for having incited his tribesmen to the battle of Culdrevny as a result of his quarrel with Finnian of Moville. This is the account given by Adamnan. It apparently implies that the old penalty of exile

1. Robinson, *loc. cit.*
2. Poenit. Vinn 23, Poenit. Col. B. I, B. 13.
3. O'Curry, Lectures on the Manuscript Materials, p. 252. Cf. Joyce, Social History, Vol. I, p. 253.
4. Anc. Laws, Vol. I, pp. 112, 216, 236, 258, 264, Vol. II, pp. 14, 98, 228, 362 etc.
5. Cours, Tom. 7, p. 83.

for homicide was applied by the Synod, although Adamnan speaks of their action as excommunication [1]. Other early accounts, however, ascribe the departure of Columba to the fact that his *anmchara*, St. Molaisi, (Molash, or Lasrianus,) when consulted by him, imposed the penance of perpetual exile from Ireland with the injunction that he should make amends for the loss of life occasioned by the battle for which he had been responsible, by converting as many souls as had perished in the battle [2]. Very similar is the command of St. Ita to Brendan, whose negligence has caused the death of a youth by drowning. He is to become a wanderer in the earth, teaching others and bringing souls to Christ [3]. On receiving this command he goes to Britain and consults Gildas who sends him into a neighboring wilderness (*disertum*) inhabited by lions, and lionesses [4] ! Penitent clerics seem frequently to have been given a wandering commission, and probably the practice accounts largely for the Irish *peregrini* or wandering saints, who often followed an active, if rather irresponsible, missionary career. The sons of Ua Corra in their voyages find on an island a solitary ecclesiastic who tells them he has been expelled from his community for neglecting matins, that he set out to sea in a boat and was cast ashore on the island alone [5]. The Litany of Œngus the Culdee invokes the sons of ua Corra and other pilgrim saints in a liturgical prayer. This prayer desires the aid of " the thrice fifty Gaedhils of Erinn in holy orders, each of them a man of strict rule, who went in one body into pilgrimage under Abban the son of ua Cormaic" [6]. The " *Imram* " of the sons of Ua Corra, however, indicates that they were penitents sent by their *anmchara*. St.

1. " Sanctus excommunicaretur Columba " Reeves, Adamnan, p. 193.
2. Visitavit S Lasrianum, confessorem suum. . . petens ab eo salubre consilium. Lasrianus imperavit ut perpetuo moraretur extra Hiberniam in exilior etc. Reeves, Adamnan, App. to Pref., p. lxxiv and p. 252.
3. Terram peregrinam debes visitare ut alios doceas et animas Christo lucrifacias. Vita prima S. Brendani, lxxxi, in Plummer Vitæ SS. Hib., Vol. I, p. 141.
4. *Ibid.*, p. 142.
5. O'Curry, Manuscript Materials, p. 293.
6. *Ibid.*, p. 381.

Finnian of Clonard became their *anmchara*, and ordered them to be placed for a year under the instruction of a divinity student. They then received further sentence to go and restore the churches they had destroyed; and, having, completed this, they start on a voyage of the ocean [1].

In Adamnan's life of Columba that saint several times administers the penance of exile. An incestuous sinner, Feachnus, comes from Scotia to Iona to confess his sins, and casts himself at Columba's feet weeping *coram omnibus*. Columban sentences him to twelve years penance among the Britons, and perpetual exile [2]. He sends another Irish inquirer, Libran from Connaught, to "Ethica Terra" (the island of Tiree) for seven years. This man had committed murder and his fine had been paid by a rich relative of the deceased, to whom in turn he had bound himself to life-service. He had then fled, that he might "obey God" rather than a "carnal master", thereby, however, breaking his solemn oath of service. The punishment inflicted is therefore for perjury, not for murder. Columban also prescribes exile for this offence [3]. The etablishment at Iona was provided with a nearby penal colony to which recalcitrants were sent. St. Baithene, successor of Columba was during Columba's lifetime *praepositus* of this colony, — the "Campus Lunge" [4]. The *Collectio Canonum Hibernensis* enjoins penitential exile for violation of the relics of bishops and martyrs — (vii annis peregrinus peniteat) [5]. The Brehon code recognizes the authority of the *anmchara* to send penitents on pilgrimage. The expression "performing penitential service to God" is glossed as "doing service to God in penitence, i. e. in pilgrimage" [6]. And the *anmchara's* rights are implied in the words "if it be pilgrimage that his *anmchara* has enjoined

1. *Ibid.*, p. 291.
2. Adamnan, lib. II, c. xxx.
3. *Ibid.*, lib. II, c. xxxix. *Poenit. Col.* B. 20.
4. Adamnan, lib. I, c. xxx, xli. Cf. Mrs. Concannon. Life of St. Columban, p. 148.
5. *Collectio*, lib. xliv, c. 8, — Wasserschl. Die irische Kanonensmmalung, p. 203.
6. Ancient Laws of Irel., Vol. III, p. 31.

upon him "[1]. Columban is simply continuing a familiar Irish custom when he says of one who refuses to make amends to the relatives of a slain man, "nunquam recipiatur in patriam sed, more *Cain*, vagus et profugus sit super terram "[2].

4. —Singing the Psalter : Nocturnal Vigils.

Another notable feature of the penitentials, as we saw in Chapter I, is the nocturnal vigil, often accompanied by psalm-singing. It is true that this practice resembles closely the use of psalmody by certain classes of Eastern monastics ; and it may have been brought to Ireland from Gallic monasteries like Lerins, where Eastern customs prevailed. But here again it is instructive to remind ourselves of native Celtic customs.

The use of forms of incantation seems to have been a prominent feature in druidism, both as a means of divination and as a means of magic. Tacitus speaks of the "vain and superstitious songs"[3] of the Gallic druids. Both the druids and the *fil* used incantations for magic, and in their verses they habitually introduced the name of a god to procure his intervention[4]. That the recitation of verses as a penitential exercise was a feature of the Indian branch of Aryan religion is attested by frequent references in the Brahman codes[5]. The singing of the *samans* by way of penance is commanded[6]. For an offence closely connected with primitive *tabu*, that of involuntary pollution during sleep, the *Excerpta quaedam* and the *Prefatio Gildae* command the singing of psalms[7]. For the same offence the *Dharmasastra* of Gautama order the recitation of verses[8].

A notable use of singing in Aryan religion was in the funeral lament and panegyric[9]. The early adoption of set forms for this rite is indicated by the evidence of Homer,

1. *Ibid.*, p. 73.
2. Poenit. Col. B. I.
3. "Superstitione vana Druidae canebant". Historia, liber IV, c. 54.
4. MacCullough, Relig. of the Ancient Celts, p. 325.
5. E. g. Apast. I, 10, 28, 9; Gaut. xxxiv, 1; xxv.
6. Gaut. xxvi.
7. *Excerpta quaedam*, can. 8 ; *Prefatio Gildae*, can. 22.
8. Gautama xxiii, 3.
9. See Schrader, Aryan Religion, in Hastings C. R. E., Vol. II.

and by the statement of Plutarch that Solon forbade their use [1]. The custom is abundantly attested among the Celts both of Britain and Ireland. Poseidonius of Apameia, who probably visited Britain about 100 B.C., makes note of the Brythonic "poets whom they call bards (βάρδους) who sing songs of eulogy and satire" [2]. It was the function of the bards to recite poems in honor of those who had fallen in battle [3]. The bardic poetry of Wales, such as the work of the sixth century bards Taliessin and Aneurin contains much of this material. Apparently in Ireland the same function, sometimes at least, appertained to the druids. "In the burial rites, which in Ireland consisted of a lament, sacrifices, and raising a stone over the grave, druids took part. The druid Dergdamsa pronounced a discourse over the Ossianic hero Magneid, buried him with his arms and chanted a rune [4].

In the Irish monasteries in early times it was customary to sing a requiem for a deceased brother [5]. In the *Vita Comgalli* Comgall on returning to his monastery finds that one of the brethren has died, and that the relatives of the deceased have come to the monastery to bewail him according to their custom, — "et plangentes fecerunt saeculares exequias". This perturbed the monks, who, no doubt would have used other incantations [6]. The funeral lamentation is referred to in the case of the death of Ethne and Fedelm, the daughters of Lœghaire, after their conversion by Patrick. Their friends, we learn, "bewailed them greatly" [7]. The singing of a solo-chant was very common, and the practice, called "keening", is "mentioned in the most ancient writings and continued to the present day" [8]. A modern example of the keening is des-

1. *Ibid.*, p. 19.
2. W. Dinan, Monumenta Historica Celtica, Vol. I, p. 304. The statement of Poseidonius is quoted by Diodorus Sicilus, Bibl. Hist., lib. V, c. 31. Strabo, Geography, lib. IV, c. li 4 uses similar langunge.
3. Holmes, Ancient Britain, p. 266.
4. MacCullough, Relig. of the Ancient Celts, p. 309.
5. Stokes, Lives of Saints from the Book of Lismore, p. 307. Anc. Laws of Irel., Vol. III, p. 33.
6. Plummer Vitae SS. Hib., Vol. II, p. 110.
7. Stokes, Tripartite Life, Vol. I, p. 103; Vol. II, p. 317
8. Joyce, Social History, Vol. II, p. 540.

cribed by O'Curry [1]. Wood-Martin has a similar account, and gives the words of the passionate song of praise and grief, and anger at the enemies of the dead [2]. The poet Crabbe described the keening dirge as "deeply melancholy" and "pure paganism" [3]. The night vigil, or 'wake', for the dead is a familiar survival of Irish and Welsh paganism. The period of watching varied, but was usually, in pagan Ireland, seven days and seven nights [4]. This period was characterized by a continuation of the mourning and was spoken of as "the days of lamentation", "*dies ululationis*" [5]. The church did not suppress the pagan funeral customs, but, within the monasteries, substituted the psalms for the native incantations. This is evident from an incident in the *Vita Fintani*. Here an account is given of the procedure when a monk died. In this case St. Fintan himself was absent; but the monks gathered in the place "where Fintan with his brethren used to sing psalms, about the body" of a dead member [6]. In the "Tidings of the Three Young Clerics" the surviving cleric sings the requiem (*ecnairc*, intercession) for his departed brothers [7]. Thus a Christian equivalent was found for an insuppressible pagan custom. The singing of the requiem within the monasteries was not confined to the death of monks, but was extended to all members of the tribe [8]. It was sometimes, at least in the case of distinguished persons, prolonged over a considerable period. We are told of King Danum Dam Argait that

1. Manners and Customs of the Ancient Irish, Vol. I, p. cccxxiv f.
2. Traces of the Elder Faiths, Vol. I, p. 309.
3. Quoted, ibid., p. 312.
4. Peractis, ut moris erat gentilium, diebus septem exequarium. De Smedt und de Baker, Vitae S. S. Hib. ex. cod. Salmant., col. 909. St. Patrick's wake lasted twelve days. Joyce, Social History, Vol. II, p. 540.
5. Laithi na canti (hence "keening"). Stokes, Trip. Life, Vol. I, p. 104; et consumpti sunt dies ululationis filiarum regis et sepelierunt eas. Ibid., Vol. II, p. 317. Cf. Joyce, Social Hist., Vol. II, p. 540.
6. Ubi Fintanus cum fratribus circa corpus psalmos canebat Vita Fint § 20, in Plummer, *op. cit.*, Vol. II, p. 105.
7. See Ancient Laws of Irel., Preface, p. liii.
8. Stokes, Lives etc., p. xi.

"the clerics are singing his requiem", although he appears to have been dead for a considerable time [1].

The prominence of the psalms in the life of the Celtic Church is remarkable. Psalms and hymns were used as charms. The Lorica of St. Patrick is supposed to have been used as a charm for disguise. It made Patrick and his companions appear as deer to their enemies; the title, *Feth Fiada*, given to it in the Irish version, is to be translated in the sense of "a spell peculiar to druids and poets, intended to produce invisibility" [2]. The emphasis on the singing of the psalter in the Celtic church can best be accounted for by the hypothesis that the old magical ideas connected with native incantation were largely retained [3]. Knowledge of, and ability to sing the psalms, were important accomplishments for the monastic; and a very high value was placed upon copies of the psalter [4]. It is generally assumed that the psalms were sung nocturnally for liturgical as well as for penitential purposes. One of the pupils of Columban, Deicola, established a *laus perennis* at Lure; and it may have been inaugurated at Luxeuil by *Columban* [5]. But was the *laus perennis* not itself penitential? Offences against the 'Rule' which were of so trivial a character that they must have been frequent (such as non-appearance at table in time for prayer before the meal, sleeping during prayer, coming to mass in the morning in night clothes, or coming late to prayers) were, according to the *Regula Coenobialis* of Columban, punished by the offender being required to sing six, twelve, fifteen, twenty-four, thirty or fifty psalms [6]. It will readily be seen that even a small number of such offences would produce virtually perpetual singing of a purely penitential kind. The protracted singing of the psalter by Egyptian monks is des-

1. *Ibid.*, p. 307.
2. Bernard and Atkinson, The Irish Liber Hymnorum, p. 209.
3. Cf. Plummer, *op. cit.*, Vol. I, p. clxxix.
4. This is evident e. g, in the quarrel between Finnian of Moville and Columba. Reeves, Adamnan, p. 192 f.
5. Acta SS. Boll., Tom. II (Jan. II) p. 563 f., Montalembert, Monks of the West, Vol. II, p. 254 and note; Margaret Stokes. Six Months in the Forests of France, p. 44.
6. Migne, P. L., Tom. 80, col. 216 f.

cribed by Cassian [1]. It is possible that the Celtic monastics were imitating those of Egypt, since it is evident that they knew the works of Cassian [2], while they gave to the practice a new penitential character. At the same time it appears probable that the Celtic monks bore in their minds memories of the nocturnal singing of the period of mourning, designed to protect the deceased on his outgoing journey [3]. There is extant an ancient "rule" of the Church of Iona which has been ascribed to Columba, in which the monks are enjoined to sing the hymns for the dead standing (the posture required in the penitentials) [4], and exhorted to "fervour in singing the office for the dead" [5].

1. Institutes, Bk. II, Ch. 2. f. Especially, Ch. 11, 12. (The description is not of a complete *laus perennis.*)

2. See above.

3. In Marie Trevelyan's Description of the *Gwyenlos* or welsh wake, the purpose of the latter is to protect the soul from evil spirits who are trying to prevent its passage to the blessed life. Folk-lore and Folk-stories of Wales pp. 274, 275. Probably the primitive fear of the dead and desire to keep his spirit from returning to trouble the living is to be kept in view as well. Cf. Wood-Martin, Traces of the Elder Faiths, Vol. 2, p. 309.

4. Excerpta quaedam, can. 8 (surgat canatque xii psalmos); Prefatio Gildae, can. 22 (xxviii aut xxx psalmos canat stando).

5. Haddan and Stubbs, Councils etc., Vol II, p. 220.

CHAPTER V

The Spread of the Celtic Penance on the Continent of Europe.

I. — Celtic monks on the continent.

In order to understand the process by which the Celtic penitential books became the models for the practice of penance in the Frankish Empire, it will be necessary briefly to indicate the extraordinary force of the Celtic influence on the continental church during the period from the sixth to the ninth century.

This influence was due to the labors of some British and many Irish monks, who, in the period named, penetrated to almost all regions of the Continent. In many instances they anticipated all other Christianizing enterprises; in others they revived the *morale* of the lax Frankish Church. Not infrequently, as itinerant missionaries they came into conflict with the settled clergy who regarded them as intruders. Thus they constituted both a stimulating and a disturbing factor in the church life of the Franks. The influence of the Celtic teachers on the Continent began with some early representatives of the British Church. Pelagius, as we have seen, was most probably a native of Britain, though he may have been a Goidel by race [1]. Some of his fifth century continental followers, such as Fastidius of Sicily and Faustus of Riez, are generally regarded as Britons [2]. Patrick, probably a native of Wales [3], made good his country's debt to orthodoxy, incurred

1. See above, p. 70.
2. Haddan and Stubbs, Councils, etc., Vol. I, p. 16; Vol. II, p. 73. L. Gougaud, "L'Œuvre des Scotti dans l'Europe continentale", in Rev. d'histoire ecclésiastique, Tom. IX (1908), p. 22.
3. Bury, Life of St. Patrick, p. 322 f.

by Pelagius, by taking a leading part in the Christianization of Ireland. But it was probably Armorica that felt most strongly the influence of British Christianity. Montalembert held that the Bretons of Armorica owed their Christianity to monks from Britain who accompanied a British migration in flight from the Saxon invaders in the fifth century [1]. This view receives some support from the documents given by Haddan and Stubbs [2]. Maglorius, who came with a migration c. 566, became Abbot, perhaps Bishop, of Dol. After the period of the English conquest the surviving portion of the British Church continued to send missionaries across the sea, especially to the related Celts of Armorica. A reciprocity of monastic leadership is indicated by many references in the lives of saints [3]. The Celtic church literature was apparently largely common to Ireland, Britain and Armorica. Bradshaw found evidence that the *Collectio canonum Hibernensis*, an Irish document containing Welsh elements, was preserved through the Armorican church [4]. Two British bishops of Armorica, Paternus and Samson, signed the decrees of the third synod of Paris, c. 555 or 557 [5]. Of British missionaries on the Continent outside Armorica we have scant information. We know that some Britons were busy in Gaul and Germany, but in few cases do we know their names. Jonas refers to a Briton Gurganus as a disciple of Columban. St. Gall. numbered a Briton among his followers [6]. A century and a half later (a.d. 739) we find their activities in Bavaria and Switzerland condemned by pope Gregory III, who warns the Bavarian and Allemannic bishops against British teachers in their midst, describing them as "false and heretical priests". This notice apparently belongs to the

1. Montalembert, Monks of the West, Vol. II, p. 143 f.
2. Councils, etc. Vol. II, p. 76 (Immigration of Britons into Britanny) and p. 86 f. (List of Breton saints who were natives of Britain and Ireland.)
3. Numerous instances are found, e.g. in Rees, Cambro-British Saints; Very many occur in Baring-Gould and Fisher, Lives of the British Saints.
4. Early Collection of Canons known as the Hibernensis, Two unfinished papers, p. 14.
5. Haddan and Stubbs, Councils etc. Vol. II, p. 75.
6. *Ibid.*, Vol. I, p. 157.

widespread effort of the English missionary Boniface and the popes to uproot Celtic Christianity on the Continent [1].

The Irish monks soon eclipsed their British cousins as continental missionaries. By the sixth century they began to spread in considerable numbers over the Continent. Among Irish predecessors of Columban are to be reckoned Fridolin, who in the reign of Clovis preached in Austrasia and in the territory of the Allemanni [2], Caidoc and Fricor who together accomplished a notable work in Picardy [3], and possibly Trudpert, who labored in the Münsterthal in the Breisgau.

The direct influence of Columban was so great as to be inestimable. Accompanied from the first by twelve monks of like devotion, he was soon joined by a large number of his fellow-countrymen. The Rule of Columban was imposed likewise on many Frankish pupils. Annegray, Fontaines, and especially Luxeuil became the parent institutions of a system of monasteries in Austrasia, Burgundy and Neustria. Miss Stokes gives a list of sixty-three names of early pupils of Columban who spread his Rule from Luxeuil [4]. The vast influence of their work is apparent from the account given by Montalembert of the "Colonies of Luxeuil" [5]. Some of these leaders bear unmistakably Frankish names; but they were all alike loyal disciples of the Irish teacher. St. Wandrille, who before becoming a monk had been a Frankish count, after an influential religious career in Gaul, followed Columban to Bobbio [6]. St. Gall, one of Columban's original twelve, with his master toiled up the Rhine, and settled among the Southern Allemanni on Lake Constance. The monastery of St. Gall became in the following centuries a rich repository of Irish MSS., a fact which furnishes one indication of the volume of Irish life which passed through it for generations. Another of the twelve was St. Deicola, or Die,

1. *Ibid.*, p. 203.
2. Vita S. Fridolini, Boll. A.SS. Mart. I, p. 433.
3. M. Stokes, Three Months in the Forests of France, pp. 75-79.
4. M. Stokes, *op. cit. App. VI*, p. 254.
5. Monks of the West, Vol. II, p. 307 f.
6. Gougaud, L'Œuvre des Scotti, Rev. d'hist. ecclés. Tom. IX, p. 26.

who established an important monastery at Lure (Lutra) [1].

After the departure of Columban to Italy the Irish missions continued to expand. The Irish workers increased in numbers as newcomers arrived from the crowded monasteries of Ireland. In course of time their schools appear to have become largely of the "double monastery" type. These institutions were so called (*monasteria duplicia*) because they accommodated in near proximity both monks and nuns. It is probably a mistake to suppose that the double monasteries were Irish in origin, although the foundation of Brigid and Conled at Kildare is a striking Irish example. They probably developed merely as a convenient economical arrangement. Examples of the type were well known on the Continent prior to the period of Irish influence; but they had given occasion for such scandalous abuses that they were restricted or formally suppressed. Their success under the Irish abbots in proof of the ascetic devotion which characterized Irish monasticism. "Wherever the apostles of Irish monasticism went," writes Mary Bateson, "this form of organization followed,-not because it was one that originated with and peculiarly belonged to the Irish, but because it could live only in the purest spiritual atmosphere [2]".

The most brilliant meteor of Irish monasticism of the century after Columban, is the ecstatic St. Fursa who after activities among the Anglo-Saxons came to Gaul, labored at Lagny and died at Peronne (c. 650) [3]. O'Hanlon notes an extraordinary number of MSS. of the *Vita* (or *Visio*) *Sancti Fursei*, indicating the greatness of his mediaeval fame. Peronne, where Fursa's relics lay, became a haunt of pilgrims and a centre of Irish influence. Hence it was frequently alluded to as "*Perrona Scottorum*". Fursa's successors in the abbacy of Peronne were Irish without exception at least to 744. Distinguished in this succession was the learned and

1. Boll. ASS. Tom. 2 (Jan. 2), p. 563 f.

2. "Origin and Early History of the Double Monasteries." Transactions of the Royal Hist. Soc., N.S. Vol. XIII (1899), p. 197.

3. Bede, Hist. Eccles., III, 19; Boll. ASS. Tom. II (Jan. 11), p. 399 f. O'Hanlon, Lives of the Irish Saints, Vol. I, p. 222 f.

poetic Cellanus (d. 706) a correspondent of Aldhelm of Malmesbury [1].

Würzburg on the upper Main witnessed the martyrdom of its Irish apostle Kilian and two of his twelve Irish companions (c. 689) [2]. Southeastward into Bavaria Columban's successor Eustathius (d. 624) had already made his way [3], sowing Celtic Christianity along the Danube, where it was soon to be championed by Rupert of Worms (696 f.).

In pioneer fields the Irish were the ardent apostles of Christianity. But where the church was already organized and possessed an established clergy, the insular saints were often most unwelcome visitors, and were regarded as disturbers and perverters of religion. The loose episcopacy of the monastic church of Ireland, which at this period knew no dioceses, explains the phenomenon of the despised *episcopi vagantes*, or itinerant Irish missionaries. To the annoyance of the diocesan bishops the Irish " bishops ", (of whom each Irish monastery could boast one or more) assumed the right to consecrate to orders on their own initiative. The fact that action was taken against them in a number of Frankish councils [4], indicates the seriousness with which their inroads were viewed by the Frankish prelates. Indeed it is clear that in the seventh and eighth centuries the Roman church was confronted in the Frankish domains by a powerful, if poorly organized, movement on the part of Celtic individualistic leaders, the main tendencies of which were recognized as disruptive of Roman solidarity and inimical to papal dominance. This

1. Traube, " Peronna Scottorum ", Sitzungsber. der König. Akad. München, Philos-Philol u. Histor. Classe, 1900, p. 469 f. especially p. 477 f.

2. Boll. A.SS. Tom. 29 (July 2), p. 612; S. Riezler, " Die Vita Kiliani ", Neues Archiv. Bd. XXVIII (1902), p. 232 f. Ozanam, La Civilisation Chrétienne, p. 134; O'Hanlon, Lives of the Irish Saints, Vol. VIII, p. 432.

3. Mon. Germ. Hist., Script. Rev. Merov., T. IV, p. 122. " Plurimus eorum ad fidem convertit, " says Jonas.

4. Concil. Cabillon. II. (a.d. 813) can. XLIII; Mansi, Concilia, Tom. XIV, col. 102. Wm. Levison, " Die Iren und die Fränkische Kirche ". Histor. Zeitschr. Ser. III, Bd. 13 (1912), p. 1 f.

movement drew upon itself a crushing response in the career of St. Boniface. An English monk of the school of Wilfrid, devoted to the principle of Roman control, Boniface found to his embarrassment that the Irish missionaries had pioneered many areas before him, and had attained considerable prestige among the native populations. Their attitude to Rome was one of respect but not of obedience. Columban had ventured to address Gregory the Great in terms that are the reverse of filial, and to bring Boniface IV to task for scandalous negligence in regard to heresy [1]. It must be remembered that the Scots of South Ireland adopted the Roman Easter early in the seventh century (636), and the same reform was brought about in North Ireland at the end of the century (Synod of Derry 697). Thenceforth the church of Ireland underwent a process of Romanization, which was interrupted before its completion by the Norse invasions of the ninth century. Missionaries from Ireland who came after Columban no longer took his attitude to the papacy; but their views of church authority were defective from a Roman standpoint.

This insular independence was not soon overcome, and Boniface seems to have regarded the Celtic church on the Continent as his and the pope's sworn enemy. He heroically undertook to suppress Celticism in Germany. This is the real meaning of the famous oath of Boniface, taken at Rome on the tomb of St. Peter, c. 722 [2]. It is a solemn engagement on the part of Boniface to give no quarter to the opponents of the papacy, who, in Germany, were principally the representatives of the Celtic tradition. With all his idealism and devotion, St. Boniface was more the suppressor of anti-papal Celticism than the torch-bearer of Christianity to the Barbarians; an organizer rather than a missionary, and with much of the spirit of the inquisitor in him [3].

1. M.G.H., Ep. Merov. Aevi, Tom. I, p. 156 f.; p. 170 f.
2. M.G.H. Epistolae, III, p. 265; Migne, P.L., Tom. 89, col. 803.
3. J.W. Thompson has pointed out the sordid economic aspect of the movement under Boniface, who gave an extraordinary attention to tithes. — "The German Church and the Conversion of the Baltic Slavs" Amer. Jour. of Theol., Vol. 20 (1916), p. 211 f.

In the time of Boniface (d. 755) Ireland was sending to the Continent men who distinguished themselves as much for their learning as for their religious zeal. Of these Vergil the Geometer is especially famous. Vergil was an abbot, possibly a bishop, in his own country [1]. He came to Germany and became abbot of a monastery near Salzburg. He taught scientific ideas, manifestly suggested by Greek studies. Boniface laid information against Vergil before pope Zachary, charging him with a heresy which seems to have been the doctrine of the earth's antipodes. The attempt to crush Vergil failed however; he long outlived Boniface and become Bishop of Salzburg (767-784) [2].

Investigation has made it increasingly clear that the contribution of the Irish schools to education and learning in Europe during the eighth and ninth centuries was a highly important phase of mediaeval history [3]. The instruction of the Irish teachers was so highly regarded in England in the seventh century that Aldhelm (himself the disciple of an Irishman, Maildulf) playfully speaks of young Englishmen going over to Ireland "in fleets" to pursue their studies [4]. Bede makes frequent reference to this intercourse [5]. Not a few also found their way from the Frankish kingdoms to the Irish monasteries. "Dagobert II was sent to Ireland for his education. Innumerable foreign ecclesiastics came to Ireland in that age to improve themselves in the study of scripture [6]".

1. Aghaboe, Queens Co. Ireland. Todd, St. Patrick, p. 64.

2. Sandys, Hist. of Classical Scholarship, Vol. I, p. 452 f. Gilbert, Le Pape Zacharie et les antipodes. Rev. des quest. scientifiques, tom. XII (1882), p. 478 f.; G.T. Stokes, Ireland and the Celtic Church, p. 224 f.; Healy, Insula Sanctorum, p. 566 f.

3. Stokes, Ireland and the Celtic Church; Meyer, Learning in Ireland and the Transmission of Letters; Zimmer, The Irish Element in Mediaeval Culture; Gougaud, L'Œuvre des Scotti, *op. cit.*, p. 255 f.; Sandys, Hist. of Classical Scholarship, Vol. I, p. 452-495.

4. Hibernia, quo catervatim isthinc lectores in classibus advecti confluunt. S. Aldhelmi Ep. III, *ad Eahfridum*. Migne, P.L., Tom. 89, col. 94.

5. E.g. Hist. Eccles., III, 3; III, 7; III, 27; V, 9; V, 10; V, 15. (Of these four refer to Englishman studying in Ireland, the other two to Franks.)

6. Zimmer, Irish Elem. in Med. Cult., p. 45 n. Cf. Levison, *op. cit.*, p. 5.

In the times of Charlemagne the phenomenal learning of the Irish won the high commendation of Alcuin, who speaks of the *doctissimi magistri de Hibernia* [1] who have distinguished themselves in Brittany, Gaul and Francia. But the greatest influence of Irish learning abroad was reserved for the ninth century. As a consequence of the devastations of the Northmen in Ireland, large numbers of the population fled to Gaul, and there many scholars found a home and eager pupils. "Almost all Ireland" says a monk, Hericus, writing to Charles the Bald to dedicate to him his *Vita S. Germani*, "despising the sea and its perils, is transporting itself to our shores, with its troop of philosophers [2]". Amid this "troop" there stand out a few names of men of the largest intellectual calibre. These include Dicuil the Geographer, who, about 825, tells of Irish missionaries in Iceland; Sedulius Scotus who loved Greek and good wine and taught for many years at Liége prior to 860; and Moengall who promoted the teaching of music at St. Gall. Overshadowing all for learning and originality is John Scotus Erigena, who was protected by Charles the Bald from a heresy trial at Rome over his book, *De Divisione Naturae*, in which he had exalted reason above authority [3].

The impression of widespread Irish influence on the Continent is confirmed and deepened by the testimony of paleography. The prevalence of abbreviations formed by suspension and by contraction, in mediaeval MSS, has been traced to an Irish origin. The adoption of this method in Ireland is regarded as due to the necessity of economizing parchment — a very scarce commodity in that region of the world. The fact that Irish scribes succeeded in imposing their manner

1. M.G.H. Epistolae Carol. Aevi. Tom. II, p. 437 (ep. Alcuini 280).

2. Quid Hiberniam memorem contempto pelagi discrimine, pene totam cum grege philosophorum ad littora nostra migrantem. Migne, P.L. Tom. 124, col. 1133.

3. For a brief account of these and other Irish scholars see Zimmer, Irish Element in Mediaeval Culture, pp. 46-102. A less critical account is given in Healy, Insula Sanctorum et Doctorum, pp. 566-589. See also Sandys, Hist. of Classical scholarship, Vol. I, p. 464 f.

of writing on Europe indicates the preeminence of the Scots in letters, and supports the view held by Zimmer, K. Meyer and others, of the rich scholarship of Ireland from the fifth to the ninth century [1]. Students of the Canon Law, no less than students of paleography, concede a dominant influence to the Scots. It is to a professor of law (Wasserschleben) that we are indebted for the best work on the penitentials. Hinschius gives them considerable attention in his masterly treatise on ecclesiastical law [2]. Paul Fournier ascribes to Irish canons the biblical element which entered into the law of the Church during the Carolingian period. "En tout cas," this writer remarks, "ces faits démontrent suffisamment qu'à l'époque carolingienne, de toutes parts les textes bibliques envahissent les collections canoniques ; or ce sont, à mon avis, les missionnaires irlandais qui ont été les premiers auteurs de cette invasion [3]."

There is another equally pronounced and more important "invasion" to consider — that of the Celtic penance.

2. — The Introduction of the penitentials on the Continent.

The aggressive Celtic missionaries whose labors have been briefly sketched above, introduced into Europe the penitential literature and practiced the administration of penance according to Celtic usage. Within the Frankish territories it is clear that before the time of Columban penitential discipline was in almost total neglect. This fact is plainly stated by Jonas of Bobbio in the seventh century [4]. It might by suspected that Jonas is here exaggerating conditions in Frankish Christianity

1. W.M. Lindsay, *Notae Latinae* : An Account of Abbreviation in Latin MSS. of the Early Minuscule Period c. 700-850, Cambridge, 1915, *passim*. Cf. Review in Nation, New York, Vol. 104 (1917), p. 659.

2. System des Kathol. Kirchenrechts, Bd. IV, p. 824 f.

3. Paul Fournier, " Le Liber ex Lege Moysi " in Rev. Celt., Tom. XXX (1909), p. 221.

4. See above, p. 44.

in order to extol his hero. But the pages of Gregory of Tours, Columban's contemporary, reveal an almost total absence of what Jonas (quoting the language of Gildas [1]) calls *medicamenta poenitentiae.* The extraordinary "History of the Franks" [2] reveals, to be sure, cases enough of crimes which elsewhere would have called for penance. It is replete with incidents of the most ghastly cruelty. Homicide is recorded almost on every page [3]. But for these crimes there is no attempt to exact penance. Murder is followed by revenge, not by penitential discipline. The hands of Clovis are stained with many murders, but he does no penance and is not asked to do any [4]. Punishment is largely left to God, and death or misfortune is interpreted by Gregory, who is "almost as superstitious as a savage" [5], in the light of a miraculous recompense for sin. This applies even to lesser crimes than homicide, as when Sigivald duke of Auvergne is punished by Heaven for taking church property [6]. In one instance we read that parties guilty of rioting in a church "atoned for their evil conduct" and were taken back to the communion of the church by Ragnemod Bishop of Paris [7]. What was done by way of expiation is not stated. In another instance in point we have a fuller statement of the process. As Gregory had a personal quarrel with count Leudast, he tells the story of this adventurer in some detail. In one episode Gregory pardons the count without any suggestion of penance. Ultimately Leudast is excommunicated by the bishops and outlawed by an edict of the king. There is no appeal to written or traditional rules. The word *penance* is not used, and the only fasting in the case is done voluntarily by

1. Williams, Cymmrod. Rec. Ser. No. 3, pt. 2, p. 178, note.
2. Ed. by Wilhelm Arndt and Bernard Krusch in M.G.H., Script. Rer. Merov., Tom. I, pp. 1-450, and by René Poupardin, Grégoire de Tours, Histoire des Francs.
3. E.g. in lib. III.
4. Lib. II, c. 41-43.
5. E. Brehaut, History of the Franks by Gregory of Tours, N.Y., 1916, p. XI.
6. Lib. III, c. 16. Poupardin, Grég. de Tours, p. 94.
7. *Ibid.*, liv. V, c. 32, *op. cit.*, p. 186.

the innocent queen out of grief and sympathy with the Bishop who has been maligned [1]. This is as near as we get to penance in Gregory of Tours. The rampant barbarity of the Franks had not been tamed to discipline by the feeble and inefficient Merovingian church. The Celtic penitentials came, not to conflict with an established penitential discipline but to fill what was almost a total vacuum, and to inculcate penance among those who had not been accustomed to it in any form.

Fragmentary as are the materials for the history of the Frankish Church, it is possible to trace through the seventh, eighth and ninth centuries the gradual introduction of the Celtic penitential books. Some time between 644 and 656 there was held a synod at Châlons-sur-Saône under Clovis II, which recognized the new practice of penance with private confession to priests [2].

It is notable that at this stage the new penance is received apparently without suspicion, and that no mention is made of penitential books. As yet the confusion resulting from the use of variations in these books had not appeared. Nor was there, so far, any attempt to make confession obligatory by act of council. Lagarde points out that a number of the bishops present "had felt the influence of Columban" before becoming ecclesiastics [3].

We may be sure that the rapid spread of Irish influence, which by the time of this council had already begun, bore with it generally the introduction of the Celtic type of penance. Even writers who minimize the influence of the severe monastic rule of Columban recognize the more per-

1. *Ibid.*, lib. V, c. 49, *op. cit.*, pp. 201-204.

2. De poenitentia vero peccatorum quae est medela animae, utilem hominibus esse censemus, et ut poenitentibus a sacerdotibus data confessione indicatur poenitentia, universitas sacerdotorum noscitur consentire. Mansi, Concil., Tom. X, col. 1191 (Concil. Cabillon, c. 650 A.D. can. 8). Hinschius observes that the statement of universal opinion in favor of this way of conducting penance cannot refer to earlier times, but can only be connected with the new (Celtic) penitential practice. System des Kath. Kirchenrechts, Bd. IV, p. 826. Cf. Levison, *op. cit.*, p. 12.

3. Latin Church, p. 57.

manent influence of his *poenitentiale* [1]. And not only the monks of Columban, but all the Irish missionaries, had passed through a training in the same type of penance and were accustomed to the use of penitential books.

The spread of Irish canons is well illustrated by the instance of the celebrated code, the *Collectio canonum Hibernensis.* This compilation soon found a wide vogue on the Continent, probably in the form of excerpts. Fournier supposes that a number of sections of considerable length were separately circulated about the end of the eighth and beginning of the ninth century [2]. Later, widely used Frankish penitentials contained many borrowings from the Hibernensis. The *Poenit. Martenianum*, for example, has sixteen passages from it [3], and the *Capitula Theodori* published by Jacques Petit show a similar influence [4].

The Irish collection was adopted with satisfaction by those who were working for the reform of the ill-disciplined church of the Franks, as it sanctioned some of the principles which the reforming clergy advocated. It refused to princes the right to judge the bishops, and took the causes of clerics out of the hands of lay courts. It made stringent regulations against simony.

With these factors which rendered the Hibernensis agreeable to the reforming element in the church, came also the more distinctly Celtic phase of the work, viz. its penitential canons. When hostility to the penitentials became pronounced the influence of this collection waned ; its reforming tendencies were taken up in a more papalistic strain in the forged decretals [5]. Boniface, as we observed, was a consistent opponent of the Celts. As an Englishman he was no doubt familiar

1. Molinier, in Rev. historique, Tom. IX, p. 97 f.; reviewing Malorny, Quid Luxovienses monaci, discipuli Sancti Columbani, ad regulam monasteriorum atque ad communem profectum contulerint (Paris, 1895).

2. " De l'influence de la collection irlandaise sur la formation des collections canoniques. " Nouvelle Revue historique de droit, 1899, p. 27 f.; p. 34.

3. Wasserschl. Bussordn., p. 282 f.

4. *Ibid.*, p. 145 f.

5. Fournier, *op. cit.*, p. 75.

with the private, and largely Celtic, penance of Theodore, perhaps even with that of Bede. As we have seen, the Frankish church possessed no rival system with which to combat. that of the Celts. If the ancient public penance had ever been introduced among the Franks, it was evidently long since discorded. Boniface was anxious to make good this defect. On the ground of his general antagonism to the Celts, he might be expected to hesitate before committing himself to sanction their penitential books, even if he had secretly approved the latter. It is very probable too that he had seen in England, if not among the Franks, evidence of the abuses that invariably sprang from the adoption of the principle of commutation in penance.

Already before the middle of the eighth century, these abuses prevailed in England, to the alarm of earnest churchmen. The synod held at Clovesho in 747 expressed a vigorous denunciation of certain outgrowths of the system of commutations. These abuses were largely connected with almsgiving, which had been perverted into a mitigation of penance, and was evidently popularly regarded as purchasing immunity from punishment. The synod decreed that alms were not to diminish or change the satisfaction of fasting and other "works of expiation" imposed by a priest [1]. Another abuse early combatted in England was that of vicarious penance. The *Poenit. Cummeani* in its closing paragraph specifically provides for the employment of a 'righteous man' to perform penance for persons who do not know the psalms, and are not able to fast [2]. This passage has evidently suggested the language used in the additions to the *Poenit. Bedae : Et qui de psalmis hoc quod superius diximus implere non potest, elegat justum, qui pro illo impleat et de suo precio aut labore hoc*

1. Bonum est eleemosynas quotidie dare; sed pro his non est abstinentia remittenda, non est jejunium impositum semel, juxta ecclesiae regulam, sine qua non remittuntur ulla peccata, relaxandum. Concil. Cloveshoviae (a.d. 747) Can. 26. Mansi, Tom. XII, col. 404.

2. Et qui psalmos non novit et jejunare non potest, elegat justum, qui pro illo hoc impleat et de suo precio aut labore hoc redimat, id est per unumquemque diem de precio valente denario in pauperibus eroget.

redimat [1]. Whether from the application of this canon, or from the adoption of the principle of vicarious penance directly from Cummean or from some other source, the same council of Clovesho was led to pronounce against the acceptance, in fulfilment of penitential requirements, of vicarious psalm-singing. This pronouncement was called forth by the shocking statement of a certain rich man, who in applying for reconciliation, asserted that he had already through the psalm-singing, fasting and alms-giving of others, rendered satisfaction sufficient for all his sins, though he should live for three hundred years [2]. The fathers of the council ignore the penitential regulation which apparently the rich man was merely abusing, and appeal to scripture, shrewdly quoting Matt. 19.23, "How hardly shall they that have riches" etc.

It is not improbable that acquaintance with some of the abuses of penance in England, in addition to his Romanizing zeal, predisposed Boniface against the Celtic penance. He did not attempt however, although he desired, to set up among the Germans the ancient system of penance. Such an attempt after a century of the Celtic practice must have proved a fantastic failure. Yet ecclesiastical interests dictated some reform of the Celtic administration of penance. The Celtic penitentials based on that of Columban, gave no importance to reconciliation. Apparently their terms were fulfilled without actual excommunication, and the transaction did not involve any formal reconciliation. In England, however, reconciliation had a place. Theodore's penitential disavows public reconciliation, thus taking away the real character of that feature of penance; but it contains provisions for a sort of private reconciliation. This is to be delayed to the completion of the term of penance [3], or at least for six months or a year [4].

1. *Poenit. Bedae*, sect. X, can. 8.

2. Ut per aliorum psalmodiam et jejunium et eleemosynas persolutum esset, etc., *ibid.*, can. 27. Mansi, Concil., T. XII. Col. 406. (De Sanctae psalmodiae utilitate.)

3. *Poenit. Theod.* I, XII, 2.

4. Poenitentes secundum canones non debeant communicare ante consummationen poenitentiae, nos autem pro misericordia post annum vel menses sex licentiam damus, *ibid.*, I, XII, 4.

The *Poenit. Cumm.* has taken this milder provision word for word from Theodore [1].

The attitude of Boniface, as well as the action which he took on penance, are revealed in the *Statuta* which he promulgated at the Synod of Lestines in 743. This document indicates that he regarded the ancient penance, with its open reconciliation, as desirable but impracticable. He therefore makes a very generous, because necessary, compromise. The passage with which we are concerned reads as follows :

"Since we are prevented by a variety of circumstances (lit. a various necessity) from observing in full the canonical regulation regarding the reconciliation of penitents, nevertheless it should not be entirely dropped. Every priest will take care, immediately after receiving the confession of penitents, to reconcile them severally with prayer. To those who are dying the communion and reconciliation are to be offered without delay [2] ".

In reality this represents an almost total surrender to the Celts. There is not a word to suggest that the ceremony of reconciliation was public; in fact *statim* and *singulos* seem absolutely to preclude this. Tixeront, with his theory of private confession and public reconciliation, as the uniform rule of the church, cites this as a case in point [3]. But not only does the language of the document in itself expose the error of such a supposition ; the historic background makes it impossible. Boniface certainly knew the practice of the English church, and probably knew the words of the *Poenit. Theod.* I, XIII, 4. " Reconciliatio ideo in hac provincia publice statuta non est quia et publica poenitentia non est." These words might have been written into the *Statuta* of Boniface

1. Poenit. Cumm. XIV, 6.

2. Et quia varia necessitate praepedimur, canonum statuta de conciliandis poenitentibus plenitur observare, propterea omnino non dimittatur. Curet unusquisque presbyter statim post acceptum confessionem poenitentium singulos data oratione reconciliari. Morientibus vero sine cunctamine communio et reconciliatio praebeatur. — Concil. Leptinense (743 a.d.), Statuta Bonifacii, can. XXXI. — Migne, P.L. Tom. 89, col. 823 ; Mansi, Concilia, T. XII, col. 386.

3. Le Sacrement de Pénitence, p. 4 f.; p. 53.

without conflicting with the context. As Lagarde remarks, "This reconciliation granted directly after private confession, and therefore private itself, had scarcely anything except the name, in common with the former reconciliation, which put an end to the excommunication which was pronounced before all the people, and was prolonged for weeks, months or even years [1]." Boniface feels compelled to make terms even more favorable to the Celtic penance than Theodore had done, and grants reconciliation without delay. His canons bear testimony to the fact that the new penance had secured its entrance. They are significant not so much for their attempted modification of the Celtic penance, as for their substantial recognition of it. They show that the penitentials and the penitential method which they represented, had already ceased to be exercised merely by Irish monks and *episcopi vagantes*, and had been taken up by the church in general.

The process in which the *Statuta* is a milestone had already been in operation for a century and a half. Morinus puts the dividing date for the entrance of private penance about 700. No exact date is valid, for, as Morinus himself states, the change was not brought about in a moment of time or by decree of any general council, but gradually and with tacit consent of the churches [2]. As usual in such historic evolutions, men of the time did not realize the significance of the movement. It was only later when the penitentials multiplied and their conflicting precepts brought confusion, that Frankish bishops took up arms against them.

Next to Boniface among illustrious churchmen of the eighth century may be reckoned Chrodegang Bishop of Metz. He was made an Archbishop on the death of Boniface (755), and died in 766. He is famed for the semi-monastic organization of the clergy of his diocese. The Rule which Chrodegang prepared for his canons (c. 744) has passed through several recensions. In all its forms, however, it recognizes the practice of private confession. Emphasis is laid on the

1. Latin Church, p. 58.

2. Sed paulatim et tacito quodam ecclesiarum consensu. Commentarius lib. VII, c. I (p. 437).

frequency of confession; it was the duty of each canon to confess at least twice a year [1].

It is probable that Chrodegang was consciously or unconsciously influenced by the Celtic practice. In the case of Benedict of Aniane the connection can be definitely established. The researches of the learned Benedictine, Dom Bruno Albers, have opened up the history of a number of rules related to that of St. Benedict [2]. From these studies it appears that the famous rule of Cluny was mainly taken from the work of Benedict of Aniane (fl. 779-817; d. 821), author of a *Concordia Regularum* and of the Capitulary of Louis the Pius of 817 in which his reformed Benedictinism was (unsuccessfully) promulgated [3]. Benedict of Aniane made confession a part of the daily routine of the monastery. The monks went in by turns to their confessors, during the hour appointed for the purpose [4]. The *Concordia Regularum* of Benedict indicates that the Aquitanian reformer was considerably influenced by Columban. This influence on Benedict is mediated through Donatus, a pupil of Luxeuil, the founder of a cloister at Vesontio in Burgundy, who wrote a revision of the rule of Columban, c. A.D. 643-651 [5]. In his *Concordia* Benedict quotes Donatus on daily confession [6]. Frequency of confession was carried to such excess in some of the Columban monasteries that the same writer refers to the rule of St. Fara, abbess of Evoriaca, as authorizing confession three times in

1. The Regula of Chrodegang is given by Mansi, Tom. XIV, col. 313 f. This provision is in col. 320.
2. Untersuchungen zu den ältesten Mönchgewohnheiten, Münich, 1905. Cf. Mary Bateson, "Rules for Monks and Canons", Engl. Hist. Rev. Vol. IX (1894), p. 690 f.; Rose Graham, review in Eng. Hist. Rev. Vol. XXIV (1909), p. 121 f. I am indebted for this reference to J.W. Thompson, "Church and State in Mediaeval Germany," Amer. Journ. of Theol., Vol. 22 (1918), p. 396, note 3.
3. Graham, *op. cit.*, p. 123; cf. Lagarde, Latin Church, p. 92. Albers, *op. cit.*, especially, p. 123 f.
4. Bateson, *op. cit.*, p. 696.
5. Seebass, Über Columba von Luxeuils Klosterregel und Bussbuch, p. 37 f.; also his Über das Regelbuch Benedikts von Aniane, Zeitschr. f. Kg., Bd. 15 (1895), p. 244 f.
6. Migne, P.L., Tom. 103, col. 854.

the day [1]. This is the holy nun frequently referred to by Jonas as Burgundiofera, who was blessed by Columban in her infancy, and became a devoted follower [2].

The earliest attempt to make confession obligatory on the part of the laity appears early in the reign of Charlemagne. Charlemagne was so impressed with the disciplinary value of penance that in 789 in a Capitulary of Aix-la-Chapelle, he made it incumbent upon priests to admonish the people to confess their sins [3]. In connection with the government of Saxony Charlemagne gave private confession special recognition. His *Capitulatio de partibus Saxoniae* encourages Saxon criminals to come to confession with the promise that on testimony of their confessors that they have done so, their lives will be spared [4]. In this instance it is explicitly indicated that the crimes were secretly committed. Confession, however, was a matter between the culprit and the priest alone. The priest notified the authorities not necessarily of the acts confessed, but simply that confession had been made, — the implication being that penance was imposed.

This recognition of private penance in state jurisdiction is noticeably similar to that which obtained under the ancient laws of Ireland. During the eighth century the spread of the penitential books in the Frankish empire was virtually unopposed. Irish writers and their followers were chiefly responsible for the penitentials of this period that have come to light. Six of the eight printed by Wasserschleben as "Penitentials related to that of Columban", are ascribed by that investigator to the seventh or the first half of the eighth century [5]. These are named respectively, Poenitentiale Roma-

1. *Ibid.*, col. 855.

2. See especially Jonas, Vitae Discipulorum Columbani, § 11. M.G.H., Script. Rev. Mer., Tom. IV, p. 130.

3. Capit. Carol. Mag., Aquisgran. Anno. 789, c. 81; Migne, P.L. Tom. 97, col. 184.

4. Si vero pro his mortalibus criminibus latentur commissis aliquis sponte ad sacerdotem confugerit et confessione data agere poenitentiam voluerit, testimonio sacerdotis de morte excusetur. Capit. de Partibus Saxoniae (775-790), c. 14. M.G.H., Leges, Tom. II, Capit. I, p. 69.

5. Bussordn., p. 58.

num [1], Hubertense, Bobiense, Parisiense, Floriacense, Sangallense. The connection of these early continental penitentials with Columban's is a clear indication of the fact that Irish influence was dominant in the development of the penitential literature. Even where the influence of the *Poenit. Theod.* is more obvious than that of *Poenit. Col.* as in the Bigotianum, Irish influence is still very prominent [2] ; while Cummean's work, also closely related to Theodore, was written by a Scottic abbot. The *Poenit. Cumm.* became the parent of considerable group of eighth century penitentials [3], in which the characteristics of Celtic penance were retained.

Early in the ninth century Roman churchmen were startled to discover that the Celtic monks had succeeded in making their type of penance general in the Frankish Church.

3. — Opposition to the Penitentials.

During the late eighth and the early ninth century the progress of the new penance was no longer viewed with equanimity by the Frankish prelates. A serious conflict now began. On the one hand the Irish writers and their followers produced and circulated broadcast their *libri pœnitentiales*. These booklets, while agreeing in their main principles, represented much individual judgment in detail, and the discrepancies naturally caused confusion. On the other hand, the Frankish bishops, harassed by the ubiquitous Scots, and envious ot their fame of saintliness and learning, were inclined to view with disfavor the discipline which these missionaries had inaugurated. The attitude of the lower clergy was, however, quite the reverse. The priests, enjoined by royal command to minister penance to their flock, a duty for which they had but

1. Identified by Wasserschleben with the penitential published by Haltigar., ibid. See below p. 169. The texts ot these documents will be found in Wasserschleben, Bussord., pp. 360 f.

2. See the evidence for connection with the Irish treatise *De Arreis*, Chapter I, p. 64.

3. Cf. Wasserschl. Bussordn., p. 493 f.

small training, welcomed the friendly authority of a book ot ready-made judgments, and used such versions as fell into their hands. Bishops frequently attempted to substitute the practice of public penance for the current system. But the private penance of the penitentials subjected the priest to less embarrassment in its enforcement. The bishops were of course, better informed on the history of the church and the writings of the Fathers, and could approach the subject of public penance more intelligently. They identified the cause of public penance with their episcopal rights, since it was the bishops who controlled the discipline of the ancient church. No less did the lower clergy cling to private penance because it rendered them more independent of their bishops.

In the main, it was the priests and not the bishops who had the better of the contest [1]. In spite of the efforts of the hierarchy public penance obtained but slight recognition. Rome, following the views of Gregory the Great, supported the public form of penance, and maintained it in the neighboring churches. But "except probably within the immediate jurisdiction of Rome" [2] public penance was almost totally neglected.

The attempt to combat the influence of the penitentials and establish public penance in the Frankish empire is largely a matter of the ninth century. In England, as already noted, opposition to the provisions of the penitentials, or to abuses flowing from these, had reference mainly to the matter of commutations. These evils were apparently not so prevalent in the Frankish church. Morinus affirms that this practice (redemptio pœnitentiæ) beginning in England, was not frequent in Italy, Gaul or Germany before the end of the ninth century [3]. At any rate, it was not this feature that invited the attack upon the penitentials with which we are now concerned. The basis of this attack lay rather in the confusion introduced by the variant books in use, and their unauthoritative character. The ninth century, — the century of the

1. Lea, Hist. of Auric. Conf. and Indulg. Vol. II, p. 98.
2. Lea, *op. cit.*, p. 73.
3. Commentarius, lib. X, c. XVII (p. 760).

Forged Decretals, — craved, amid political disorder, spiritual authority. The ancient public penance, never repudiated by Rome, could claim acceptance on the ground of old authority. But who had written the penitentials? Who had authorized them?

Early in the century appears the demand for open confession of open sin. The ancient penance demanded the exposure of secret sins as well [1], but this could hardly be expected of the Franks. A capitulary of Charlemagne of the year 813 contains the formula "open sin, open confession" [2]. And in the canons of the synod of Arles of that year this provision is accompanied by the phrase "secundum canones" [3]. Two canons of Châlons held in the same year deal with penance in the same spirit. The bishops regret the neglect of the ancient form of public penance, and resolve to beg the Emperor to aid in the reform of the discipline so that public sinners may perform public penance, and be excommunicated and reconciled according to the canons [4]. By the reference to "the canons" in the above citations, we need not doubt that the authority specially alluded to is that of the collection of Dionysius Exiguus (d. 556) which, with additions, had been presented by Pope Hadrian I to Charlemagne, c. 787, and was accepted by a Council of Aix-la Chapelle in 802 [5]. The canons are taken from the fourth century councils, and sanction only the ancient public discipline, which made no distinction in the manner of penance between public and private sins. Their acceptance in the Frankish Church did not, of course, bring

1. Lea, Hist. of Auric. Confess., Vol. I, pp. 21 f.

2. Mansi, Concil., Tom. XIV, App., col. 346.

3. Mansi, Concil., Tom. XIV, col. 62. Concil. Arelat., can. 26.

4. Pœnitentiam agere juxta antiquam canonum institutionem in plerisque locis ab usu recessit et neque reconciliandi antiqui moris ordo servatur; ut a domino imperatore impetretur adjutorium, qualiter si quis publice peccat, publica mulctetur pœnitentia et secundum ordinem canonum pro merito suo excommuniceretur et reconcilietur. — Mansi, *op. cit.*, Tom. XIV, col. 98, — Concil. Cabillon II (813 a. d.), can. 25.

5. The *Codex Canonum* of Dionysius is in Migne, P. L., Tom. 67, col. 134-230. Cf. Hefele, Conciliengesch, Vol. 3, p. 704; Mansi, *op. cit.*, Tom. XIII, col. 1101; cf. Art. "Canon Law" in Schaff-Herzog, Encyc.

public penance immediately into effect. But they could be appealed to by those who sought this reform.

It was realized, however, that public penance, even in the modified character, in which it was now advocated, could not be successfully introduced while the universal circulation of the penitentials continued. The Celtic booklets were therefore the objects of episcopal condemnation. Canon 38 of the same synod of Châlons repudiates and inveighs against the "*libelli* which are called penitentials, and of which the errors are certain, the authors uncertain" [1]. While there was probably good reason for the strictures of the bishops, we need not conclude that their motives were all stated in these words. They were jealous for their authority as bishops. Canon 43 of the same synod vehemently condemns the Scots who irregularly assumed episcopal functions [2]. This jealousy was not felt merely toward the Scots, but also to some extent toward the priests, who conducted private penance. Yet at this date, confession in private is not attacked but supported [3]. The action of this council in stigmatizing as unauthorized and condemning the penitentials, apparently had little effect upon their use. The bishops therefore resolved on more drastic action, and returned to the fight in the synod of Paris of 829. The statement of this synod on the subject informs us that "many of the priests, partly from indifference, partly from ignorance, were imposing penance in a manner at variance from the canon law, using for the purpose certain booklets written against canonical authority, which they call penitentials". It is therefore commanded that "each of the bishops shall diligently search out these erroneous booklets in his diocese, and give the flames those which are discovered, to that unskilled priests may no longer deceive men" [4]. It is interest-

1. Repudiatis ac penitus eliminatis libellis quos pœnitentiales vocant, quorum sunt certes errores, incerti anctores, de quibus recte dici potest, mortificabant animas quæ non moriuntur et vivificabant animas quæ non vivebant. Mansi, Concil., Tom. XIV. Col. 102.

2. See above, p. 146.

3. *Ibid.*, can. 33. Mansi, Concil. Tom. XIV, col. 101.

4. Quoniam multi sacerdotum partim incuria, partim ignorantia, modum

ing to find the ninth century hierarchy seeking reform by methods which became familiar in the age of the Inquisition and the Index. There is no record to show what was accomplished in response to this decree. Certain it is that the books claiming distinguished authorship did not perish ; and the same statement applies to a large number of those whose origin historians might still describe by the phrase *incerti auctores*. There were difficulties in the operations of the ninth century "Index" almost as great as those which arose with the printing press. Lea has ascribed the growth in popularity of the penitentials to "the size of the dioceses, the insecurity of the roads, and the troubles of those centuries of transition", facts which rendered it impossible for bishops to hear confession in person, and so left the task mainly to the priests [1]. The same conditions would make any general destruction of the offensive books equally impossible.

Amid the forgeries of the ninth century stands a document purporting to be a decree of Pope Calixtus I (217-222) in the form of a letter to the bishops of Gaul. This forged document sanctions the formula of the bishops, and authorizes public penance for those whose sins are open and scandalous [2]. The public exercise of penance for public sins was forcibly advocated also by Hincmar of Rheims [3]. Benedict the Deacon, who published a collection of "Capitularies" which belong to the pseudo-Isidorean movement, likewise championed this theory

pœnitentiæ reatum suum confitentibus secus quam jura canonica decernant, imponunt, utentes scilicet quibusdam codicillis, contra canonicam auctoritatem, scriptis, quos pœnitentiales vocant... omnibus nobis salubriter in commune visum est, ut unusquisque episcoporum in sua parochia eosdem erroneos codicillos diligenter perquirat, et inventus igni tradat, ne per eos ulterius sacerdotes imperiti homines decipiant. Concil. Paris. VI, can. 32. Mansi, Tom. XIV, col. 559.

1. Hist. of Auric. Confess. and Indulg. Vol. I, p. 120 f.

2. Manifesta peccata non sunt occulta correctione purganda. Ep. pseudo-Callixt., incorporated in Pseudo-Isid., Migne, P. L., Tom. 130, col. 134.

3. Publicus peccator... juxta traditionem canonicam publicam pœnitentiam accipiat. Hincmari Capitula, lib. III, c. 1, Migne, P. L., Tom. 125, col. 793.

of penance [1]. His influence appears in the reassertion of the principle "public penance for public crimes" in the Council of Mainz of 847 [2]. At the same time the influence of the penitentials is felt in the use of the seven-year term for greater offences [3]. The persistence of this ancient Irish penitential provision may perhaps be explained by the fact that in Frankish customary law, as in Irish, the payment for a freeman's life was the price of seven female slaves [4].

Even among the opponents of the penitentials the influence of the system they inaugurated was in fact unavoidable. Not only does this appear in the restriction of public penance to public offences, and in the acceptance of such secondary features as the seven year term. It appears also in the attitude to the entire subject of commutations. Here again Frankish and Celtic native practice were closely allied. In the English Church abuses arising from the penitential practice in this regard were condemned, as we noted, before the middle of the eighth century. The Frankish synods took no special action to combat such evils; and the abuses referred to were apparently later in manifesting themselves in Gaul [5]. A compromise attitude on the question of compositions in penance appears in the canons of a synod held at Thionville in 821, in which

1. The collection is in M. G. H., Script. T. IV, and in Migne, P. L., T. 97. These capitularies make public penance less formidable by announcing the heaviest fines for the murder of the public penitents — a humane precaution since they were unarmed. — The rule : Qui hominem publicam pœnitentiam agentem interfecerit, bannum nostrum in triplo, componat, et wergildum proximis suis persolvat, appears twice (can. 107 ; can. 234).

2. Concil. Mogunt., I, can. 31. Mansi, Concil., Tom. XIV, col. 912.

3. *Ibid.*

4. Il se suit de là que le tarif du meurtre dans la loi salique semble avoir été le résultat de la conversion en sous et en deniers d'un tarif plus ancien, dans lequel l'homme libre était évalué sept fois le prix d'une femme esclave, comme dans le droit irlandais. H. d'Arbois de Jubainville, *Revue Celtique*, Tom. 8 (1887), p. 511.

5. Morinus, Commentarius, lib. X, c. XVII, (p. 760). I fail to find any evidence for Lagarde's statement that " Carolingian councils which attacked certain penitentials, had especially in view the "redemptions ". (Latin Church, p. 78.)

there appears a demand for penance *plus* a fine. For the killing of a subdeacon five *quadragesimae* are to be spent in penance and the sentence is to be completed by the payment of 400 *solidi*, together with other payments described as "three-fold composition and three-fold Episcopal banns", which are to be given to the bishop [1]. For the murder of a bishop the amount is nine hundred instead of the four hundred *solidi*. The *bannus episcopalis* seems to refer to the penalty incurred by violating the sentence of excommunication during penance which the bishops now sought to enforce. This penalty apparently, had a money equivalent, which is here referred to in connection with satisfaction for another offence [2].

The typically Celtic commutations of penance obtained a foothold generally. St. Boniface is himself credited, in an addition to the *Pœnit. Egberti*, with the authorisation of commutations [3]. By the terms of this note on penance a seven year term can be reduced to one year, thirty to three days, etc. Singing one psalter is equivalent to a three-day penance and fifteen paternosters. Prostrations are acceptable instead of singing. Penance may be vicariously performed. Penitents not guilty of capital crimes may have masses sung for them by a priest. One mass is good for twelve days' penance, ten masses for four months, thirty for a year, etc. No money-commutations are referred to. Although Boniface, owing to the necessities of the time, went a long way in approving Celtic

1. Si autem mortuus fuerit singulas subdictas (i. e. quinque) quadragesimas cum sequentibus annis pœniteat et cccc solidos cum tripla sua compositione, et episcopalibus bannis triplicibus episcopo componat. Concil. ad. Theodonis Villam, 821, Mansi, Concil., Tom. XIV, col. 389.

2. Cf. Hinschius, System des Kathol. Kirchenrechts, Bd. V, p. 295. Hinschius quotes a late ninth century synod : Quincunque per contemptum banni episcopalis ab ecclesia eliminantur, et ex hac distinctione pœnitentiæ subiciuntur, quadaragesimam in pane et sale et aqua ita jejunent, aute foras ecclesiæ nudis pedibus laneis induti, communione privati. This represents the reaction against private penance, and illustrates the *bannus episcopalis*. Cf. note 1, above.

3. The paragraph is attached to the *Pœnit. Egberti* as *de dictis S. Bonifacii Archiepiscopi*. Wasserschleben, Bussordnungen, p. 246. It is included in the works of Boniface, under the title *De Pœnitentia*. Migne, P. L., Tom. 89, col. 887.

penance, it is not probable that this paragraph is really from his pen. Nor is Hildenbrand's suggestion that Alcuin is the author of the *Capitula Theodori*, (a document showing a strong influence from the *Pænit. Theor.*) more than a rough guess [1]. In fact no notable Frankish ecclesiastic can be cited as author of a penitential, at least before Haltigar; and there is some uncertainty about the nature of his connection with the *pseudo-Romanum*.

4. — VICTORY OF THE CELTIC PENANCE.

The Synod of Paris of 829, just referred to, marks the most determined attempt to combat the influence of the penitentials. The failure of the methods adopted was early perceived. The new penance had gained the position of widely established custom; and even if the books in question had all been destroyed, others would no doubt have immediately come into use, and the practice of penance would have been little affected. Nearly four centuries of evolution were still required before the Celtic penance was to find itself quite at home in the papal church; and in the meanwhile it was to undergo changes which left it a poor instrument of discipline or of religion.

But currents favorable, in the main, to the system of the penitentials were setting strongly in. Certain ecclesiastics turned from the futile attempt to uproot it, and began a movement to harmonize it with the rising conceptions of Roman authority. They lamented, with the councils, the confusion and lack of authority which were, in their minds, the most serious defects of the penitentials. The main principles of the latter — a codified penance [2], private confession and reconciliation, and even composition in money — they approved, or at least did not flatly condemn. Their point of view was that the authority in which the penitentials were deficient might be supplied through the promulgation of a new code

1. Hildenbrand, Untersuchungen über die deutschen Pœnitentialbücher.
2. *La pénitence tarifée* is the more exact French expression.

of penance bearing the claim of Roman origin and sanction. There were, probably, difficulties in the way of obtaining a genuine approval from Rome. But the literary ethics of the ninth century made possible a short-cut to the objective in view.

The name *Pœnitentiale Romanum* had already appeared. Its precise use is difficult to discern, since Rome, loyal to early tradition, still maintained the practice of public penance. The expression may have been used for a type of penitential favored by Rome, no example of which can be definitely pointed out among extant penitentials [1]. By Cummean it was ignorantly or loosely (in the sense of "authoritative") used of a familiar and entirely non-Roman work. Cummean quotes *Pœnit. Theod.* with the note *De romano pœnitentiale* [2]. An attempt was now made to give specific content to this expression, in the production of a penitential designed to supersede, by the claim of Roman authority, all rival treatises.

Haltigar became Bishop of Cambrai in 817, and died in 831. He was a man of personal eminence, and was appointed to act in a diplomatic capacity for the Emperor at the court of Constantinople in 828. In the following year he was present at the Council of Paris which decreed the burning of the penitentials. About 830 he received a letter from Ebbo, Bishop of Rheims, on which complaint is made of the confusion resulting from the use of the penitentials owing to their differences and discrepancies and unauthoritative character, and Haltigar is urged to undertake a new work that will enable the priests to adjudge penance properly [3]. Haltigar in his reply, records his amusement at the request; mindful of his own infirmity and burdened with his tasks, he cannot undertake literary work at present; but with the difficulty of the task enjoined he recognizes the authority of him who was enjoined it; he does not wish, nor ought he, to give a total refusal [4]. About a year later, Haltigar died.

1. See above, Ch. I, p. 65.
2. *Pœnit. Cumm.*, c. VII, can. 11; *Pœnit. Theod.*, liv. II, 10, can. 5.
3. Ep. Ebonis ad Haltigarium, Migne, P. L., Tom. 105, col. 651.
4. *Ibid.*, col. 654.

Two works on penance are connected with Haltigar's name. One is his *De pœnitentia libri V.* Part of this work is a treatise on the deadly sins, in which Gregory the Great and Prosper of Aquitaine are much quoted. The penitential part consists of prohibitions and anathemas, and does not possess the character of the current penitentials. It makes no special claim to authority. This work can hardly have been called forth by Ebbo's letter, as it does not attempt to provide a detailed guide to priests in the exercise of penance such as might have replaced the confused Celtic books.

The other work [1] is of an entirely different character. It bears the legend : *Incipit liber pœnitentialis ex scrinio Romanæ ecclesiae assumptus* ; thus professing, to combine the strain of the *libri pœnitentiales* with Rome. In one text a short preface contains the words, *Pœnitentiale Romanum quem de scrinio Romane ecclesie assumpsimus* [2]. It is written in the form rendered familiar by the Celtic models, and makes free use of the earlier penitentials. Wasserschleben notes in all twenty-two correspondences to *Pœnit. Col.* (A and B), and twenty-nine to *Pœnit. Cumm.* Gildas and the Collection of Dionysius, are among other authorities which are more sparingly used. Immediate reconciliation is taken for granted [3]. The prologue, as in *Pœnit. Cumm.* fully authorizes money-redemptions of penance, confining these however to persons who cannot undergo fasting, and making careful distinctions between rich and poor : " si quis forte non potuerit jejunare, et habuerit unde dare possit ad redimendum, si dives fuerit, pro septem hebdomadibus det solidos XX ; si autem, non habuerit tantum unde dare possit ad redimendum, si dives fuerit, pro septem hebdomadibus det solidos X, si autem multum pauper fuerit, det solidos III ".

The writer anticipates objections to this tariff on the part of those called on to pay the highest fine, by adding : " Nemi-

1. Wasserschleben, Bussordn., p. 360 f. ; Schmitz, Bussbücher, Bd. I, p. 719, f. ; Bd. II, p. 242 f.
2. Migne, P. L., Tom. 105, col. 693.
3. E. g. in II, 7, and in the *orationes ad dandam pœnitentiam* by which the work is preceded.

nem vero conturbat, quia jussimus XX solidos dare, aut minus, quia, si diues fuerit, facilius est illi dare solidos XX, quam pauperi solidos III ".

A caution to confessors is added on behalf of serfs (*servi vel ancillae*) who are not in their own power and cannot fulfil harsh terms of penance.

The essential features of the Celtic penance are fully retained in this work, and its dependence on Celtic sources disproves its claim to a Roman origin. This is not to state flatly that it had not come, as claimed, from a book-repository of the Roman church. Such books may frequently have found their way to Roman book-shelves; in Rome, however they were not accepted as guides to penance. But the book is manifestly contemporary or nearly contemporary, and Frankish in origin; and Haltigar could not have believed it to be a Roman book. The existence of Ebbo's letter, together with Haltigar's *ex scrinio Romanae ecclesiae* must inevitably direct conjecture to Haltigar himself. At least he was undoubtedly involved in the misrepresentation conveyed in the phrase just quoted. The book, wich appears in all MSS. of Haltigar's works, must have been promulgated by him. It preceded the pseudo-Isidorean decretals by about twenty years, and cannot therefore reflect the propaganda of the pro-Ebbo, anti-Hincmar pseudo-Isidorean party. Yet it is not impossible that Ebbo himself had a hand in its production. Ebbo has been, with great probability, connected with the Forged Decretals [1]. It is curious that the aim of Pseudo-Isidore as expressed in the opening sentences of that compilation. is very similar to that which appears in Haltigar's reply to Ebbo's letter in regard to penance [2]. But if Ebbo wrote or assisted in writing the pseudo-

1. Cf. E. Seckel, Pseudoisidor, in Realencycl. (3rd ed.). Vol. 16, pp. 265-307 ; H. Carrington, Pseudo-Isidorean Decretals, New Schaff-Herzog, Vol. IX, pp. 343-f.

2. Cf. Hinschius, Decretales Pseudo-Isidorianæ et Capitula Angilramni, (Leipsig, 1863) ; Prefatio, I, (p. 17); (Migne, P. L., Tom. 130, col. 7). « Compellor a multis, tam episcopis quam reliquis servis Christi, canonum sententias colligere et uno in volumine redigere et de multis unum facere. Cf. Haltigar's reply to Ebbo's letter (ut) "pœnitentialem in uno volumine aggregerem". Migne, P. L., Tom. 105, col. 654.

Romanum, he must have changed his mind on the subject of penance before he collaborated in the pseudo-Isidore; for that work supports the contention for public penance in the case of public sins [1], a position foreign to the *Pœnit. pseudo-Romanum*.

The attack upon the penitentials in the ninth century did not seriously affect their inflence. The promulgation of the *pseudo-Romanum* was a victory for the Celtic penitential type; pro-papal Frankish churchmen found it necessary to copy the Celtic models in a work for which Roman authority was claimed. From this time on protests against the use of the books of penance rarely appear. The status of the penitentials was generally recognized, and not only tacitly. In 866 the missionaries whom Nicholas I sent to Bulgaria were supplied with a *Judicium Pœnitentiæ* which, it seems, had been requested by the converts in that field [2]. We are left uninformed as to whether Pope Nicholas used one of the current penitentials or had a new schedule of penitential judgments prepared. Regino, the learned abbot of Prüm (d. 915) in his *De ecclesiasticis Disciplinis et Religione Christiana*, gives a long series of regulations for an inquiry into the qualifications of the clergy. The final clause of the ninety-five requirements reads: « Si habet pœnitentiale Romanum, vel a Theodoro episcopo aut a venerabili presbytero Beda editum; ut secundum quod ibi scriptum est interroget confitentem, aut confesso modum pœnitentiæ imponat [3] ».

Thus the accommodation of the penitentials with the papal church order proceeds, in a manner characteristic of the age, by intentional or unitentional misrepresentation. Boniface is credited with a series of typically Celtic commutations; Hal-

1. Cf. the Ep. pseudo-Callixti, and Concil. Carthag. III, can. 32, Migne, P. L. Tom. 130, col. 334.

2. Nicholai Papae Responsio ad Consult. Bulgarorum, sect. LXXV, — Judicium pœnitentiæ quod postulatis episcopi nostri quos in patriam vestram misimus in scriptis secum utique deferent. — Migne, P. L., Tom. 119, col. 1008.

3. Regino, De eccles. Discip., Inquisitio, Migne, P. L., Tom. 132, col. 191.

tigar issues a work based on the Celtic books with the claim of a Roman origin ; and Regino authorizes the penitentials of Theodore and Bede, describing them as editions of the *Pœnitentiale Romanum* [1].

1. The Roman adoption of Theodore's penitential was so complete by the later mediaeval period, that Lea càn point to evidence of its ascription in the twelfth and in the fourteenth century, to *Pope* Theodore (642-649). Hist. of Auricular Confess. and Indulg., Vol. II, p. 103. Similarly, Jerome is credited with the authorship of the *Pœnit. Cumm.* See article by G. M. on the Penitentials in Dict. of Christian Antiquities, p. 1611, and cf. the reference in the Prologue of the *Pœnit. Egberti* to "Hyeronimus".

CHAPTER VI

How the use of the Penitentials affected the Discipline of the Continental Church.

The position of Celtic penance in the Continental Church was rendered virtually secure in the ninth century. So far was it already a *sine qua non* of the priestly ministry in the Frankish church that, as we have seen, Archbishop Haltigar, in becoming sponsor for a penitential, the terms of which are mainly Celtic, adroitly represents it as emanating from Rome. (c. 830.) The Church as a whole had, of course, given no pronouncement annulling canonical penance or authorizing the use of penitential books. Much difference of opinion prevailed. In Britain and Ireland, and among the Eastern and Western Franks, the Celtic penance was strongly in the ascendant. In Spain and Italy the invasion was only beginning, and the struggle against it was maintained to the opening of the thirteenth century.

1. — Private Penance wins Official Acceptance.

There remains the task of indicating the effect of the invasion on the customs and discipline of the papal church. As one result private confession and penance obtained official acceptance. This result was not reached without conflict and long delay. In the Frankish territories the opposition to the penitentials actually bore some fruit. The demand for "open penance for open sin", advanced as we saw in 813, was not enforced by Charlemagne. It was supported however by the example of

Louis the Pious, who himself voluntarily submitted to this humiliation for cruelty to his nephew Bernard, in 822, and was induced or compelled to accept a new sentence in 833[1]. Similar instances were not infrequent. While priests might use the handy penitential, bishops often strove to exact a public performance of penance. Rodulf of Bourges reiterates (c. 840-850) the old demand for public penalty in the case of public sins, with canonical excommunication and reconciliation, — repeating or anticipating the phraseology of the Council of Mainz of A.D. 847 : qui publice peccat publica mulctetur poenitentia[2]. The doctrine of public penance was reasserted in the Synod of Worms in 868, which decided that the murderer of a priest should be deprived of weapons and should stand at the church door during worship for a period of five years, "orans et deprecans Deum"; afterwards he was to appear in the congregation during another five years, at the close of which he was to be reconciled[3].

This represents a vigorous attempt to enforce public penance with all its humiliating features, as a deterrent to assaults upon the clergy. It must have been virtually impossible during the stormy times of the Norse invasions to put so drastica discipline into effect. For the most part we may be sure such regulations remained a dead letter. Yet undoubtedly public penance occasionally occurred, in cases where piety or policy induced a desire to give public proof of repentance. Outstanding examples of this in the centuries following are the penance inflicted by the recluse St. Romuald upon Otto III in 998[4], the famous scene at Canossa, 1077, the penance performed by Thomas a Becket for his connection withthe Constitutions of

1. Mansi, Concil., T. XIV, col. 652-3; Migne, Patrol. Lat., T. 98, col. 659.

2. Capitula Rodulfi, 34. Mansi, Concil., T. XIV, col. 959; Concil. Mogunt. anno. 847, can. 6, *ibid.*, col. 911.

3. Concil. Wormat. anno. 868, can. 56. — Mansi, Concil., T. XV, col. 874,

4. The Emperor was not yet out of his teens, but according to Peter Damiani had been guilty of perjury, murder and adultery — Peter Damiani, Vita S. Romualdi, 22, Migne, Patrol. Lat., T. 144, col. 975.

Clarendon, 1164 [1], and that of Henry II for the murder, by his partisans, of Becket, 1172 [2].

In most cases of this kind it is manifest that the church was playing for political and economic privileges. And it is to be observed also that the exercise of public penance where it occurred differed widely from that which obtained in the early church. It showed the influence of the system of the penitentials in the fact that it could be repeated as often as a sinner lapsed and confessed. Moreover it was not, as in the ancient period, understood to cover private as well as public sins. This distinction is sometimes explicitly drawn, as for example in the admission to private penance of those guilty of secret incest by the Mainz council of 825, which, in the following canon, insists on a severe public penance for public homicide [3]. In both these peculiarities of the occasionnal public penance, we are probably justified in recognizing a concession to Celtic practice.

A treatise entitled *De excommunicatis vitandis, de reconciliatione et de fontibus juris ecclesiastici*, which appears as the work of Bernald of Constance (d. c. 1100) [4] has been shown Thaner and Saltet to be a plagiarized edition of an otherwise lost work by Hincmar, originally entitled *De concordantia canonum* [5]. This document reverts to the doctrine of the ancient church that penance can be accorded only once, but admits the fact of the modern neglect of this rule [6].

Public penance in its weakened medieval form was seldom attended by the necessity of confession before the congrega-

1. Dean Hook assignes this act to the desire of Becket " to make a good impression on the public mind ", Lives of the Archbishops of Canterbury, Vol. II, p. 397, based on Anonymus Lambethiensis.

2. *Ibid.*, p. 414.

3. Concil. Mogunt, anno. 852, Mon. Germ. Hist., Capit. II, 189.

4. Migne, Patrol. Lat., T. 148, col. 1181 f.; Mon. Germ. Hist., Libelli de Lite, T. II, p. 112 f.

5. L. Saltet, Les réordinations, une étude sur le sacrement de l'ordre.

6. Apud modernos tamen locus pœnitentiæ illis non negatur, quia adeo usquequæque humana pravitas invaluit et jugum antiquæ disciplinæ abiecit utsancta aeclesia jam multum gauderet, si vel ita modo respicere vellent. — Libelli de Lite, T. II, p. 115.

tion, although the sentence was publicly rendered [1]. The annual season of reconciliation, which in the early period took place regularly on Holy Thursday, was only rarely observed, although its observance was frequently demanded. The ancient discipline was most nearly copied in what was now known as "solemn penance ", which was reserved for the worst cases, and confined to laymen [2]. It could be imposed only once in a life-time, and involved the humiliation of a public appearance on Ash Wednesday and Holy Thursday during each Lent of the period of the sentence [3].

Down to the era of the crusades public penance, largely owing to the urgent efforts of the bishops, maintained itself side by side with the later systems of the penitentials. The Roman church has never repudiated the practice ; but in the decisions of the Council of Trent a frequent custom was recognized in the provision that public can be commuted to private penance [4]. Of the rival forms of penance, that introduced by the penitentials was by far the easier to enforce. It gave more consideration to the disinclination of human nature to undergo public shame. While it was the crusading movement which virtually extinguished the public discipline, the victory of the rival system was manifestly inevitable before that period.

The production of new petitentials seems to have declined during the tenth century [5]. But the large number of existing books could be relied upon to extend the application of their principles till a later day when, incorporated in the sacramental system, private penance was to become the normal practice of the church, and the other features of the Celtic books were to exert a powerful (and mainly injurious) influence on mediaeval Christianity.

1. Lea. Hist. of Auricular Confession and Indulgences, Vol. I, p. 48. (The view of Watkins is that confession was *always* private. See his Hist. of Penance, Vol. II, p. 769.)

2. Regino, De Eccl. Discip., lib. I, c. 291 : Migne, P.L., Tom. 132, col. 245.

3. Lea, *op. cit.*, vol. I, p. 48 ; Vol. II, pp. 79-80.

4. Concil. Trid., Sess. XXIV, De Reformatio, can. 8.

5. Cf. Wasserschleben, Bussordn., p. 90.

The tendency of the eleventh century may be illustrated from the writings of a German and an Italian bishop of that period, Burchard, bishop of Worms, (d. 1025) and Peter Damiani, cardinal-bishop of Ostia (d. 1072). The former, in his so-called " Corrector ", represents the general acquiescence of Northern Europe in the system of the penitentials, of private and codified penance. He warns priests against violating the secrecy of confession, on pain of deposition and exile for life [1]. The latter, a generation later, is the most vigorous opponent of the penitentials, which by now are evidently in vogue in the Roman region. The unauthorized books are anathema to him. " Who indeed ", he asks wrathfully, " complied these canons ? " " Spuria canonum vitulamina " he calls them, in almost untranslatable sarcasm. One says of a penitential, it is Theodore's, another, it is the Roman Penitential, another, it is the Canons of the Apostles ; thus the variant claims of authorship take away all authority [2]. Yet the same writer did not refuse to hear confession privately, or to impose a penance dovoid of any public humiliation. This in exhibited in the case of the Marquis Ranierus whom Damiani does not excommunicate, but sends on a pilgrimage. Neither absolution nor reconciliation in the ancient sense, is suggested [3].

It is clear from such a protest as that of Damiani that the use of the penitential books, by whomsoever compiled, was regarded by conservative piety in Italy as a degrading innovation. But it is equally clear that the practice of penance in private, which derives from the use of these books, was becoming customary. The church was happy to secure any sort of

1. Si quis sacerdos palam fecerit, et secretum penitentiæ usurpaverit... ab omni honore suo in cunctum populum deponatur, et diebus vitæ suæ peregrinando finiat. Wasserschleben, Bussordnungen, p. 478; Migne, Patrol. Lat., T. 140, col. 949.

2. Migne, Patrol. Lat., T. CXLV, col. 170. (The two passages here referred to are put in juxtaposition by Watkins. Hist. of Penance, Vol. II, p. 723 f.)

3. Migne, Patrol. Lat., T. CXLIV, col. 455. " In this instance ", says Watkins, "it is not easy to determine whether the penance is of the more ancient or more modern type " (Watkins, Vol. II., p. 740). To the present writer it appears to be essentially the latter.

penitential discipline after the tenth century debauch of the papacy. Better private penance with all its abuses, than no penance at all. Everywhere there was a sense of confusion in respect to penance. Variations in the ancient canons and in the current penitentials, with the lack of any authoritative pronouncement by the church, left the administration of the discipline largely to the clergy as individuals to do what they would or what they could. The total absence of system and uniformity called forth awkward questions from the laity, who were asking, as Hugh of St. Victor notes, by what scriptural authority confession was demanded [1].

The popes of the age had opportunity to bring definite legislation to bear. Such a reform would have been difficult, but if successful, would have incalculably strengthened the discipline of the church. Had complete new authoritative legislation been undertaken in the age of Hildebrand, it might have accomplished much toward the moral betterment of clergy and laity, and offset the evil tendencies of the later middle ages. But the popes had no program of penance. When Alexander II is requested by two priests to grant them permission to hear confessions and impose penances, he accedes to their request on condition that the bishops in whose dioceses they are operating do not forbid them [2]. In another letter the same pope allows the confessor discretion in the matter of the duration of penance, with attention to the sinner's contrition, sorrow and good works [3]. The tendency of such utterances was to increase the disorder. No sort of uniformity was any longer demanded or maintained.

Even the penitential books lost their importance. It is true that they had transformed the practice of penance. But they were no longer held in esteem. Whether the condemnation

1. Date auctoritatem. Quæ scriptura hoc præcipit ut confiteamur peccata nostra? Hugh of St. Victor, De sacramentis Christianiæ fidei, Migne, Patrol. Lat., T. 176, col. 549, Cf. Moeller, Church History, Vol. II, p. 338; Watkins, Hist. of Penance, Vol. II, p. 727.

2. Nisi episcopi, in quorum parocchiis estis prohibuerint, licentiam damus; Löwenfeld, Epistolæ pontificum Romanorum ineditæ, p. 54; Watkins, History of Penance, Vol. II, p. 724.

3. Löwenfeld, *op. cit.*, p. 55.

of priests like Peter Damiani contributed to this result in any marked degree it would be hard to say. The fact is that their very multiplicity was their condemnation. A single penitential might have commanded respect; the comparison of many with their variations and inconsistencies was destructive of the authority of all. The right of the priest to use his discretion is emphasized more and more in the later penitential books, such as those of Peter of Poictiers and Alain de Lisle [1]. The latter has indeed a scant knowledge of the history of penitential literature. Why, he asks, was a seven-year penance formerly common? And in reply he ascribes it to Old Testament references to a seven-year period [2]. There were almost as many standards of penance as there were priests to administer it. For Peter Lombard (c. 1150) the subject of penance is a "quaestio multiplex", owing to the confusing variety of opinion and practice [3].

The church as a body, and the papacy, its head, having so far failed to take action on penance, not a few efforts were made on the part of provincial authorities to overcome the confusion. A council held under Bishop Odo of Paris in 1198 issued a series of canons in which guidance is given to the priest in administration of penance. The confession is to be held in the church and the confessant is to be questioned minutely and personally. Absolution is given only on the latter's promise to abstain from mortal sin. Although the place of confession is in full view of any who may be in the church, it is clear that the interview is entirely private. There is no suggestion of a public satisfaction. In can. 13 priests are ordered to enjoin confession on their flocks, especially at the beginning of Lent [4].

Similarly in England more definite standards were being

1. Morinus, Commentarius, lib. VII, c. 22; Migne, Patrol. Lat., T. 210 col. 279 f.
2. Migne, Patrol. Lat., T. 211, col. 298.
3. P. Lombardi Sententiæ, lib. IV., Dist. 17; Migne, Patrol. Lat., T. 97, col. 897.
4. Mansi, Concil., T. XXII, p. 678; Watkins, Hist. of Penance. Vol. II, p. 732; Lea, Hist. of Auricular Confession and Indulgences, Vol. I, p. 216.

set. In the year 1200 London council prescribed a careful investigation of all the circumstances of sin (tempus, locum, moram in peccato factam, devotionem animo poenitentis, etc.), and went so far in guaranteeing secrecy as to require the imposition on married persons of only such penalties as would not expose them to the suspicion of their partners in marriage [1]. In both these instances the use of penitential books is discarded, but the principle of private penance is recognized. They exhibit the tendencies of the late twelfth century, aud mark a departure from the codified penance of Burchard, in the direction of the Lateran Decree of 1216.

It was left to the Fourth Lateran Council (1215-16) to frame for the whole church laws for the uniform administration of penance. This long overdue legislation was the plan of Innocent III. himself. It has been suggested that his primary object was to strengthen the means of bringing to light lurking heresy [2]. But the use of the confessional for this purpose would mean the violation of the seal of confession which is guarded in the Lateran decree.

The famous canon 21 of this council, enacted in 1216, has often been quoted and often translated [3]. Its principal terms may be stated as follows: —

1. Annual confession on the part of all the faithful of years of discretion, each to his own priest.
2. Refusal to perform assigned penance calls for expulsion from the church and the refusal of Christian burial.
3. On permission from his own priest one may confess to another priest.
4. No scale of penances is prescribed, the priest being simply warned to be discreet.
5. The decree is to be frequently published that no one may plead ignorance.
6. In accord with Burchard's "Corrector" the severe sentence of deposition and perpetual penance is prescribed for betrayal by the priest of matters confided in confession.

1. Mansi, Concil., T. XXII, p. 715; Watkins, Hist. of Penance, Vol. II, p. 733.
2. Lea, *op. cit.*, Vol. I, p. 228.
3. Migne, Patrol. Lat., T. XXII, col. 1008.

This is vigorous legislation, armed with heavy penalties for irregularity of people or priest. The question for our interest is : In what degree is the Celtic tradition here represented ? Three statements will suffice to answer this question.

In the first place to make any general and uniform regulation of penance was foreign to Celtic tradition. Synods in Wales and Ireland had at one stage formed penitential canons ; but the more influential penitential books owed their influence primarily to the authority of their individual authors. This however, is but a formal difference. The Celtic practice of penance was, in all probability, more uniform and more universal, than that secured by the legislation of Innocent III.

Again, the penitential books are ignored. They are neither prescribed nor rejected. Their specific prescriptions have passed, like those of the fourth century canons, into desuetude. The silence of the Council here shows that the use of this or that or any penitential was no longer an issue.

But, in the third place, the private and secret nature of the penance is a simple projection into the Latin church of the practice of the Celts. The violation of the seal is an offence attended by the greatest penalties. The Celts regarded it as an unpardonable sin [1].

The three-cornered conflict between Celtic penance, ancient penance, and no penance at all, ended in this stern and specific act of legislation. Confession and penance were to be obligatory. The priest was given a large measure of discretion in assigning penalties, a feature which departs as far from the canons of St. Basil as from the penitentials of Finnian and Columban. But the Celtic principle of inviolable secrecy was triumphant.

2. — Sacramentalism and Private Penance.

The sacramental theory of the mediaeval church was in process of formulation in the twelfth century. Of the variant

1. See above, p. 96.

view-points of the writers of that period in regard to the number of the sacraments and their relative importance it was the judgment of Peter Lombard that finally prevailed. The Lombard belonged to the generation after Abelard, of whom he was a pupil, and flourished about the middle of the century, (d. 1160). In his famous "Sentences" he enumerates seven sacraments, the list adopted by the great scholastics after him, — baptism, confirmation, the eucharist, penance, extreme unction, ordination, marriage [1].

There would be no advantage in recounting the complicated story of the progress of theological opinion on the question of the sacraments in the twelfth and thirteenth centuries [2]. It is with penance alone that we are here concerned. Something of a supernatural meaning may have been attached to penance even by the early church. Reconciliation, restoration to communion by the imposition of hands, partook of the nature of the later absolution and gave the restored penitent a feeling of security which he could not possess while under the discipline. No doubt under the Celtic system the completion of the penance brought a similar sense of relief. Here the lack of any formal reconciliation was a natural result of the fact that excommunication had not taken place. The acceptance of a penitential duty after confession in itself constituted an important step toward complete reunion with the church : but the church as a body of worshippers was not informed of the sin, the confession, the discipline undergone, or the termination of the sentence. While the oversight of the confessor during penance was not excluded, there was not even in private a formal and authoritative release from the results of sin.

Gradually in the continental development there emerged a more ecclesiastical conception. Formulas for the administration of penance begin to exhibit the phraseology of an authoritative release. At first the language used is intercessory only. Authority for the practice may be traced to the *Statuta* ascribed to Boniface [3]. In order not to ignore entirely the ancient

1. Petrus Lombardus, Sententiæ, IV., 2.

2. The reader may refresh his memory by reference to Lagarde, Latin Church, p. 32 f.

3. See above, p. 156.

canons, says this document, the priest should reconcile singly with prayer those whose confession he has just received [1]. The rule of St. Chrodegang enjoins the confessor on assigning canonical penances [2] to pour forth prayers for the penitent. From the eighth to the twelfth century the practice of an intercessory private reconciliation on the assignment of penance was customary. It is to be contrasted with the ancient reconciliation by imposition of hands on the completion of penance, as also with the Celtic omission of any formal ceremony. The author of the *Statuta Bonifacii*, likely enough Boniface himself, rightly recognized the practice as a compromise [3].

Occasional substitution of the term absolution for reconciliation occurs not long after the age of Boniface. Alcuin is able to use the words *absolvere* and *reconciliatio* in a letter of uncertain date advocating the observance of confession to the church of Septimania [4]. Reference to "prayers of reconciliation" which appear in the sacramentary, acquaintance with which on the part of his readers, Alcuin assumes, indicate that the accustomed language of absolution was intercessory. This fact in itself sufficiently defines the doctrinal assumption on which the act was based. The priest did not grant absolution: he supplicated God for it. It may be assumed however, that the intercession is regarded as prevailing, where the other conditions have been fulfilled. Alcuin's emphasis is on the essen-

1. Curet unusquisque statim post acceptam confessionem pœnitentium, singulos data oratione reconciliari. — Mansi, Concil., T. XII, p. 386.

2. Tunc da illi pœnitentiam canonice mensuratam et postea effunda super eum orationes et preces. — Migne, Patrol. Lat., T. LXXXIX, col. 1073.

3. Et quia varia necessitate præpedimur canonum statuta de reconciliandis pœnitentibus pleniter observare, propterea omnino non dimittatur. — Statuta, 31, *loc. cit.*

4. Cur etiam et in secundo pœnitentiæ baptismate, per confessionem humilitatis nostræ, ab omnibus post primum baptisma peractis eodem divina miserante gratia sacerdotali similiter auxilio non debemus absolvi peccatis? Si peccata sacerdotibus non sunt prodenda, quare in sacramentario reconciliationis orationes scriptæ sunt? Quomodo sacerdos reconciliat, quem peccare non novit? — Alcuin, Ep. 138, Ad Fratres in Provincia Gothorum, anno incerto. Mon. Ger. Hist., Ep. Karol Aevi, T. II., p. 118; Migne, Patrol. Lat., T. 100, col. 339 (no. CXII).

tial need of confession. " How ", he asks, " can a priest reconcile one whom he does not know to be a sinner ?"

With the prevalence of sacramental ideas the power of the priest as an intermediary was considerably extended, especially in the view of those theologians who were at once mystical and ecclesiastical. Whereas Abelard regards the priest's function in confession as that of a physician [1], and thinks confession itself may sometimes be safely omitted [2], Richard of St. Victor (c. 1150) urges sinners to seek priestly absolution [3]. Peter Lombard is none too sure of his ground on the question of the necessity of confession, but in one passage reaches the conclusion that confession is to be made first to God and then to a priest, and if such confession is possible and is not performed, the sinner is barred from entering Paradise [4]. In this passage Peter cites the recent sacerdotal tract *De Vera et Falsa Penitentia,* to which the influential name of Augustine had been fraudulently attached. The republication of this tract in Gratian's Decretum gave a false authority to its provisions, and helped to make general the view that the priestly absolution was divine [5].

Richard of St. Victor indeed distinguishes between the priest's power of remitting sins in respect to their *poena* or penalty, and God's power of releasing from guilt, *culpa* [6], a distinction which naturally remained in the region of theological thought, and did not concern the layman anxious about future penalties.

The increasing prominence of the priestly act in the conception of penance, rendered obsolete the intercessory formulas of absolution, and called for the use of a simple pronouncement

1. Abelard, Ethica, 25. Migne, Patrol. Lat., T. 173, col. 668-669.

2. *Ibid.*, 25, col. 669-670.

3. Vera pœnitentia est abominatio peccati, cum voto cavendi, confitendi, et satisfaciendi... (quoting Jas 5 : 16, Confess your sins one to another) ... eget ergo sacerdotis absolutione quamdiu datur hoc posse. — De Potestate ligandi et solvendi, c. 5. Migne, Patrol. Lat., T. 196, col. 1163.

4. Petrus Lombardus, Sententiæ, lib. IV., Dist. XVII, § 3, 4.

5. Cf. Moeller, History of the Christian Church, Middle Ages, p. 337, p. 339 f.

6. Richard of. St. Victor, *op. cit.*, c. 12.

in the indicative mood. So, about the time of the Fourth Lateran Council, the declaratory formula becomes a favored innovation. Its adoption was promoted by the support of Thomas Aquinas and the scholastic teachers generally. The examples cited by Lea indicate the manner in which the transition was made [1]. The earliest phase merely involves an authoritative announcement in the third person, the act of absolution being ascribed to God or to St. Peter [2]. Then the first person is used with a limiting phrase, or with ascription of derived authority [3]. Before the middle of the thirteenth century [4] the new form, *ego absolvo te*, was coming into use. Alexander of Hales defended it in his Summa, (c. 1245) [5]; the University of Paris favored it; Aquinas in his *Opusculum* (c. 1270) gave it his unqualified approval [6]; and three centuries later it was prescribed by the Council of Trent.

3. — Private Penance, Individualism and Fanaticism.

The settlement of penitential practice made by the Fourth Lateran Council was that of a government which prudently aims to secure obedience by granting concessions. The mediaeval period, it is generally agreed, was one of universalism. Yet it made large concessions to individualism where the latter was entrenched by custom. Just as the feudal nobility habitually asserted their virtual independence of the greater units of government, so the erring layman, through the penance system, secured his exemption from the humilations imposed by the ancient church upon his class. It is quite erroneous to see in the legislation of 1216 a one-side triumph. Instead, that

1. Lea, *op. cit.*, vol. I., p. 481, quoting a work of Garofalo. Cf. also Moeller, Hist. of the Christian Church, *loc. cit.*

2. Ipse te absolvat; absolvat te sanctus Petrus et beatus Michæl archangelus.

3. Ego absolvo te auctoritate domini Dei nostri Jesu Christi et beati Petri Apostoli et officii nostri.

4. Lea says 1240.

5. Pt. IV., Quest. XXI, I.

6. Opusc. XXII, 5.

legislation represents a compromise to which the practice of the previous six centuries naturally led. The universal institution succeeded indeed in asserting the right to search consciences. But in the seal of confession it expressly disavowed the right to expose the penitent's shame. The official adoption of private penance may truly be regarded as the greatest concession to individualism in the Middle Ages. Through it one great phase of mediaeval religion was recognized as sacredly private; and we will hardly be mistaken in the conjecture that the total result was favorable to the growth of private conceptions of religion itself, and ultimately inimical to the solidarity of the centralized church. Whatever the intention, and whatever the influence of councils and authorities, it is a fact that penance in the high Middle Age is characterized by individualistic interpretations and practices, by private variations, excesses, and fanaticism.

It was not till the Council of Trent that the sacramental character of penance was asserted to be *de fide*. Till that decision it was only a favorite opinion sanctioned by the best doctors. The duty of confession was of course on a different basis. A campaign to make confession universal followed the Fourth Lateran Council. The inviolable secrecy of the confessional was emphasized as an inducement to the laity. Pope Innocent himself invited the confidence of the masses in their priests by taking the highest ground on the sanctity of the seal. He denounced the confessor who reveals a sin confided to him, as worse than the penitent who has commited it [1]. Heightened statements of the merits of confession itself in the issues of time and eternity, were freely made by the propagandists of the reform [2]. This insistent demand of the church combined with the general religious revival of the early thirteenth century to produce an emphasis on the efficacy of confession which outwent the sober dicta of the theologians.

1. Gravius enim peccat sacerdos qui peccatum revelat quam homo qui peccatum committit, — Innocent III, Sermo L, de Consecratione. Migne, Patrol. Lat., T. 217, col. 652.

2. See especially Lea's references to Caesarius of Heisterbach and Pseudo-Augustine. Lea, *op. cit.*, Vol. I, p. 234.

While the latter were developing doctrines of merit and explaining priestly absolution, the popular mind was often obsessed with the oft-proclaimed importance of confession itself.

The strain of this emphasis is to be found in the older theology, and in certain writers of the previous century. In the early days when confession was a public humiliating exomologesis, it was rightly regarded as an important part of the satisfaction. Such a theory also accommodated with the practice of immediate absolution, and with the light penalties involved in the composition system. Abelard was far from being a fanatical advocate of confession and does not demand that it should be universal, nevertheless he regards it as *magna pars satisfactionis* [1]. Peter Cantor, late in the century, uses the superlative adjective : *oris confessio maxima est pars satisfactionis*; and even quotes with approval an unnamed author who enjoins confession to as many priests as possible in order the more promptly to secure absolution [2].

Long practiced in the use of the remedies for sin provided by the penitentials in which confession was the first essential, assured by some of their teachers that confession itself had enormous value in satisfaction, and urged by the hierarchy, as an unavoidable duty, to confess at least once a year, the devout adopted an exaggerated and even fanatical view of the importance of confession in the discipline of penance.

One of the most interesting features of the extreme stress laid on confession appears in the wide-spread practice of confession to laymen. This practice was, as we have had occasion to note, not unknown in the early church [3]. It was somewhat extensively revived in the Middle ages, and was believed by many to be efficacious as a remedy for post-baptismal sins.

1. Abelard, Ethica, 19. Migne, Patrol. Lat., T. 176, col. 665; cf. col. 668.

2. Unde sicut auctoritas habet : Quanto pluribus sacerdotibus confiteberis sub spe veniae, tanto celeriorem consequeris absolutionem culpae. —Peter Cantor, Verbum Abbreviatum, c. 143. Migne, Patrol. Lat., T. 205, col. 342.

3. See above, p. 86.

References to it are found as early as Thietmar's Chronicle (c. 1015) [1]. It was favored by Pseudo-Augustine, and not condemned by Thomas and Albert [2]. In cases of necessity, such as that recorded by de Joinville of Gui d'Ybelin, it was confidently resorted to [3]; and its occurrence in normal situations is well authenticated [4]. From the examination of the subject made by a modern investigator [5], it would appear that the decline, already noted, of "la pénitence tarifée", and the reduction of actual penalties through composition, directed greater attention to confession, regardless of its sacerdotal aspect. The act of confession to whomsoever addressed, was meritorious, and availed to efface the sins accumulated since baptism or since a previous confession. The practice antedates the rise of the doctrine of priestly absolution, the tendency of which was to render valueless lay confession. It may indeed be the case that the Lateran canon was directed against this and other irregularities as much as against open neglect. Still confession to laymen was in some measure tolerated by the scholastics, and long survived the Fourth Lateran Council.

Scenes of emotional repentance accompanied the work of the Mendicant Orders. In the course of the thirteenth century, as everyone knows, having obtained papal authority to administer penance, the friars virtually thrust the seculars, while they excluded the regulars, from the confessional and from the pulpit. The abundant ministrations of the friars no doubt largely attracted those confessants who had formerly resorted to laymen, and so extinguished what had been a common custom.

Confession itself, however, even if multiple, failed to satisfy the more ardent. Amid the phenomena of mediaeval fanati-

1. Georg Gomer, Die Laienbeicht im Mittelalter, ein Beitrag zu ihrer Geschichte, Munich, 1909, p. 11.

2. For the references see Gomer, p. 47.

3. Threatened with Danish axes, d'Ybelin confessed his sins to de Joinville, who managed to pronounce a modest form of absolution : "I absolve thee as far as God gives me power". Ethel Wedgewood, Memoirs of the Lord of Joinville, p. 177.

4. Cf. Lea, *op. cit.*, Vol. I, p. 220.

5. Gomer, *op. cit.*

cism nothing is more remarkable than the craze for self and mutual flagellation, which, shortly after the middle of the thirteenth century, seized whole populations in various parts of Europe. The origin of the flagellant movement is not simple but complex. No doubt it is to be related to the various means of self-mortification usually practiced by peoples who hold a religion of satisfactions as did the mediaeval man [1]. Flagellation was not unknown in early monasticism, and appears as a recognized means of correction in the Benedictine rule. Benedict, however, does not appear to make it a penitential exercise, but a form of corrective punishment for boys who make repeated mistakes in the services (ch. 45) and for monks who have proved otherwise incorrigible [2]. The ordinary form of penance was probably labor [3].

In the rules of the Celtic monks, on the other hand, this feature was given great prominence. Montalembert, in his discussion of the rule of Columban, has perceived this distinction. "The rigid discipline used in the monasteries of Scotland and Ireland" says the French historian of monachism, "is here manifest by the prodigal use of beating, which is reserved in the Benedictine code for incorrigible criminals, and prescribed in the penitentiary for the most insignificant omissions" [4]. The prodigal use of beating spread with the Celtic influence, and became a common form of monastic penance. A penitent who had been sentenced to be whipped might receive the discipline from his confessor, or from another, or he might inflict it upon himself. St. Pardulf, who died about 737, was in the habit of receiving frequently during Lent, in a state of nakedness, a flogging from his obliging

1. The worship of the Scythian Diana, as well as that of Isis in Busiris, was characterized by severe flagellation — in the latter case mutual. Cf. Anon., Hist. of Flagellations, Lond., 1883, p. 23. Similar in motive and character was the worship of Baal on Mount Carmel as described in I. Kings 19

2. If any brother has been frequently convicted and excommunicated and still does not mend his ways, let the punishment be increased by the laying on of blows. — St. Benedict, Regula Monachorum, ch. 28.

3. *Ibid.*, ch. 25.

4. Monks of the West, Vol. II, p. 288.

pupil Theodenus [1]. Early in the following century flagellation came to be so frequently imposed in the monasteries, that the Council of Aachen (817) in which the reforms of Benedict of Aniane were enforced took action against it and forbade the nude flogging of monks [2]. The rule of Cluny, however, which in abolishing field labor and increasing the nocturnal psalmody, distinctly leans toward Celtic usage, restores the once condemned practice in even more humiliating form, and orders scandalous offenders to be stripped, bound and flogged in the public street [3]. Regino of Prüm (c. 900), in a list of penitential commutations, makes one hundred strokes (percussiones) correspond to a day's penance on bread and water [4]. The scale is significantly identical with that in the penitential part of the rule of St. Columban [5], where two hundred strokes are the stated equivalent of two day's penance.

Regino's extension of flagellation, in the passage just cited, to laymen as well as monks, is regarded by Pfannenschmid as marking the beginning of the flagellant movement [6], although it was not till the thirteenth century that the movement attracted great numbers. From about the time of Regino the scourge has its place in most cases of the occasional public penance. About a century later, and still long before the first crusade, Fulk Nerra, Count of Anjou, a man whose record for violent crimes is a distinguished one, made satisfac-

1. A. S.S. Boll., T. 51 (Oct. T. 3), p. 435.

2. Ut monachi nudi non verberuntur, istius modi usus apud nos nunquam fuit, nec, Domino adjuvante, in antea erit. Concil Aquisgran., anno 817. Mansi, Concil., T. XIV, p. 352.

3. In medea platea nudatur, ligatur, et verberatur. Udalrici Consuetudines Clun., lib. iii, c. iii. Migne, Patrol. Lat., T. 149, col. 735.

4. De Eccles. Discipl., lib. 2, c. 44. Migne, Patrol. Lat., T. 132, col. 197.

5. This part of Columban's rule, known as the Regula Coenobialis, is given in Migne, Patrol. Lat., T. 80, col. 216 f. Seebass has published a critical text in the Zeitschr. f. Kg. Bd. XV (1895), p. 366f. As previously noted Seebass was of opinion that the section has become detached from the Penitential of Columban.

6. Pfannenschmid, Heino, in Runge, Paul, Die Lieder und Melodien der Geissler des Jahres 1349, p. 39 f.

tion for his sins by submission to the rod, in Jerusalem [1]. In the penance of Becket after his acquiescence in the Constitutions of Clarendon, and in that of Henri II after Becket's death, this again is the outstanding feature. Peter Damiani, perhaps the greatest exponent of penance in the Middle ages, is also the most renowned exponent of flagellation. He was the centre of a group of flagellants whose self torture, as recorded by him, almost passes credence. Here it is to be noted that the penalty is inflicted in private, or in the presence only of the pious necessary attendant who applied the scourge. Damiani stirred his readers to emulate the deeds of the heroes of his *vitae sanctorum* ; — of St. Rodulph who castigated himself with a brace of twigs in either hand [2], or if beaten by others, exulted if the discipline were administered by two instead of one of the brethren [3]; and of St. Dominic of the Cuirass, who for endurance in self-flagellation was *facile princeps*. For the commutation of tedious penances into brief but bitter floggings, Damiani with his zealous pupils worked out a system of equivalents quite in the spirit of the penitential books against which the Italian saint was so incensed. St. Dominic was able, through his astonishing power of endurance, fully to discharge an a single lent, a penance of a thousand years, which had been imposed at his own request [4].

With the Crusading era, men like Peter the hermit and Fulk of Neuilly endured and induced others to endure the scourge. With the thirteenth century popular revival, the infatuation increased. It is not our purpose to describe the spread and suppression of the Flagellants [5], but only briefly to indi-

1. Wm. of Malmesbury, Gesta Regum Anglorum, lib. III, § 235, in Rolls Ser, 90, pt. 2, p. 292.

2. Armata scopis utraque manu

3. Damiani, Vitae SS. Rodulphi et Dominici Loricati, c. 3. Migne, Patrol. Lat., T. 44, col. 1011.

4. *Ibid* ., col. 1015.

5. For a succinct account see Haupt's article "Flagellation, Flagellants' in the New Schaff-Herzog, Vol. IV, p. 233 f. (As immediate causes of the outbreak of 1260 Haupt gives : A penitential disposition inspired by St. Francis, tension and disorder due to the imperial-papal strife, a violent epidemic, and above all the apocalyptic of Joachim of Fiore).

cate the antecedents of the movement. That the penitential literature directly inspired the violent outbreaks of the thirteenth and fourteenth centuries, is extremely unlikely : but that through Columban and Regino it originally gave vogue to the practice of penitential flagellation, can hardly be doubted.

It may here be remarked, however, that the Flagellants of the later period became markedly anti-sacerdotal and anti-ecclesiastical. Protesting against ecclesiastical corruption, and in the heat of their enthusiasm despising ecclesiastical usages, they formed a sect under Conrad Schmid in Thuringia, which rejected all the sacraments of the church. John Gerson inveighed against these sectaries before the Council of Constance in 1417, charging them with contempt for sacramental penance [1]. Lax tendencies had by this time rendered ecclesiastical penance incapable of satisfying the demands of the sincere devotee. The Flagellant sect, revolting from these tendencies, expressed an extreme mystical individualism. The form which their devotion took was originally derived from Celtic monastic penitential practice. That the very features of corruption which alienated these zealots, were in themselves largely the product of the system of the penitentials (la pénitence tarifée), will appear in the following pages.

4. — Commutations in Money, Vicarious Penance, and Indulgences.

"Prima relaxatae poenitentiae occasio est poenitentiae canonicae redemptio". Such is the judgment of the learned Morinus [2]. It is probable that in the redemption of penance by composition, commutation, and vicarious satisfaction, lay the most profound as well as the most damaging influence exerted by the penitentials upon the discipline of the western church. In consideration of this phase of the influence of the penitentials, we are led to agree with M. Tixeront when he says, "Leur influence n'y fut pas heureuse [3]".

1. Contemnuntur confessiones et poenitentiae sacramentales. Mansi Concil., T. XXVIII, p. 381.
2. Morinus, Commentarius, lib. X, cap. 16.
3. Tixeront, Le Sacrement de pénitence, p. 44.

Attention was called in a former chapter to the source of these prominent elements in the penitential literature. They were borrowed from Celtic and supported by German tradition, in which crimes were considered as torts and compensated for by payments according to a fixed tariff. The purpose of the following paragraphs on the other hand is to indicate the nature of the generally recognized [1] connection between this feature of the penitentials and the indulgence system. The rise of indulgences has been discussed by Gottlob with special reference to early papal documents in which the evolution or the system is partly illustrated [2]. This investigator finds the earliest genuine plenary indulgence given for the building of churches in the Spanish March in priveleges issued by Pope Serguis IV. c. 1011 [3]. In this case the penitents, who profit by the indulgence, give payment for it not in money but in labor on church construction. Now the tenth century Anglo-Saxon sinner needed no special papal letter in order to obtain the same privilege. It was written in the laws or "canons" of King Edgar, a set of interesting regulations no doubt due to the activities of St. Dunstan, but largely reflecting the Penitential codes. In a passage "of Penitents" this code states: —

> Penances are devised in various ways and a man may also redeem much with alms... He who has ability let him raise a church to the glory of God...facilitate the people's journeying by bridges over deep waters and foul ways [4]...

The service was not rendered in labor but commonly in goods or money, and involved as in "indulgences" proper,

1. Loofs, Leitfaden zum studium der Dogmengeschichte, 4 Aufl. Halle 1906 p. 495f. Hinschius, das katholische Kirchenrecht, vol. 5, p. Harnack, Hist. of Dogma, Vol. V, p. 325f.

2. Adolf Gottlob, Kreuzablass und Almosenablass, Ein Studie über die Frühzeit des Ablasswesens, Stuttgart 1906, in Stutz, Ulrich, Kirchen geschichtliche Abhandlungen.

3. Den erste wirkliche vollendete Ablass den es überhaupt gab. Gottlob, *op. cit.*, p. 198. The document is in Migne, Patrol. Lat., T. 139, col. 1509 f.

4. Canons of King Edgar in Thorpe, Ancient Laws of England, vol. II, p. 283. "Of Penitents", 13, 14.

a relaxation or omission of the ascetic discipline otherwise required. For the Anglo-Saxon church provided ways by which the penitent might "Distribute for the love of God all that he owns"... "to help poor men, widows, step-children and foreigners, etc. [1] " A sick man might redeem his fast at the rate of one penny a day, or thirty shillings for twelve months [2].

Direct compositions in money were accepted by Regino of Prüm, who, as we saw, was instrumental in the circulations of the penitentials [3], in language that is simply an expansion of passages in Cummean's and other Celtic codes of composition, and in Haltigar's pseudo-Romanum [4] :

> If perchance one cannot fast, and has the means of redeeming it, if he is rich, for a seven weeks fast he should give twenty solidi. Should he not possess the means of giving so much, he should give ten solidi. If, however, he is very poor, let him give three solidi. Moreover, let no one be perturbed because we have commanded to give twenty solidi or less : since, if one is rich it is easier for him to give twenty solidi than for a poor man to give three. But let everyone direct his attention to that to which he ought to give, whether for the redemption of captives, or over the sacred altar, or to the servants of God, or to the poor in alms. For a month which one is under obligation to spend in penance on bread and water, let him sing 1200 psalms kneeling, or without kneeling, 1680... One who really does not know the psalms, and cannot fast, for a year during which he is to fast on bread and water, let him give in alms 26 solidi, and fast till the ninth hour one day in each week, i. e. on Wednesday, and one day, Friday, till vespers : and let him estimate what he receives in three forty-day periods, and contribute a moiety of it in alms... for one day in autumn, winter, or spring, a hundred strokes or fifty psalms. In summer one psalter or a hundred strokes.

1. *Ibid.*
2. *Ibid.*, can. 18, p. 285.
3. See above p. 171.
4. See above p. 169.

The singing of one mass is enough to redeem twelve days; teh masses, four months, etc. [1]

This significant passage is quoted at length by Morinus in his study of redemptions [2]. It reveals the working of the system about the beginning of the tenth century. The plan of commutations is remarkable for variety and flexibility. The prescriptions are designed to meet any demand that may arise, and especially to enable the layman, unpracticed in fasting and psalmody, to compound for his penance as agreeably as may be. As noted in a recent paragraph, the passage contains the first extension of flagellation to the laity.

It is obvious that this unblushing transmutation of penance into fines or exercises more agreeable than protracted fasting, is essentially similar to the familiar operations of the indulgence traffic. There can be no question that in the prevalence

1. Si quis forte non potuerit jejunare et habuerit unde possit redimere, si dives fuerit pro septem hebdomadibus det solidos viginti. Si non habuerit tantum unde dare possit, det solidos decem. Si autem multum pauper fuerit det solidos tres. Neminem autem conturbet quod jussimus dare solidos viginti aut minus; quia si dives fuerit, facilius est illi dare solidos viginti quam pauperi solidos tres. Sed attendat unusquique cui dare debeat, sive pro redemptione captivorum, sive supra sanctum altare, sive Dei servis seu pauperibus in eleemosyna. Pro uno mense quod in pane et aqua poenitere debet aliquis, psalmos decantet mille ducentos genuflexo, an sinon genuflexo, 1680... Qui vero psalmos non novit et jejunare non potest, pro uno anno quem jejunare debet in pane et aqua, det in eleemosyna XXVI solidos & in unaquaque hebdomada diem unum jejunet usque ad nonam, id est, feriam 4 & unum, id est, feriam 6 usque ad vesperam : & in tres quadragesimas, quantum sumit, penset & medietatem tribuat in eleemosyna... Pro uno die in autumno, hyeme, vel verno, 100 percusiones vel psalmos quinquaginta. In aestate psalterium unum vel percussiones centum... Cantatio unius missae potest redimere duodecim dies ; decem missae quatuor menses, etc.

Regino Prumensis, De Eccles. Discipl., lib. 2, c. 44 ; Migne, Patrol. Lat., T. 132, col. 197.

2. Morinus, Commentarius, lib. x, c. 16. Very similar are the terms of a penitential ascribed to Egbert of York : Et qui unam hebdomadam jejunare debeat in pane et aqua, cantat trecentos psalmos genuflectens, vel quadringentos et viginti sine genuflectione... Et qui psalmos non novit nec jejunare potest, distribuat quotidie denarium unum vel denarii valorem pauperibus... Et qui annum unum talem poenitentiam agere debeat, distribuat XXVI solidos in eleemosynas et quaque hebdomada jejunet II dies.

of these practices lies the foundation of what appears in the developed stage of indulgences. Lindsay, in his History of the Reformation, states the matter in general terms:

"So books were published containing lists of sins with the corresponding appropriate *satisfactions* which ought to be demanded of the penitents... From the seventh century there arose a practice of commuting satisfactions or penances. A penance of several years' practice of fasting might be commuted into saying so many prayers or psalms, into giving a definite amount of alms, or even into a money fine and in the last case the analogy of the Wehrgeld was frequently followed. This was in every case the commutation or relaxation of the penance or outward sign of sorrow, which had been imposed according to the regulations of the Church laid down in the penitentiaries (relaxatio de injuncta poenitentia). This was the real origin of Indulgences... It will be seen that Luther expressly excluded this sort of Indulgence from his attack" [1].

The commutations of Regino, however, make no explicit appeal to the conception of vicarious merit, a conception closely bound up with the later practice of indulgences. But here also the penitentials are prophetic of, and influential in the later development. We have seen that in the early penitentials, as in primitive law, the offender was identified with his kindred, and the latter were held responsible if the amount of the *éric*, *galanas*, or *wergeld*, remained unpaid [2]. The eighth century penitential of Cummean, authorizes, as has been noted, vicarious singing and fasting to be paid for at the rate of a penny a day [3]. It soon became a recognized custom for the rich and powerful to redeem penance through the services of their friends or of their serfs. Attention has been called to the serious abuses of this kind that came to the notice of the Council of Clovesho, 747 [4]. Ideas of vicarious merit were early applied to penance. Harnack is speaking of the late Caro-

1. Lindsay, Hist. of the Reformation, Vol. I, pp. 218-219.
2. See above, p. 122 f.
3. Wasserschleben, Bussordnungen, p. 463
4. See above, p. 154

lingian epoch when he says: "Accordingly the whole institution (of penance) was included under the conception of merit, from of old connected with works and alms" [1]. The adverse decisions of a fews councils did not hinder the general acceptance of the principle of vicarious penance. In England it was powerfully enforced by the national legislation. The laws of King Edgar (959-975) show that Dunstan viewed it with unreserved favor. One passage will illustrate this:

"Thus may a powerful man, and rich in friends, greatly lighten his penance. Let him take with him xii men and let them fast three days on bread and on green herbs and on water, and get, in addition thereto, in whatever manner he can, seven times cxx men who shall also fast for him iii days; then shall be fasted as many fasts as there are in vii years".

Following this naïve legislation, the poor man is reminded: Scriptura est enim: Quia unusquisque onus suum portabit [2].

The solidarity of the tribe has here given place to the solidarity of the manor or the feudal complex, as tribal conditions have given place to feudal. Harnack in his History of Dogma in an illuminating footnote remarks: "The Church looked upon Christians as forming a clan with the saints in heaven [3]". Harnack is misleading, however, in stating in the same place that the mediaeval discipline was "evolved on Latin ground". A generation later Anselm gave the world his immensly influential satisfaction theory of the atonement. The presuppositions of *Cur Deus Homo* are feudal [4]. Feudal relations of obedience, ideas of honour and service, and of graded personal values, are assumed. Equally are the current ideas of penance and satisfaction assumed. Man cannot make satisfaction for the offended honour of God, his infinite suzerain. Christ offers hmself, an infinite sacrifice, on behalf of helpless

1. Harnack, Hist. of Dogma, Vol. V, p. 327.
2. Canons of King Edgar, Thorpe Ancient Laws of England, Vol. II p. 287 (Dunstan, who was Edgar's ecclesiastical and temporal adviser, was educated at Glastonbury, where "the wandering scholars of Ireland had left their books" Green, Short History, p. 56.)
3. Hist. of Dogma, Vol. V, p. 330.
4. A. Foley, Anselm's Theory of the Atonement, p. 113.

man. " His death excels the sins of all men [1]". The Father owed a reward to the Son for this sacrifice; but having all things already, the Son hands over the reward to men [2]. To this measureless supererogatory merit of Christ was added by later theology, that of the Virgin, the Saints and the martyrs, and the whole regarded as the *thesaurus meritorum ecclesiae.*

This theory was not yet available in the time of King Edgar. The poor man's questionings are anticipated only with a soporific quotation from Scripture. But many must have asked of the strange inequalities of penance : How can these things be ? Perhaps even the fortunate landlord who set his serfs, or others " obtained in whatsoever manner he could" to fast for him, may have marvelled at the wondrous ways of Providence that made it possible for him to discharge seven years of penance with only the slight inconvenience of going three days without meat. And the more enlightened of the clergy must have felt keenly the need of an explanation of what they were authorized to sanction.

The writers of the penitentials, under the influence of tribal custom, had not felt it necessary to encumber their works with theological explanation. Yet under the guise of commuted penance they prescribe something essentially the same as the liberal indulgences of the crusading era. When one recalls the universal belief in the communion of the faithful, living and departed, it appears but a short step from the vicarious fasting of 852 English laborers to the vicarious merit accumulated by the whole army of martyrs and saints who had mortified the flesh in their day. It need not therefore surprise us that the penitential literature itself begins to hint strongly at the solution which Alexander of Hales was long afterwards to give in the doctrine of the *thesaurus meritorum.* In one of those *ordines* for absolution which by the ninth century began to be attached to the penitentials, there occurs a distinct suggestion of a fund from which the absolving priest is able to draw for the benifit of the sinner :

1. Cur Deus Homo, lib. II, c. 14.
2. *Ibid.*, c. 20.

"Ex parte Dei et omnium sanctorum bonum quod fecisti ab infantia tua, et alii pro te facient et sacrificia et officia quae a catholicis per universum mundum aguntur, habeas partem, ut boni Christiani, et si ad aliam penitentiam non poteris pervenire, hanc penitentiam et confessionem, sis salvus ante Deum [1]".

Thus the rigours of penance were escaped through the superabundant merits of the faithful. It was left for Anselm and Alexander of Hales to explain and systematize in their theories of atonement and of the treasury, a view which was already universal, — the natural product of the adjustment of penance to tribal and feudal usage. The scholastic teaching is only the logical development of this general conception, under the influence of increased sacerdotal and centralizing tendencies. Hales defines the nature of the Treasury of Merits. Albertus, removing the treasure from connection with the sacramental system, relates it to the power of the Keys, and hence is able to restrict its distribution to the pope alone. Aquinas more insistently asserts sole papal control [2], and adds the application of the benefits to those in pergatory [3]. But these are after all, only aggravations of tendencies already patent; variations of principles already recognized. The evil genius of the Latin Church, having corrupted its discipline through the very guides to repentance, might long ago have exclaimed in triumph :

Mischief, thou art afoot,
Take thou what course thou wilt !

1. Poenit. Vallicell. II, Ordo Poenit., in Wasserschleben, Bussordnungen, p. 557.

2. The pope may authorize whom he will, even laymen, to act for him. The only restriction placed on the papal control of the Treasury is a clause involving a moral judgment, and left to the pope to interpret : Solus papa ob plenitudinem pontificalis potestates quam habet plenarias indulgentias pro libito suae voluntatis, legitima tamen existente causa, facere potest. — Supplementum, Q. 26, A1, A4.

3. Supplementum, Q. 25. A1.

CONCLUSION

We have now reached a point where the further pursuit of the influence of the penitentials would probably be fruitless. Our search has led us through seven centuries ending with the thirteenth, and has involved numerous references to phenomena of an earlier age. Many facts germane to our subject have been deliberately omitted as being of only remoter interest. Doubtless many others that might have been considered with advantage, have escaped the writer's notice, or have been by him inadequately appreciated. The treatment has been adapted to the space desired, and is admittedly far from exhaustive.

That the Celtic penitentials represent a unique usage which exhibits the impress of pre-Christian racial custom ; that they were instrumental in the transformation of Christian penance, and that the practices which they sanctioned promoted certain processes of decay in mediaeval Christianity, — these have been the main contentions. The author ventures to hope that the defects of the work may not prevent its making some contribution toward the charting of a field of history which has not attracted attention commensurate with its importance.

PROTAT BROTHERS, PRINTERS, MACON (FRANCE)